AS THEY REALLY WERE

As They Really Were

The Citizens of Alnwick 1831

Keith Middlemas

F

FRANCES LINCOLN LIMITED

PUBLISHERS

Frances Lincoln Ltd
4 Torriano Mews
Torriano Avenue
London NW5 2RZ
www.franceslincoln.com

ISBN: 978-0-7112-3290-7

Printed and bound in China

9 8 7 6 5 4 3 2 1

Special thanks are due to the Paul Mellon Foundation for
their assistance with the publication of this book.

TITLE PAGE *Plate 1. Percy Forster,
self-portrait (n.d., late 1820s). He
wears the still-fashionable Regency
wing collar with cravat high.
Although the son of a gamekeeper, he
has evidently established fashionable
status by his late twenties.*

RIGHT *Plate 2 [21]. James
Bamforth sexton [with keys] ditto
verso.*

CONTENTS

NORTHUMBER-LAND,

Drawn from an Actual SURVEY;

By Tho: Kitchin, Geog.

Explanation..
Borough Towns with the N.º of Members they send to Parliament by Stars.
Market Towns.
Parishes or Villages.
Parks.
Roads.

English Miles.
4   8   12

PART OF SCOTLAND

Berwick
Orde
Norham
Morton
Wessel
Tilmouth
Bowesden
Coldstreme
Dudda
Fennick
Tweed R.
Brankston
Barmore
Holy Island
Carram
Learmouth
Ford
Detchon
Staples
Kelso
Pressan
Doddington
Ross
Kilham
Horton Cast
Belford
Castle
Farne Is.
Kirk Newton
Till R.
Wooler
Bambury
Jedborough
Akeld
Chatton
Warnford
Tuggel
Sunderland
West Lilburn
Chillingham
Ellingham
Ilderton
W. Ditchburn
Cheviot Hills
Benwick
Embleton
Hartside
Eglingham
Dunstan-brugh Cast
Crawley
Honick
Houghton
Coquet R.
Shawdon
Hull Abbey
Lesbury
Yeldow
Whittingham
Alne-wick
Whitside
Une R.
Aylnmouth
Skirnwood
Over Truit
Newtown
Gemblespeth
Lalenton
Edlingham
Buston
Blackburnhaugh
Wharton
Shilbottle
Warkworth
Uninhabited
Read
Moor
Hingle
Rothbury
Whitley
Ambel
Butterhaugh
Ground
Durtree
Tosson's Mag.
Bramshaugh
Acklington Park
Thecam
West
Elsdon
Wingates
Felton
Togsden
Cragshele
Garetshild
Grounds
W. Thurston
Coquet I.
Bellin
Hollinhead
Raylees
N. Witton
Horsley
Withrington P.
Corvenside
Catchaside
Rothley
Trittington
Olgham
Emothough
North Tyne R.
Target Nuke
Stanton
Woodhorn
Desert
Dalle Castle
Woodburrs
K. Whelpington
Mitford
Bothal
Newbiggin
The Wast
Chestrum
Hartburn
Melton
Morpeth
Wansbeck R.
Billingham
Bellerley
Throcking
Bolham
Netherton
Cambo-ise
Hawthorn
Ramshaw
Butchester
Kirk Harle
Whalton
Bedlington
Heinley steel
Greenley Clu
Chin Chace
Colwell
Stanington
Horton
Blyth
Lowes Forrest
Symondbury
Chollerton
K. Heaton
Belsey
Shotton
Blyth R.
Iverton
Haydon
Ward
Bingfield
Pont Eland
Dennington
Seaton Road
Haltwesell
Johnly
Halton
Stannerton
Witchsteds
Monkseaton
Plainmiller
Hexham
Corbridge
Kenton
Whitley
Tinmouth Castle
Langley Cast
Oningham
Newburn
Gofford
L. Benton
Walls End
Lambley
Toddswood
Plank
Park
St. Andrew
NEWCASTLE
S. Sheilds
Eiles
Winnelran
Whitfield
Grundridge
St. Peters
Mickley
Knarsdale
Alston Town
Sleley
Shotley
Ouston
Newbiggin
Espenshiles
Whittin-sul
Kirkhaugh
Alne
Haw
Cuple
Blanchland
Allonheads Cole Clugh
Sunderland
PART OF THE
BISHOPRICK OF DURHAM

PART OF CUMBERLAND

THE GERMAN OCEAN

FOREWORD

We are used to seeing portraits of family members or famous people in history but Professor Middlemas's book of Alnwick portraits is a wonderful snapshot of ordinary people going about their business in a small town in the 1830s. The skill of the artist and the quality of the reproductions give us a clear view of their clothing whilst character is etched on weathered faces. No doubt the descendants of these characters now roam the streets of Alnwick and will welcome this insight into the daily lives of their ancestors.

The Duke of Northumberland
January 2010

Percy Forster's drawings give a remarkable insight into the people of Alnwick in the 1830s – their occupations and trades – and also the individuals who made up that society. But rather than produce 'types' or caricatures, Forster observes each individual with care, and delineates them with great felicity. This is a fascinating portraiture of the everyday world, focussing on those whose lives are rarely seen prior to the emergence of photography later in the century.

Sandy Nairne
Director, National Portrait Gallery

OPPOSITE *Plate 3.*
Thomas Kirchen's map of
Northumberland, from The
Antiquties of England
and Wales *(1786) by*
Henry Boswell.

CHAPTER 1
PERCY FORSTER AND ALNWICK'S PEOPLE

A BATTERED FOLIO VOLUME, its blue cover falling away, some of its pages stained or crumbled: it holds just over a hundred pencil sketches, mostly numbered (irregularly), each hinged on to the book's pages, so that the handful of portraits *verso* can also be seen; with brief titles, dates and comments in the artist's hand (repeated later but more clearly and below, probably by my father in the 1920s). Some of the portraits have decayed with damp: two or three have been irrevocably lost.

I inherited it from my grandfather, a country solicitor, more than thirty years ago, from his office in a mid-eighteenth century building in Alnwick's main street, Bondgate Without, in Northumberland, where it had lain for a century and a half among piles of documents reaching back to the sixteenth century, covered in soot from the local coal fires, unexamined except by George Tate, the Alnwick historian in the 1860s, even then unacknowledged. I put it aside on a safe, dry shelf, to be shown as a curiosity to friends. But over the years the portraits crept up on me like Pirandello's *Six Characters in Search of an Author*.

They had to wait. There were more urgent books, and a professional career in what came to be known as contemporary history. But gradually they became a louder voice, almost an obsession, forcing the question, what were these people really like? I began to look at Alnwick, the town where I was born a century after the artist's project ended, to ask, why did he undertake it, what did he mean to do, and what sort of community was it that they lived in?

Preservation became the first priority. Thanks to the help of a gifted Sussex photographer, Colin Baxter, who spent days teasing out clarity by digital means, they can now be seen as strongly as when Percy Forster, the artist, selected, numbered and bound them up. The second priority was to work out how to present them, and this gave focus to other questions: what were his intentions, his principles of selection, in a town of over 5,000 adults and children, with another thousand in its rural hinterland? What was each one's social and working place within the geography of a small but politically very important county town? Were they chosen, mostly in the year of the first wholly national Census 1831, to represent, or to be representative of a community?

Behind these lurked a far more difficult question. Was there any means in the twenty-first century by which we could understand them as they really were? The barriers to doing so are huge. We cannot 'know' them as we might our neighbours; the letters, newspapers, advertisements of the time reveal only disparate elements of their daily lives, since these fragments all need interpretation, a metaphorical Rosetta stone connecting the languages of history. If it is possible to imagine them, is our interpretation enhanced by the portraits, as if they were 'visual aids'?

⬦

The sketches were done by a talented local artist, son of the Duke of Northumberland's gamekeeper, living in Hulne Park, outside the actual

OPPOSITE *Plate 4 [2]. Female standing [member of Forster's family, probably his sister Mary].*

ABOVE *Plate 5 [6]. Charlotte Forster, sister to the artist Percy Forster, Hulne Park Alnwick, April 26, 1833.*

BELOW *Plate 6 [88]. My mother aged 88 January 31 1840, lived Hope Terrace Alnwick.*

town; born, October 1799, the fourth son (after Joseph, 1786, Ralph, 1791 and Charles, 1792) with two sisters, Mary 1794 and Charlotte 1801. As was then the custom, christening came later, so that he and Charlotte were christened together in St Michael's Church on 10 October 1801. His father John had married Mary Greyson of Haltwhistle in 1783, so that both his parents were by the time of Percy's birth nearing early middle age.[1]

There is a sketch of Charlotte (Plate 5) and another of his mother Mary in old age (Plate 6) and a watercolour which, from its position in the folio and the fact that it is not captioned, is probably Percy himself (Plate 1) in wing collar and cravat. Another (Plate 107) depicts the whole family with relations going on a fishing picnic near Wark on the Coquet river. Apart from these, Marshall Hall's dictionary *Artists of Northumbria* (2005) gives a full column, next to Myles Birkett Foster, describing him as 'sporting, animal, genre and still-life painter in oil and watercolour . . . [he] practised as a professional artist in Northumbria, the Scottish Borders and Cumbria, first exhibiting publicly in Newcastle while working in Alnwick'.[2]

Despite these achievements, he was, like Van Gogh thirty years later, almost entirely self-taught. But from his late twenties he became a regular exhibitor across the North East, being made an honorary member of the Scottish Academy in 1828. From his studio in Chapel Lane Alnwick, he worked to private commissions and listed himself in Pigott's *Directory for Northumberland* in 1822 and 1829 as 'portrait painter'. His life spanned almost exactly the same era as that of Eugène Delacroix in France, 1798 to 1863.

In his early career, his name is sometimes written Foster, which adds to the obscurity. The only record of his schooling comes in no. 61 (Plate 71) depicting George Barkas, his much-loved schoolteacher; and nothing of academic training.

But from his later life there is no doubt that he was well educated, probably at the Borough School, reserved for children of Freemen of the town; and his talent was recognised by the Newcastle critics, one still life in the Northern Academy 'bearing comparison with almost any fruit piece ever painted', according to the *Tyne Mercury* (1828).

Forster's rise in the social order can be see in his self-portrait (Plate 1), which shows, even in his late twenties, a degree of dandyism, and in the implication of changing the spelling of his name, Forster having an illustrious Northumbrian history. In the same vein of social climbers comes another Northumbrian, John Martin, painter of vast apocalyptic canvasses, born in 1789 in a one-roomed cottage.

Aged forty-two, Forster settled briefly in Kelso, then Coldstream and Carlisle, before moving permanently to Newcastle. An oil *The Leading Hounds* appeared in the Royal Academy in London in 1845; two at least at the British Institution in 1854, and *The Greenland Falcon* at the Suffolk Street Gallery 1859 — after which nothing is known of him except that his work now commands high prices: one mezzotint of his 'celebrated short-horned cow, Bracelet' being engraved by no less than Thomas Landseer.[3]

All Forster's exhibited oils were typical of the period: posed portraits, bowls of fruit, still lifes, dead game, birds, hounds and the inevitable large, squarish prize cattle grazing on the surrounding great estates. Like most of his contemporaries, his clients were local gentry and well-to-do farmers and professional families in the town. His style evidently owed much to Thomas Bewick, the great naturalist engraver, whom he knew professionally from the editions published by William Davison, the Alnwick publisher/printer; and possibly from meeting him during Bewick's

summer holidays at Chillingham, 15 miles away. One drawing in this folio, 'Evening' (no. 110) closely resembles a Bewick endplate. Like Bewick, he refused to bolster his clients' pride in great fat farm beasts by making them larger than they were by putting, as Bewick said, 'great lumps of fat here and there to please a few cattle-makers', as his drawing of a cow at Alnwick market demonstrates.

But the pencil portraits in this folio, done for his own pleasure and the family's amusement, are very different from the work of often-repetitive still-life painters of the mid-nineteenth century. They are very well drawn and skilful, the character of each face showing through with economy of line, sharply delineated and entirely without the sentimentality or anthropological curiosity of most early nineteenth-century studies of working men and women — in no way resembling the Victorians' cosy views of smiling cottagers outside their hovels.

Mostly of men, unsurprisingly for the period, they show people as they appeared to him while he drew, or as he finished them off shortly afterwards, being meticulous to note 'from memory',[4] standing, sitting reading the paper, walking in the street, coming home from work laden with firewood to light the stove for supper, ready to go out fishing, ferreting or hunting, in their day-to-day clothes and tall hats, often with their dogs at heel. Details of clothes and the subtle grading from homespun fabric to tailored cloth, fob watch and chain with seals, emphasise the status or show the subject's work: the fardel of logs on a labourer's shoulder and the eels hanging from a street crier's hoop.

There is none of the obsequiousness to the Duke's high status and that of his friends for which most contemporary portraitists were paid, nor the woodenness of what is now admired as naïve art — which continued under another discipline in the early studio-posed daguerreo-types and photographs which were to follow in the later 1840s. Instead, the influences which shaped these portraits took account of what had seeped into the North East, not just from late eighteenth-century classicism but the early nine-teenth-century illustrated travels in Italy, and the discoveries made after Napoleon's conquest of Egypt in 1798–9. There is also a recognisable link to Samuel Palmer, in the sense that, for both, there was a common world of toil, humble and hard work from dawn to dusk, that was not yet overlaid by the more overtly moralistic approach of Courbet and Jean-François Millet in the mid-nineteenth century.

By coincidence, at just this period, at Shoreham in Kent, Palmer (who was the same age) was hiding away never-published watercol-ours, in what he called his 'Curiosity Portfolio'. Like Forster, this decade saw most of his best work, before economic necessity drove him to more routine commercial work.

Alnwick in 1831 remained an important centre of the North East economy, culture and politics, and not only because the Dukes of Northumberland, owners of 160,000 acres, had their main country residence in the huge castle overlooking the town (complemented by the great Adam-designed Sion Park outside London and Northumberland House at the capital's smart centre). The town did not simply live off its 600-year history since it had been besieged by William the Lion, King of Scotland. Within an unusually large agricultural parish, it provided the marketing and transport systems for an agricultural region served by large numbers of traders and artisans, still organised in ten separate guilds. It gave substance to a growing number of professional groups who provided legal contracts and banking or insurance facilities for their busi-nesses, relatively up-to-date medicine for those families who could pay, and the comforts of reli-gion, either through the Established church or its Presbyterian, non-conformist and Dissenting competitors—who by the 1830s were in the major-ity. Beyond that, it was becoming provincial focus for two of the great reforming movements: the Parliamentary Reform Act, 1832 and Municipal Corporations reform 1834–5.

According to the Census of 1831, which gave only numbers not individuals' names, Alnwick's parish boundaries covered 16,250 acres; that is, its large extent comprised many farms, moor-land, the Duke's park, and small villages such

LEFT *Plate 8 [73]. Ald Molly Todd 1831 from memory October 14 1831. Long hostess at Coal Eglingham.*

children out of 103. Apart from his sister and his mother, the women are engaged on domestic jobs in their homes; or like 'Old Peg Downison', selling fruit in the streets (Plate 7). The exception, Old Molly Todd, hostess at the tavern (Plate 8) displays the only female with some authority — at least over her guests.

Since men of mature age were his focus, seventy-nine portrayed from a headcount of 1,350 adult males, represented approximately one in sixteen. But what were his aims and reasons for selection? The majority are tradespeople, professionals, artisans, with a smaller number of labourers from the mainly rural working class; but these are at least numerically proportionate to the seven members of the aristocracy or gentry.

This is a quite different agenda from those of painters and cartoonists of the 1790s and Napoleonic War era. Gillray's and Rowlandson's often savage caricatures looked for their sources to a very turbulent time of street protests going back to John Wilkes, and the images of the French Revolution, caring only that their victims should be recognisable by name and exaggerated physiognomy. (c.f. Gillray's cartoon of Charles James Fox, in which the great Whig statesman appears as 'a Democrat' a creature of bloodstained, hairy animal body, a murderous mob leader.) The milder cartoons of Bunbury or Tenniel and Leech, mocking illustrations of upper class pretensions and folly, are scarcely ever specific portraits.

John Kay's later eighteenth-century drawings of notable figures from the Scottish Enlightenment fall in between caricature and portrayal: these were published by Hugh Paton of Edinburgh in monthly instalments after 1830. Yet Kay and his later editors still used the word 'caricature'.[6] According to Kay's *DNB* biography, his contemporaries extolled his portrait-caricatures

as Denwick. Its population of 6,788 lived nine-tenths in the urban area. Of the total of 3,141 males and 3,647 women, roughly half were under sixteen, a proportion comparable to Third World countries today. Within the town itself, expanding to new Regency streets radiating out from the traditional centre, there were roughly 2,700 men, 3,200 women. The average number of children per family was 4.3 per cent. Yet of the 2,950 people over twenty, only 182 men, rated as freeholders, had the right to vote under the old unreformed parliamentary system, of whom no more than forty-two were actually resident in the parish.[5]

Forster's project largely ignored those under twenty years of age, apart from a few sketches of children playing, and concentrated heavily on men. He drew only eleven women and thirteen

ABOVE *Plate 9 [80]. Wise Willie from memory 1832. A well-known character in Alnwick. Woodman.*

BELOW *Plate 10 [82]. Edward Stamp March 14 1840. Banker.*

for their 'likeness' to the originals, displaying 'intimacy as well as quaintness'. Never published, Forster's portraits have no such testimonials, and therefore cannot, in themselves, answer the question why these, and to what end?

Forster's people are not caricatures. Neither are they what might be termed early social-scientific illustrations, like John Dempsey's watercolour portraits of men of the working class and underclass, posed as if for a police inspection, ranging from a Jamaican beggar in London and a gardener from Durham to fishmongers, lunatics and war veterans, which one commentator describes as 'almost a scientific presentation – specimens like butterflies on pins'.[7]

But Forster's approach is strikingly similar to that of Henry Vandyke Cooper, the illustrator of *Gray's Anatomy*, first published in 1858.[8] Like him, but thirty years earlier, Forster sought anatomical accuracy, not only in his faces but in his people's deportment – which is technically accurate, from the Duke's high bearing to the stooped shoulders of the day-labourer Wise Willie (Plate 9). He achieves the perception of personality without exaggeration, gives clues to character and status almost without need for captions. His lively, painless dissections have none of the static sadism of his immediate predecessors.

Indeed there is no exact parallel in British art until the twentieth-century work of Edward Ardizzone in the pubs of Maida Vale.

Like Cooper's work, the perception of class or status lies in the clothes, the boots, the type of headgear, the back, crooked or straight. There is a certain technical equality, unusual for the Regency period and the reign of William IV, in which as much care, attention and skill are devoted to Willie the Woodman and Old Meg as to Hugh Percy 3rd Duke – possibly more. The

Duke is obviously better dressed, but not more carefully drawn, and a certain blandness suggests the smooth outward face of power (Plate 97). The corn factor Billy Smith (Plate 56) sitting with his newspaper, the banker Edward Stamp (Plate 10) surveying the town, the draper and the fisherman in his vast leather boots and oilskins Robin Patterson (Plate 11) are more perceptive in the social sense than anything else of the period, if one leaves aside the later fictional characters of George Eliot or Elizabeth Gaskell.

They are also equal in another sense, not simply because Forster selected them to draw, but because he chose to put them all on the same paper of the same size (like today's A4), using the same techniques and format. There is no technical specialisation, there are no backgrounds for example, except for two or three family parties, focus being wholly on the figure, whether indoors or in the street. Yet unlike the photographers

who soon followed, there is no 'civil contract of portraiture' which would entitle the viewer to meet them as 'witnesses for the people or events represented'.[9] Thus the gentry exist on the same level as all the others, even the little boys playing hoopla and marbles. Greater respect is reserved for the artist's mother and sister, or Foster's schoolmaster, George Barkas (Plate 71) 'I was taught at his school and never knew a better man', and Old Thew the farmer, still active in his ninety-seventh year (Plate 12) than for the notables of the town.

The subjects do not tell a story in any narrative sense, though John Thew had nearly a century of experience. A farmer all his life, he would have remembered, as a young man, the Seven Years' War and the loss of the American colonies; many of the others could have described the Napoleonic War and Waterloo to the six-year-olds running in the street. Memory's conjunction slices through chronology yet demonstrates how

LEFT *Plate 11 [89]. Robin Patterson August 12 1832, Fisherman Newton by the Sea. Note: verso: oilskin cap/blue jacket/canvas trousers/sea-burnt boots.*

RIGHT *Plate 12 [1]. John Thew, 1830, aged 91, a farmer under the Duke of Northumberland and one of his oldest tenants. Mr Thew's ancestors have rented land under the Percy family for upwards of 500 years, and he is now the last of the race! [Gilfin Farm Denwick since 1810].*

different for each, depending on age, were what modern historians conceive of as universal forces of change.

They are mostly prosperous, some evidently well-to-do. Even the poorest here are adequately fed, their eyes are not dulled, their bent backs come from labour not misery. But the pauper and the sad, often derelict inhabitants of the Alnwick Poor House or the Correction House are not shown. Those who are, do not seem to remember the awful harvests of 1816–19, nor the years of rural discontent 1830–1, which in the south of England produced the 'Captain Swing' riots, the Tolpuddle Martyrs, and rumours of revolution. Instead, some who are evidently better educated and well-read, epitomise both the Enlightenment's afterglow and intimations of

Plate 13 [33]. Tom Beasley, July 17 1831, from memory. For long, woodman to his Grace the Duke of Northumberland, died worth £7,000. The good old times!

the approaching Age of Improvement. Forster is realistic for the upper class (when set against, say, Ingres' commercial, often subservient portraits of grand tourists stopping off in Paris to sit for him on their way to Rome, Florence or the German spas), but exceptionally accurate for those in employment, from trades people to artisans, labourers to farmers.

To a great extent, photography, as developed within a decade of 1831 by Louis Daguerre's and W.H. Fox-Talbot's discoveries of how to fix an image at one moment in time with the aid of optical science and chemistry, set up a perpetual claim to being 'true to life'. Early photography indeed made subjects look 'more noble', partly because of the stiffness induced by sitting totally still for minutes on end. But, as always, the camera was not neutral or impartial, set within its own necessity of careful light, background staging and usually proper dress — what Alan Thomas called 'restrictive rigidities'.[10]

The tourist's eye tries to understand the identity of what he photographs, and lives with that afterwards as memory. The historical tourist is equally reliant, because photography's latent power is to suggest that images *are* reality, that the camera or its digital equivalent, settles what meaning is, disposes of myth, and concludes the argument about what distinguishes us from them.

The artist, on the other hand, is quite unrestricted by the moment that photography captures: he puts together simultaneously a whole range of moments, past as well as present, together with aspects which the human eye or photographer's lens can barely register — something which came much later in photography with Charles Baudelaire (called Nadar)'s attempt in the 1850s and 1860s to show people as they really were. In that sense, photographers followed artists by aiming at the same target and learning from them – until, in an Impressionist reversal, painters such as Degas (born in 1834) in turn learned from photography to understand better the natural world and the individual.[11]

Indeed it is doubtful if photographers before the late nineteenth century were able fully to capture 'character' as Forster did: compare the Sussex woodman in Briggs' *Victorian Portrait*, Edward Reeves of Lewes, *c.*1860 with Tom Beasley (Plate 13). Reeves' grainy likeness says more about his work and dress, but less about the way he looked at the world. Not till 1864 did an American photographer put it closer: 'The original should be represented under such circumstances of position, arrangement, light and shadow, and accessories, as shall suggest character, while also conducing to pictorial effect.'

Although it is obviously not intended to be comprehensive, Forster's collection possesses a collective ethos: these are not just eccentric drawings bound up in the same book. But how to assess it in the context of a progressive town, spreading out rapidly (like the former Elizabethan garrison town of Berwick on Tweed thirty miles north) beyond its largely demolished medieval wall, quite different from the cities north and south, the urban agglomerations of Edinburgh and Newcastle with their far longer histories?

After all, Forster is in the picture himself (Plate 1). He is not just an observer, able to display character from memory and vision; his knowledge as an insider in their community, someone who had grown into the professional middle class within his parents' lifetimes, is what gives them part of their life. Thus if there is a 'story' they tell,

it has to be seen through his eyes rather than through documentary evidence of what we know about them, what they wrote, read, or in some cases said. In one sense, what Forster did resembles the Inquisitor's technique taking notes on thirteenth-century Cathar heretics in the southern French town of Montaillou, put together by Emanuel le Roy Ladurie to create a community-interpretation, or Ronald Blythe's interviews with local people in his village after the Second World War (*Akenfield*, 1969).

These could merely be a collection of people whom Forster liked to draw, as a private hobby. That would make them interesting in their own right. But there is a sense of coherence about the folio, not just in place and time; and that he bound up this selection suggests more. Forster was by then in his thirties. He is the inquisitor, his subjects not heretics but the Alnwick locals, and the modern viewer has to think in terms of Ladurie's eyes rather than his pen. But what does this imply about Forster's intentions and assumptions, and the place in wider art history of a highly-skilled provincial artist able, in his private work, to compose a sort of symphony for his particular town and community?

One could assume that collating portraits dating back to the 1820s, but assembled or done from memory in 1831, the Census year, was a direct or indirect response to the increasing interest in social documentation deriving from Malthus' fear of over-population on one hand, and Bentham's designs for an ordered, highly regulated society on the other. The search to establish a factual basis on which to set up improved local, regional or even national government, armed with remedies for inefficient agrarian practice or small-town backwardness and corruption, as well as relief for disasters and provision for the old and needy, stretches back into the late eighteenth century and lies behind the practice of meticulous investigation, from travelling agricultural experts like Arthur Young to the Culley brothers farming in North Northumberland.

But inquiries, such as the Census and its decennial sequels, commanded by central government, depicting on a parish basis what communities were in terms of numbers, status, education, inhibit the fundamentally different question: what were Forster's principles of selection? In contrast, for example, to the Census' focus on productive work, household size, geography, etc., Forster concentrated on individuals, dress, posture, habits; and his people are often on the periphery of standard productive work, being those engaged in pleasant or ill-defined occupations, such as musicians, hunt servants, street vendors, or game keepers.[12]

The fact that the portraits' numbering is irregular and that pasting up the volume may have been undertaken later from a larger range of originals, before being captioned, supports the Census connection, especially since the later ones are unnumbered and in a slightly different format. But why the folio was neither recorded nor documented is unclear, even though one note on the back of no. 12 (Plate 17) shows that George Tate, the well-known historian of Alnwick, used it in his *History of Alnwick* (c.1860). No *systematic* layout is apparent, as there are no lines of class hierarchy, age sequences, or occupation and only two women married, Sally Bamforth, the sexton's wife (Plate 15) and Dolly Wilkin (Plate 47). We have to accept it as it has survived.

LEFT *Plate 14 [68]. Edward Allen July 27 1831 from the life! A native of Alnwick a celebrated singer and ventriloquist, sleight of hand, etc.*

RIGHT *Plate 15 [24]. Old Sally Bamforth the sexton's wife, both very odd characters from Yorkshire. Additional note: 'originally from Yorkshire resided many years at the corner of Fenkle Street and Narrowgate Street'.*

Forster apparently left no direct messages apart from the captions, either below or on the drawings' reverse. Some of the papers have been folded, as if to fit in his pocket for a quick street sketch, to be tidied up later, by sometimes a day or a month and in two cases (Plates 89 and 95) after an interval of years.

In many cases, he numbered the pages in pencil in the top left, and then overlaid that with a printed number (52 out of 116 in all) and five or six have a separate, different pencil figure as if from a distinct series. Nowhere is there a clue to the sequence and it is fair to conclude that, if there was one, it lay in perhaps two earlier series, collated, possibly from an old sketchbook now lost, mainly in 1831–2 in the present version, those after 1834 bearing no number at all.

The vast majority date from spring 1831, the earliest being 1827, the last 1852. Some indications, such as his inclusion of his friend and painter-colleague Hugh Watson and Watson's view of Embleton (Plate 88) show that the selection was Forster's, not his family's: why else put no caption to the probable self-portrait (Plate 1)? In any case, there is no doubt that he wrote the captions, one of which (Plate 71) is signed, two others bearing notes for his own use, reminiscent of Edward Lear's directions: Old Thew (Plate 16) 'nose in red/ eyebrows grey/wig bay/cheeks in colour/coat grey with metal buttons/topcoat drab . . .' and the fisherman (Plate 11) 'oilskin cap/blue jacket/canvas trousers/sea-burnt boots'.

So the captions bear his initials, date, full name of the subject in most cases, and comments ranging from frequent use of 'a celebrated character' to 'damn you dog' (Plate 42) and 'as strange a pair of ecclesiasts as ever graced the Established Church' – Bamforth the gloomy sexton and Thomas Patterson the Parish Clerk (Plates 74 and 75).

It was for himself then, in the first instance, part of a wider assembly, long since disassembled. Forster's intention could have been to set out a crowd of individuals — but if so, why many who could not, as potential clients, have afforded a portrait and were, to the outside

Plate 16 [26]. Old Thew, aged 93, Denwick [verso the same 'good' 1832]. Additional note 'nose end red/eyebrows grey/wig bay/cheeks in colour with the nose/coat grey with mettle [sic] buttons/topcoat drab/hazel ring.

RIGHT *Plate 17 [12].
William Cleghorn, a native of
Alnwick. From the life. Now
living April 9 1852. 'He died
in the early 1860s' [note in
George Tate's handwriting].*

world, insignificant at the time? Less than half of his hundred might have become clients; and even if some were so already, the sketches are not easily viewed as trials for a later canvas.

The note on no. 12 (Plate 17), William Cleghorn (1852) has an addendum by George Tate, noting that the man 'died in the early 1860s' — which may be an acknowledgement by the author of Alnwick's two-volume history; but again, this could relate to the folio's later history, Tate being mentor and a close friend to my great-grandfather Robert Middlemas and President of the Berwickshire Naturalists Society.

Detective work cannot go much further unless new documentation surfaces. At least we can say that Forster's intention was to create a sort of memory and preserve it, if not ever to exhibit it publicly. This is how he read them, in the street, the inn, or at home, as most of the women are — at work. Even the agricultural labourer wears a tall hat, but these rough ones differ subtly from the tall hats of the gentry, as do the latters' boots — handmade and elegant, apt even for the Duke for badly or unpaved streets, but very different for walking rather than work.

Some carry canes, some rough sticks, and many have their dogs with them, usually on a leash, for companionship, self-defence or terriers for foxholes, hounds for huntsmen — a panorama of early nineteenth-century canines before modern breeding really began, when a dog show meant obedience and skills, not groomed appearance. The archetype of a modern collie, herding sheep on television, can just be traced here, as can Forster's own dogs, the lurcher with a stick in its mouth, 'Wolf a pup of mine' and Tom 'my favourite terrier'.

Yet overall there is a distinct social balance, proportionate to what the later 1841 Census demonstrated with its lists by name and occupation; and most of his portraits are of people of working age or at their prime. Perhaps Forster thought that the gentry and middle classes were already well enough represented by miniaturists and engravers, whereas the majority of his people would have no other visual memorial. If so, he was quite radical for the times.

Why not then give space to paupers in the workhouse, house servants and the criminal fringe? It may be that for him, as for many of his contemporaries with a classical education, *demos* was the community of the *active* citizen, from which the truly indigent, the rag and bone collectors of Teasdale's yard, like Athenian helots, were excluded. Forster's repeated use of phrases such as 'a celebrated . . .', 'a well-known character' may indicate the existence of an unspecified norm for membership of a community, defining who was worth the pencil line.

On the other hand, many nineteenth-century artists were caught in a dilemma, between fascination with the underclass which, as in Gustave Doré's engravings, could only be represented to the public as acceptable reportage in black and white, and the need actually to sell their finished paintings to private clients who preferred smiling peasants in colour to slums and criminals, the workhouse and the brothel. Given the choice, these would prefer Morland or his successors in depicting a working class happy if not prosperous, well-fed and clean. Herbert von Horkheimer's workhouse is grimly monochrome in the version printed in *The Graphic* but its inmates in the 'art' version smile, are comfortable and seem relaxed. Few artists in any case made what Doré called 'the pilgrimage to Wapping', the slums of any of England's great nineteenth-century cities.

Forster may have worked for a similarly discriminating client audience; alternatively, since we know that Alnwick and its environs was not actually a rural semi-Eden, that he deliberately chose not to record what Luke Fildes saw 'from below', and may even have welcomed the new Poor Law, with its harsh discipline for those apparently outside the community, the able-bodied poor who did not wish to work.

But the volume can in any case be read as an antidote to the drabness of Census numbers and the harsh conclusions derived by both Malthus and Bentham. Forster's method of categorising community demonstrates an alternative approach: particular, lively, full of amusement or fun. It could then be seen as a counter-attack in defence of what he imagined to be the real community against the intrusion of an abstract,

Plate 18 [102]. Hound with stick in its mouth.

fundamentally alien, mathematical definition, exemplified in the Census itself.

How should they then be viewed and read today? How can the modern observer of what is undeniably an exhibition (of which I am curator) understand their position in a county market town, their customs and affiliations, beliefs and sense of identity?

Ranke's famous dictum that historians should portray the past *wie es eigentlich gewesen war* (as it really was), is impossible yet endlessly desirable. Can we know them, rather than merely know about them? Can we grasp their point of view, their relation to each other, and understand their versions of their world?

This is not the same as describing a supposedly homogenous community in terms of economic geography, like Durham miners, medieval yeoman farmers, or the 'wild geese' migrant Irish recruits to European armies. The perspectives of work and skills, important as they are, are not sufficient to assess a cross-class selection like Forster's. We have to put life into the place, into what Edmund Burke called the little platoons of family and civic association: 'To love the little platoon we belong to in society is the first principle (the germ as it were) of public affections. It is the first link in the series by which we proceed towards a love to our country and to mankind.'

A reading of fictional characters in nineteenth-century novels such as *Middlemarch* or *Bleak House* might help to interpret the biographies of those who actually lived, and, in lieu of their letters and obituaries, the context which they inhabited. Yet none of these depicted here but the gentry has a biography, neither can they now be written – for lack of documentaries other than the bare facts of birth, marriage, children, and death. In any case, literary and historical analyses have their limits: too much is open to speculation by future generations revisiting the past for their own reasons, often with agendas that their subjects probably never dreamed of, resembling early archaeologists seeking to substantiate what they already believed, like Forster's contemporary, Belzoni searching for temples of the Nile.

This is the modern historian's great conundrum, after centuries of believing that scholarly analysis of past archives and relics led with certainty to knowledge – of which David Hume and Gibbon were the exemplars best known to Forster's people. Now we doubt even documentary certainty, because of the question: why was this written and for whom? And we are infected with a devastating relativism . . .

This is so even for a distinguished exhibition like the British Museum's 'Intimate Portraits: Drawings, Miniatures and Pastels from Ramsay to Lawrence' (2009, covering the century

1730–1830). The 180 works on show were all of literate, graceful members of upper-class society; nowhere was the question of community raised. Neither is the issue of race, soon to be a staple of mid-nineteenth-century historians' analysis of how the British came to be what they were, as in Robert Knox's *The Races of Men* (1850). Even *The Times'* journalism only began to set stereotypes: English/Saxons against Irish Celts and Scottish Gaels under Delane's editorship after 1842.

We cannot know these people as Forster did, as friends or acquaintances. To us Willie the Woodman and Old Meg lie below the historian's Plimsoll line, undocumented except in the parish registers (and not always there). Except by chance, these are un-documentable. On the other hand, the 3rd Duke was an international figure, a friend of Wellington as Prime Minister, British envoy to Paris in 1830; and Alnwick Castle's archives include profuse estate records and his correspondence, some of which is quoted below, in relation to the 1830 revolution in France and its repercussions in southern England. Gentry collections of private letters also survive, despite nearly 200 years' depredations, although those after 1840 bearing the prized Penny Black (Rowland Hill's introduction of the modern universal postal service) have had a better chance.

Omitting such a handful of possible but fundamentally unrepresentative biographies has the advantage that it may preserve Forster's sense of equality in treating the 'lower orders' as individuals in the same format and size as 'those who mattered'. Even if they did exist, a hundred individual biographies would not make the exhibition any more revealing, however, for the modern viewer, who is inevitably victim of anachronism, having no choice but to look at early nineteenth-century drawings through twenty-first-century eyes. The absence of biography is in fact a liberating factor, enhancing the unity of Forster's project, hinting at the underlying associations, place, identity, and community.

It also makes it easier to try to describe as a whole the world they lived in and the intermediate structures of a civilised life; how they experienced and assessed it, and how, at each level of class structure, they related it to worlds beyond, of which only the few actually had experience: Newcastle, Edinburgh and the other great cities, Britain and the Continent, after the long Napoleonic War came to be seen as defining Britain's role in Europe.

What the curator of this collection can do is to provide the context and the frame, encouraging coherence by containing it, enhancing tones, immediacy, and a sense of proportion to the whole vivid canvas. A salami slice can be made, like Ladurie's at Montaillou, through the archive collections, newspapers, handbills and early assessments of Alnwick such as Davison's volumes illustrated with engravings from 1822 onwards,[13] which allow one to examine the intersections of long-term change and short-term fluctuations, deep currents against surface tides, as they affected each person at that point in his or her life.

Such a context would need to document Alnwick's rural economy and agricultural improvers, benefiting from Arthur Young's reports of the 1780s and those of the Cullen family, who built up a truly modern business in Northumberland farming in the early nineteenth century. It could not avoid the diatribes of campaigning radicals such as William Cobbett in his *Rural Rides*. But to construct it requires use of *all* aspects of historical documentation, not just what are commonly referred to as 'documents' – which are of course subject to prejudice, selectivity and haphazard survival.

Newspapers of the time are like sedimentary layers for the archaeologists: they were written for the present not the future and were largely irrelevant within a month of publication. They, and sources such as estate records, drapers' bills, shooting and hunting records, are available as ways to interpret each layer in which they were made, soon to be succeeded by others.

But this context has also to be interpreted to the modern viewer-reader, for whom it is not enough to state baldly 'these people lived but cannot, unlike Pirandello's characters, speak'. Whatever is taught or not taught about history in today's national curriculum, we know that all historical change still affects us, because it shaped the world we know – even if we believe that we have powers to change anything. The future is linked irrevocably, if not in a determining way, to the past. The danger is that what we understand by the past changes according to the questions we put to it.

Far too often, especially in Britain, the habit and fashion for biography distorts the past, not only because it reduces it to a specific lifetime– whereas it is continuous–but because it leaves the author free to construct a version in which his subject is central (a situation that could only ever exist for a specific moment, or a single order like Napoleon's command to fire on the Paris crowd in 1795). The dangers of confusing historical empathy with the actual emotion of nostalgia are clear. We see what we long to see, find lessons rather than explanations, and pride ourselves on being superior to our ancestors, when we have brains and creative skills no further advanced than the architects and sculptors of the pyramids in the third millennium BC.

What does distinguish us is knowledge, principles of analysis, scientific discovery, and technology. In answer to Alvin Toffler's *Future*

Shock, one should point out that, given the circumstances and knowledge of the time, the inhabitants of Alnwick in 1831 were in much the same situation as we still are, relatively just as apprehensive and uncertain about being able to react to the unforeseen.

The viewer's eye should focus not only on the composition but also on the coherence of a community and its physical construction, its history, its buildings and the town's streets. What follows is an attempt to construct such a framework by asking 'What is a community?' beneath and behind the ideology of 'national community' (foisted, later on, according to Benedict Arnold in *Imagined Communities* (2nd ed. 1991) on Britain's colonial empire in the later nineteenth century). The simplest answer is that Forster knew what his community was, how it hung together, and what were the conventions, traditions and unwritten rules ensuring social cohesion. He needed only to select in order to illustrate. But the modern curator has to decide how to portray this conjuncture as an integral part of the exhibition.

Forster's is not a group portrait but an artist's construction. The balance of gender, class, occupation is his, as if he had purchased their separate personalities to hang on his walls. Such an ethos may deceive the viewer in an audience 200 years later, which has lost those people's dimensions of local space in early nineteenth-century conditions. This curator is not selecting portraits for his own exhibition of the Dutch interior, or Renaissance magic or icons, and he must start from Forster's own choice.

Yet the reasons for the Census and its criteria remain significant in a tradition of central authority, for the same reasons as that of the Roman Empire that compelled Mary and Joseph to journey to Bethlehem: they were of the tribe and lineage of Judah, a collective designation which owed nothing except obeisance to Rome's authority. In that sense, the Census and the higher, central authority that ordained it, have to be part of the canvas, not least because any view of community has to accommodate differences between local workers and immigrant Scots, town dwellers and their rural suppliers, farmers, bankers, lawyers, and labourers, even if their behaviour also varied widely, according to prosperity or lean, bad-harvest years.

Later censuses from 1841 onwards include a heading 'where born', but whereas this in Northumberland meant town or village, for Scots migrants it was put simply as 'born in Scotland'. This imports an element of social if not actual discrimination but it says little about the linkages within the town and among its people, or the concept of nationness as distinct from nationalism. In any case, the philosophical contrast between Britishness and Englishness, for example, goes back much further than the first census of 1801 in the Border counties, once described by King James VI/I after the Union of the two crowns in 1603 as his 'middle shires'.

It may be easier to distinguish local/community identity from regional/national identities, as Linda Colley's work suggests, even though the several layers coexisted in each person alive. Alnwick's historical identity, like that of its comparators across the River Tweed such as Kelso, was and remained plural, just as its population was never stagnant but changed over the decades as migrants passed through: only a handful of Forster's characters came from families established there as early as the seventeenth century.

Alnwick's sense of community was very definitely not imagined, nor did it depend, as was once

together by the Congress of Vienna in 1815. The nature of the glue holding a community together had changed since the eighteenth century: any literate person was obviously reading the same widely available newspapers, sharing in what Anderson called 'print-as-commodity', not just for London stock prices and the dates of fairs, festivities and future race meetings, but for opinions on reform, the status of Catholics, and the campaign against slavery.

A community of the mind coexisted with other ways of expressing identity in the same town, those of labour, religion, sport, or trade. Universal print was already eroding the ancient oral culture and old Northumbrian, which had been not an accent but a true dialect, closer to what was spoken in the Friesian Islands than to the south of England. Yet any account of the community would have to include its historical inheritance, its age-old customs and traditions.

The common reader, despite what he had inherited from his parents and local gossip, was now able to take part in interpreting the wider world, in a way which had been possible only for the intellectual elite a century earlier. This was so, even if 1820s journalism tended, like its modern successors, to emphasise the bizarre or the criminal; and its close-printed columns of argument and reportage enabled generalised speculation about how deliberate change, that is Reform, might capture the future. Newspapers in a single city, Newcastle on Tyne, available in Alnwick by coach the same evening, reflected political parties' cosmology: the *Newcastle Journal* (Tory), the *Newcastle Courant* (Whig).

Thus disputes within the community, say between the Duke and Alnwick's ruling body the Four and Twenty, over rights on the Town Moor and his park's encroachment on common land, blended with wider controversies, borough and

LEFT *Plate 19 [26 verso]. Old Thew, aged 93.*

thought, on the erosion of religious commitment, (indeed in the first half of the nineteenth century, religious enthusiasm rose with the Evangelical Revival). But it was subject to continued redefinition, according to the interests, affiliations and attributes of its inhabitants. Men after all may die overseas for their country, but for their town, they die on their doorsteps and in the narrow streets. World War, as the Napoleonic conflict should properly be described, however, did not come home like that to Alnwick – not until 1914–18, when the Northumberland Fusiliers raised fifty-four battalions (four of them Scottish, two Irish), more than any regiment in British Army history.

Nevertheless, by 1831 no one alive, no community could be insulated from what had happened at national level since the French Revolution began: Old Thew's life spanned the transition from mercantile empires, through the US Declaration of Independence, to the unpicking of the Old Europe, supposedly stuck back

Plate 20. Hulne Abbey from the North East. Engraving by William Davison 1828 (from Descriptive and Historical View of Alnwick, 1829).

Yet to some extent, the community's view of itself was still set literally in stone, in monuments commemorating the Scottish wars, the liberality of various Dukes, Henry VIII's despoliation of the monasteries (Alnwick and Hulne Abbeys now being romantic ruins) and the preservation of the one remaining medieval gate, Hotspur Tower, despite its appalling constraint on traffic using the Great North Road through the town.

Thomas Davison's account, first published in 1822 and reissued in 1826 and 1829, is full of respectful references to the power and enlightenment of the Percy Dukes and the late eighteenth century improvements they made to the Castle, park and the landscape round about. But of much greater importance here are its engravings, those which the local community assumed were symbols of the glorious past – even though the Dukedom was only created in 1778 once the last surviving Percy heiress married Sir Hugh Smithson, a wealthy and eligible Yorkshire squire with a burgeoning political career.

It took forty years before George Tate, the Alnwick historian, published his two-volume history, full of scholarly research and antiquarian knowledge, based on documents and surviving tombs and artefacts. Even then, the emphasis was still primarily on the medieval, its methodology mainly chronological, stretching from the Norman de Vescis to the Percy Earls' dominance of the northern Borders. But he also analyses religious disputes, sports and pastimes, markets and fairs, and the balance of power disputes within the town and with the Castle, setting the present within the past.

Historical inquiry may have risked, in Tate's eyes, becoming antiquarianism, but it was still integral to the sense of place and belonging. Even in Darwin's day (remembering that

parliamentary reform, the cost of paupers on the rates, or the status of Catholics and Quakers in relation to the Anglican Church, not just as a matter of precedent (that was for the lawyers to argue out) but as contemporary politics at every level. The Golden Age lay not in the past but was to be born out of present political discussion.

As an unintended consequence of the central state's increasing need for information, embodied in the Census and Commissions of Inquiry, ideas about the community took physical, even mathematical shape. Accurate maps drawn by military engineers, geological and topographical surveys, all built up a scientific and unchallengeable context, to match the revised boundaries taking account of enclosures. Surveys record numbers and dwellings of pupils in schools. These in turn made ancestral knowledge and oral history less necessary and reduced to quaint relics local rituals like beating of the parish bounds. Such advances in turn made the surviving structure of Alnwick's local government look outdated and increasingly inefficient.

Charles Darwin embarked on the *Beagle* from Plymouth on 27 December 1831 to return five years later with his notebooks containing most of the great thesis, even if social and moral fears inhibited their publication for another generation), history had only recently been established as an academic discipline, the first university chairs having been appointed in Britain in 1810–12. Forster was thus working on the cusp between an old world for whom continuously updated history of humanity was still the centre of everything, and the open, more critical scholarship to come.

Being a major printer and publisher across the whole North East of England, Davison knew very well that events were not the disparate creation of individual great men but were to be understood as a series of precedents and models for discussion or action. Bound by the requirements of his readers, however, he was not prepared to abandon inevitable and respectful references to likely future patrons. His book's illustrations still have much eighteenth century flattery and social deference about it.

What is clear is that the community's identity in the 1820s was already understood as part of a historical continuum, no longer dependent solely on folk memories, whose highlights Davison emphasised (while ignoring many of the subjects that the scrupulous Tate was to include, such as poverty, old age and indigence, and others which both authors ignored, criminality, gangs, policing, whores and whorehouses from which no town of five or six thousand people in the early nineteenth century was free). French historians proved to be more logical and theoretical: as Michelet had written in the 1820s, history was to be seen as a sort of *magistrature*, demanding respect equally for all aspects of the past, not just the product of emotional

recollection. 'Ainsi se fait une famille, une cité commune, entre les vivants et les morts.'[14]

Forster can then be seen as an agent intervening on behalf of the living to prevent them from being forgotten when dead.[15] He may have tried also to achieve Michelet's far more problematic aspiration, to show what they really wanted and what their lives meant. For his hundred, there would be no 'silence of the dead'. His work and his medium, as an artist not an author, is an antidote both to forgetfulness and the argument of relativists that nothing in the past can ever be wholly 'true'.

What he achieved, if the portraits are taken individually, may be modest, and apart from the fact that they are named, not unique in art history. Taken as a whole, it is of significance, not just for local and regional studies, nor just as an encounter between disciplines, history, social sciences, anthropology, economics; but for all concerned with the past-present enigma, the local–national dilemma and the questions of common good, common purpose and identity.

Plate 21. North-west view of the Castle. Engraving by William Davison 1828 (from Descriptive and Historical View of Alnwick, 1829).

Aged 97. July 16 1835 — old Jacky from Denwick.

P.S. 18

CHAPTER 2
INHERITANCE AND TRADITION

WHAT WAS A COUNTY town a decade before Queen Victoria came to the throne? England in 1801 had only nineteen urban centres of more than 20,000 people; thirty years later, this number and their size had both vastly increased, blurring the ancient distinction between a cathedral city and an industrial sprawl like Birmingham – which was soon to be enfranchised with its own MPs and a City Council. A town proves harder to define in the early nineteenth century, geographers of the time reckoning that a population of 2,000 distinguished it from a village, and that at about 10,000 it became an embryo city.

A town's identity, however, derived not just from its size, but its function, its history, its links with the rural areas that formed its hinterland, its politics, and to a great extent what should be called its common culture. Alnwick possessed all these but in its own peculiar way, together with a pool of self-sufficiency renewed regularly since the union of English and Scottish crowns by migrants from the Borders to its north.[1] It was historically English, yet the Scots armies' occupation during the Civil War and strong Presbyterian implantation in certain North Northumberland villages ensured a lively argumentative civic culture. What the de Vesci family charter of the 1200s had called 'my Burgesses of Alnewick' retained the liberties of the manorial borough, even if at some point in the later Middle Ages it had lost its Member of Parliament – probably because later Burgesses declined to pay the expense.

Three quite distinct towns dominate Northumberland, one of the larger English counties (leaving aside Berwick on Tweed, for centuries a disputed garrison, and Newcastle, a late Georgian city, capital of the Tyne Valley): Alnwick in the north, Hexham in the southwest, Morpeth in the south. None of them can be described in the same ways one would use for French, Italian or German towns of that period, partly because of better intercommunication, transport, a lively local press and greater social mobility. None could be classified as a *pays*, as most French towns were, often into the twentieth century.

Alnwick's population, according to the 1821 Census had been 1,404 families in 823 houses, in number a total of 5,927; a steady increase on 1801 figures that continued up to the 1830s. Its size was unusually large, the Parish area being 8 miles by 9, of which 24,000 acres were agriculture, 11,000 pasture, the rest hills or marshland.

Of the three towns, all growing rapidly in the first quarter of the nineteenth century, Alnwick can least be described as a 'traditional society', even if its still-eighteenth-century administration faced the same old problems of water supply, waste, educating and feeding its urban population. It is significant too, that when scholarly nineteenth-century history began to be written, Alnwick was treated quite separately from the rest of Northumberland, and by distinctive authors, Davison and Tate.

Disputes between religious preferences, Anglican Establishment, Dissenters, Catholics or Evangelicals, had divided it for half a century before 1831; migrating families brought their

OPPOSITE *Plate 22 [83].*
Jackie Thew aged 97. July 10 1835.

own ways and dialects to the overcrowded alleys and wynds, while the poor earned a bare living as domestic servants in the new, better-built but speculative outer streets where a wholly different aura of fashion and demand ruled.

Such slums — there is no other word — contained winding footpaths in place of streets like parts of modern Mumbai, narrow doors giving on to the actual paved streets, middens rife with sewage and disease, whose tiny tenements, most being of a single room with ten or more inhabitants sleeping in rotation, many belonging to the Selby family, doubled their intensity 1800–27 and doubled again by 1849.[2]

Four roads connect Alnwick to its rural hinterland and the cities beyond. First, the Great North Road ran from York via Newcastle to Edinburgh, already much improved by the engineer Thomas Telford, carrying the post-chaises daily north and south, but constricted by the narrow bottleneck arch under Hotspur Tower. Second is the road branching off it east to the small fishing port of Alnmouth. The third runs beside the Duke's Park wall towards Wooler and the fertile plains of Tweed and Till, having crossed the Aln river by a bridge far less impressive than the main one northwards and with no statue of the Percy Lion. The fourth road runs very steeply from Clayport up over the moors, to Rothbury, and south-west on to Hexham and the Roman Wall — a turnpike from 1753, connecting south-west Northumberland with the port of Alnmouth.

Physically, the town is easy to describe. Alnwick straddles a low hill, bounded on one side by Aydon Forest, the Town Moor, on the other by the deep cleft of the Aln river and surmounted by the Castle's huge medieval bulk, rebuilt finally in the neo-Gothic style in the 1770s, fronted by gentle pastures and the park laid out by 'Capability' Brown. Nearly all of Alnwick's medieval walls and ports (gates) had already been demolished in the sixteenth and seventeenth centuries, freeing up access to local farms and the moorland-common land that had already been disputed between the town's ruling body and the Percy Earls.

But what defines it and its people? It had only briefly been a garrison town like Berwick, and was never an isolated fortress against Scottish invasion as Norham or Dunstanburgh had been. Instead, it had for seven centuries been a central element of England's defense in depth, obstructing any Scottish advance on Newcastle, at least until the Civil War, integrated with the military system and managed from York. Only with the Union of 1603 did its strategic function disappear.

But it was always an economic focal point for a vast rural hinterland, its lines of trade and wheeled transport stretching far beyond the parish boundaries, along the coast and the broad agricultural plain north and south, backed on the west by the hills and moors of the intermediate range, before the main Cheviot line. As a modern analyst puts it, 'a small service centre'[3] had grown up, cutting it off from its medieval past. It had become an artisan and craft town, its industries limited to tanning and weaving which were both by this time in terminal decline; still run nominally by ten guilds, hangovers from the earlier set of crafts. Other older distinctions also survived: eleven separate constabularies, including Hulne Park and Denwick Village.[4]

The central triangle, originally an open space, had been partly filled in by the Town Hall, the Assembly Rooms and the main shops but it still served as the marketplace for crowded stalls, all sorts of livestock sales and local manufacturers; served by the ancient Saxon thoroughfares — Bondgate/Narrowgate, Fenkle Street, and

Market Street — and surrounded by a periphery of circular roads determined originally by the now-vanished defensive walls: Hotspur Street, Green Batt, Clay Port, Walkergate, Canongate, paved (if at all) with stones from their demolition.

Subsequently, the town spread out along the Alnmouth and Clayport roads and up a rise to the south in a series of late Regency stone-built terraces, Percy Terrace and separate villas. Beyond that lay the elegant mansion of Henry Selby (1769), Swansfield House, and other copies of the late Georgian style, at least up to the 1830s mostly surrounded by extensive gardens. These were for the lawyers, doctors and local entrepreneurs, a broad category summed up in the 1831 Census heading

'capitalists, bankers, professional and other educated men' (not women) amounting to 124 people. Such building tastes 'of prosperous owners who sought the outskirts in order to have special rural surroundings and at the same time convenient access to the town'[5] grew up and lasted well into the Victorian age as later, even more substantial houses, developed along the Alnmouth road.

At the centre, new cultural monuments sprang up in the early nineteenth century: the Assembly Rooms, the theatre, the two schools founded by Duke and Duchess for girls and boys, children of the poor, the Militia Depot, a dispensary, and of course the workhouse. Well beyond the town's limits had been planted other

SOUTH WEST VIEW OF SWANSFIELD HOUSE.
The Seat of H. C. Selby, Esq.

Plate 23. Swansfield House. Engraving by William Davison 1828 (from Descriptive and Historical View of Alnwick, *1829).*

Palladian mansions of noble families or gentry like the Greys of Howick or the Claverings of Callaly.

Rapidly changing urban geography was, of course, part of its inhabitants' daily experience. In Old Thew's lifetime some of the narrow alleys and overcrowded yards had been pulled down, others filled in even more densely, while outside, the last great open fields with their inefficient run-rig strips of land, had been enclosed, hedged about and subjected to improvements by landlords and owners, managing farms and estates from their new, stone-built farm compounds, with their orchards surrounded by woods or planted coverts to protect them from the north east winter gales. Even hinds and cottars' tiny tofts (timber dwellings surrounded by a small patch of cultivatable land) were being rebuilt of local sandstone.[6]

Within the town, disruptive changes also marked the early nineteenth century. The better-off moved out of the centre to the new residential areas but then required more servants — a need supplied well into the 1830s by young Scottish migrants, adding to the regular inflow of Border craftsmen, smiths and artisans. Some welcomed this as an index of prosperity after the lean years 1816–20, others deplored it as bringing in yet more alien folk, especially Scottish, (and after the Great Famine, Irish) to compete with local craft workers, shepherds and agricultural labourers.

It is less easy to assess how these population shifts and renewed waves of migrants affected Alnwick's sense of community, as that had developed over generations. There had always been migration in and through the town southwards, which impinged on the markets for crafts, horses, carriages, land, and houses, and their values, rentals, and tenures — though the evidence suggests a steady rate of change rather than radical new developments. Attitudes to the poor, elderly and indigent also changed in the 1820s, prefiguring on one hand the harsh new Poor Law regime for the able-bodied paupers after 1834, on the other, better charitable provision for the truly needy via schools, dispensary, hospital, and church.

It would take a century before the soot from local coal stained these new buildings, stone and brick, and, as it had always done, the washing hanging out across the alleys. The contrast between the shabby, dilapidated back streets and the new terraces matched the gulf between the latter's neat gardens and the foul smell of garbage, the absence of pavements, and the slaughterhouses in the arcades under the new Assembly Rooms, next to the food and animal stalls around the ancient market cross.

A sense of community is inspired partly by a place's history, not in some abstract sense but as it was actually known and understood: what can be called its 'usable past'. Some elements of Alnwick's history are needed, first to show what its inhabitants were likely to have known all their lives — and therefore internalised through habit and custom and indeed mythology;[7] second, to compare that with what the modern viewer knows now, including aspects unvisited by nineteenth century historians.

Central to that in the 1820s was the well-known local printer and publisher Thomas Davison, who had taken over from his partner, the founder, John Catnach in 1806, and already dominated Alnwick's cultural life. He competed with the Bewick–Beilby partnership in Newcastle[8] and others for the market in well-illustrated naturalist, travel, painting and historical books aiming not only at the gentry with fine libraries who subscribed to Bewick's Natural Histories of birds and quadrupeds, or the vastly expensive folios of Audubon and Thompson's *Temple of Flora*, but at a substantial middle group, ranging from the professionals classified as 'gentlemen' to prosperous, aspiring tradesmen who might only possess a few rows of books in a locally made bookcase. But beyond these, he ran the early lending library, subscription-based, catering for a far wider audience with stock of 3,000 volumes.

Having been forestalled by the work of Hodgson and McKenzie on Northumberland's history as a whole, Davison set out in 1820 to describe the town, its history and its setting. He revised his volume three years later, followed by a definitive edition in 1829.[9] Since his acute commercial sense responded to what these audiences required, he used what would today be called 'iconic images', either described in the text or illustrated by his own workshop's engravings. These seem to have been influential precisely because he satisfied his audience's expectations, taking account of what they already knew or were prepared to assimilate as history of their town – a short cut, in fact, to what they knew as their traditions. But tradition is not an image graven on stone; it is a society's means to codify the known past while adapting to future shock. It is never fixed but it helps legitimise change.

Looking at these, and taking for granted the somewhat obsequious compliments to the Percies and other noble families or local gentry, setting out their ancient lineages and distinguished presence in the national context, an idea emerges of what was local allegiance to its history/mythology, what was acceptable to readers, what indeed they wished to hear about ancient feuds and atrocities – as if they were Balkan nationalists in the late twentieth century revisiting the civil wars of the 1900s.

Davison's work was, inevitably, attuned to the politics of the time, though it did embody up-to-date and genuine scholarship (like Hodgson on the County's history), under direction of the Antiquarian Society of Newcastle; and his work was soundly but selectively based on archives such as the British Museum's Harleian mss. The same can be said of his more learned successor George Tate's two-volume *History of Alnwick* forty years later. But he drew almost entirely on the story of great men, centred on their achievements in action, focussing on wars mainly against the Scots starting in 1093; the Northern Rebellion against Elizabeth I in 1578; and, by the eighteenth century, their magnificence, generosity and public spirit. His periods of history relate to reigning monarchs, their wisdom, heroism or depravity, and concentrate on conquest, defence, schism, and Reformation rather than the long slow transformation of agriculture, trade or local industry.

Davison was not like Fernand Braudel, the great French historian, with his still-impressive panoramic view of *The Mediterranean and the Mediterranean world at the time of Philip II* (1972), in which he examined first its climate and economic geography, then industry, trade and population changes, only in his third section dealing with the history of states bordering that sea and their political elites. In short, Davison saw no need to integrate such long trends with the shorter waves, which his audience took as common knowledge in an evolving county town. What the gentry or aristocrats had done in the past was obvious from their houses, their lands and their prestige. Lower down the social scale, however, the medieval peasant or soldier was still only known to his audience, if at all, from the margins of medieval manuscripts.

For this reason, the modern analyst has to deal with what were, at heart, political matters: rifts within an overall consensus, the resistance of commoners to legal erosion of their rights to dig for lime and coal, or pasture their sheep on the Town Moor, which critical readers of Davison's history either took for granted or remembered with bitterness; the fury against enclosure was still too recent (the latest, Canongate Township being set by Act of Parliament in 1826) and painful to set out as an antidote to the prevailing admiration for agricultural 'improvement'.

He is short on religious conflict and the animus against Dissenters after the Scottish Army of the Covenant had withdrawn its garrison from the Castle in 1645, and gives a somewhat anodyne account of the subsequent decline of the Percy family. Yet he does mention the phenomenon of ancient families dying out, just as the de Vesci's did centuries earlier: of the Alnewick family, active throughout the Middle Ages, none remained by the 1820s.

Inevitably his view of the Scots and their history is lopsided, based on warfare and noble leaders, from the first invasions of Malcolm, King of Scots, slain outside Alnwick in 1093, to his successor William the Lion's capture in thick fog outside the Castle walls in 1174, through the Battle of Otterburn of 1388, when Percy and Douglas met in almost personal combat, to the last, disastrous attempt by Scotland to fend off Henry VIII's aggressive strategy, at Flodden in 1515.

English resistance is always portrayed as defence against Scottish incursions, many of the latter being little better than raids or royal banditry. Thus there is no impartial assessment of what James VI, Scottish Stuart King, later James I of England, intended for his 'middle shires' by his 1607 proposal for real union, rather than a union of the two crowns which had been brought about by the Tudors' lack of a male heir to Queen Elizabeth. Yet James I's far-sighted, if premature aim was shot down by an English parliament unwilling to see its smaller, poorer neighbour as an equal.

Davison's book may have answered one question: what was this town for? But it must have been a confusing read, setting out as it did, first a chronological overview from the Romans to James VI's union, which concentrated on the complex dealings and wars between England and Scotland since the Norman Conquest, then moving on to the history of Alnwick Castle and the Percy family (who succeeded the Norman de Vescis in 1309) covering much the same ground, embellished however with the Percy Earl's 'lineal succession', their heraldry, and their rivalries with kings of England to the south, culminating in the Wars of the Roses, the period when Northumberland had become an almost independent entity, separate and also apart.[10]

Davison wrote as if unsure whether to trace the history of the place or of its ruling family, producing in effect a double history rather than entwine the two. But his imagery stood up to the test of what his readers required. If the Percy Earls' uniqueness is his first image, the second is of the Castle in its early-eighteenth-century decay, 'being ruinous from the lapse of time and the shocks it had sustained in ancient wars' – a state from which it had been redeemed (within the lives of some of Forster's people) after the marriage of the last Percy daughter Elizabeth, greatest heiress of her time, to the Yorkshire squire Sir Hugh Smithson, a substantial landowner whose rise under George III won him the Lord Lieutenancy of Ireland and the Dukedom in 1768.

Smithson (taking the Percy name) and his wife had to choose between two ruined Percy castles, Alnwick or Warkworth, to restore. The virtual rebuilding of the former over the next twenty years was handled with the advice and guiding hands of first Palladian, then Gothic architects, and the greatest of all landscape designers, Lancelot 'Capability' Brown. Davison describes its new lavish interior, by the 1820s financed partly by the Italian banking house Ballardi of Lucca, its ancient relics, fine paintings from the Grand Tour, Adam furniture from the brothers' workshop in Edinburgh, and the magnificent library.

Outside, he admired what Brown had done without any reservation:

> The extensive parks and pleasure grounds belonging to Alnwick Castle, are admired for their fine shady walks and their beautiful variety of scenery, combining the pleasing vicissitude of rising hills and bending vales, rude moors, inclosures, and extensive woods, clothed in their rich and varied verdure, and enfolding the most vivid tints of nature, mellowed with the ruins of Alnwick and Hulne Abbeys, the splendid column on Brislee-hill, and many other interesting objects. The Castle and the estates have been much improved by Hugh Percy, third Duke and Earl of Northumberland, &c. &c, the present owner, who succeeded to the possessions and titles of his distinguished father on the 10th of June 1817.

Nevertheless, the earlier years of Percy decline are not ignored. Davison describes the

Plate 24. Brislee Tower. Engraving by William Davison 1828 (from Descriptive and Historical View of Alnwick, 1829).

Earls' involvement in the disastrous Pilgrimage of Grace and their restoration by Queen Mary in 1557, their rebellion with other Northern Earls against Queen Elizabeth, their involvement with Mary Queen of Scots, a suspect history which culminated in the 9th Earl's fifteen-year imprisonment after the Gunpowder Plot. A measured account follows of their promotion at court by Charles I, acquisition of another estate at Petworth, and the survival strategy and success of the 10th Earl, successively the King's Captain General of the Army at the start of the Civil War in 1639, who switched to Parliament as Commissioner in 1644 and benefited, after a prudent withdrawal to Petworth House under Cromwell, by the restoration of Charles II.

All this is overshadowed by the third image: the triumphs of the 1st, 2nd and 3rd Dukes. By implication, Davison compares them with the 5th Earl's splendors as head of the entourage sent by Henry VII to accompany his daughter Margaret to Scotland to marry the ill-fated James IV 'more like a prince than a subject'. Twenty pages display the first Duke's four houses, his munificence, his role as an art collector, his request to Robert Adam to design the first Castle restoration, followed by his son's marriage, first to a Bute, then to the daughter of a Kentish landowner, Francis Burrell. Hugh Percy, the 3rd Duke, was active in the American War of Independence but then broke with Lord North and condemned Pitt as Prime Minister, demonstrating that the family once again held to Conservative power in England.

For Hugh, the current incumbent, Davison has nothing but eulogy, from the award of the Garter in 1819 onwards. That provides the fourth image: status and wealth becoming power across the whole world-view of what Forster's Alnwick citizens knew – influenced by, but not undermined by the French Revolution abroad or dangerous radicalism at home. Tate, writing at a more critical time forty years later, after the Percies had retreated into a Diehard Tory stance, against the 1832 Reform Bill, was less fulsome. But by then the town itself and its sense of community had changed.

Davison's fifth image or, rather, set of images, comprise the buildings with which everyone was familiar, whether of great antiquity like the two remnants of abbeys now encircled by the park and restored as 'noble ruins', together with

Plate 25. St Michael's Church. Engraving by William Davison 1828 (from Descriptive and Historical View of Alnwick, *1829).*

St Mary's and St Michael's Church and Hotspur
Tower (preserved on the Duke's express orders
from being demolished by the local authority, which was aiming to remove the serious
bottleneck to traffic) or the relatively modern
public buildings and monuments from the neo-
classical improvement undertaken since the late
eighteenth century.

These landmarks, old or new, even those
demolished, can be read in street names
marking long-gone fortified ways in and out:
Clayport, Pottergate, Narrowgate, Watergate,
and Canongate, itself a separate township
down by the Aln River. The marketplace had as
its centre a carved stone relic, 'a neat cross' in
Davison's phrase, but most of the old thatched
houses had by then vanished, to be replaced by
freestone ones 'judiciously disposed . . . of noble
appearance'. All that seemed needed now was
better pavements and street lighting.

St Michael's Church had been restored in 1789
at the Duke's expense (which also covered the
display of banners and hatchments, symbolising
social rankings) with spaces for 1,200 in the pews.
A Roman Catholic chapel demonstrated emancipation, a Presbyterian meeting house an end to
disputes dating from the 1640s, a Sion meeting
house, a Bethel chapel, an Ebenezer chapel, and a
Methodist one, ways for a free-thinking town to
accommodate the secondary surges of disputation
after John Wesley abandoned or was abandoned
by the Anglican persuasion, in the full flowering
of the Evangelical Awakening.

Davison then listed the non-religious public
buildings:

- The Town Hall, with its square clock
  tower, since 1831 seat of corporate
  government, courts and Council and
  meetings of the Freemen

- The Correction House, with its nine cells
  and two separate prison yards, one for
  men, one for women
- The Fire Engine House, 1810
- The Depot of the Northumberland Light
  Infantry Militia with armourer's shop and
  safe storeroom

*Plate 26 [17]. John Wallace,
weather-wise Jack, aged 70,
for many years sexton at St.
Mary's Alnwick.*

- The Shambles, rebuilt in the Gothick style in 1765, with a 'piazza' in front decorated with Percy crests and shields of arms: the Assembly Rooms being on the first floor
- The Pinfold, to guard stray cattle, taken out of the now civilised Bondgate to a new area in Greenbatt
- The Poor House, built in 1810 to accommodate and employ twenty-two in-house, 323 outside and more in the 1815–19 depression.[11]
- The Dispensary, created in 1815 by local gentry, well organised, managed and financed
- The Savings Bank, established 1816, providing for the 'industrious classes' a safe and profitable depository, accompanied by the teaching of respectable financial practice
- The Schools
  a. Borough, for Freemens' children only
  b. The Grammar School, since the seventeenth century (entry restricted, like the Borough)
  c. The English School, from the 1790s teaching the three Rs and mathematics prior to admission to the Grammar School
  d. Public: Duchess's School for fifty girls predating the Duke's or Jubilee School for up to 200 poor boys, dating from 1810–11

With a few exceptions, all these emanated from the late eighteenth or early nineteenth century Enlightenment, mostly instigated by and financed by the Duke and resident gentry. What Davison described was not, in most cases, what he illustrated as 'eye catchers': the Castle, the marketplace, the monument to Hugh 3rd Duke

set up in 1816 by a tenantry grateful for rents remission in a catastrophic harvest.[12] Davison thus depicted a dual idea about the role of the upper class within the community: forward-looking, charitable, open to scientific knowledge and learned disputation on one hand, on the other, rooted in a past now heavily romanticised by architects as well as writers in the wake of Sir Walter Scott's novels. Both aspects, in his account, culminated in the enlightened leadership of a succession of progressive Dukes.

Sharply distinguished from its seventeenth century predecessors' political turmoil and religious fervour during the Percy Earls' long absence in the south, when the town had in effect governed itself, this version appears intended to bring all sorts and aspects of community together, in a coherent, demonstrable pattern. Alnwick's medieval past had been subsumed or taken over, remodelled in the same way that other towns and cities, lacking the real history, were to be given a fictitious one: like Manchester's Town Hall, decorated by Ford Madox Brown forty years later, to impose a unifying version of the city's origins and on the heterogeneous flow of migrants.

The icons were to be a source of fuller integration and this held good even outside the urban area by a sort of appropriation process, covering the Duke's 'park and pleasure gardens' including the aviary at Hulne Abbey, the fake ruins of Ratcheugh Farm, the monument to William the Lion's capture, the Observatory and the grandiose inscription on Brizlee Tower, taken from Christopher Wren in St Paul's Cathedral.

Above the entrance to this splendid piece of masonry is the following inscription:

MDCCLXXXI
H. DVX. NORTHUMBRIÆ

A little above the balcony, under the duke's medallion, is inscribed the following: 'CIRCUMSPICE, – EGO OMNIA ISTA SUM DIMENSUS; MEI SUNT ORDINES, MEA DESCRIPTIO; MULTÆ ETIAM ISTARUM ARBORUM MEA MANU SUNT SATÆ' (Look about you. I have measured out all these things; they are my orders, it is my planning; many of these trees have been planted by my hand.)[13]

In a wider sense, they helped to define the whole economic relationship between the town and its surrounding farms and estates. Davison's portrait of Alnwick's *genius loci* says a great deal about the town's culture and, by implication, the balance of power; but is short on the daily life of its inhabitants – probably because what they did – work, leisure or intellectual and religious life – was so obvious as not to require repetition. It was a guide, an almanac, not a commission of inquiry. That absence is barely made good by piquant details set out in Sykes' *Local Records* of Northumberland and Durham.[14]

Sykes adopts a similar tone, writing how in August 1750 on the death of his wife's father, the Duke of Somerset, the newly created Earl Percy and his Countess rode from Newcastle with a large retinue to be met near Alnwick by 'large numbers of gentlemen and the principal inhabitants . . . The Earl immediately began to repair the Castle and, with the most consummate taste and judgment, restored and embellished it as much as possible in the Gothic style. Thirteen years after this time, the repairs and alterations were still going on.'

But Sykes also noted, at the May fair, that the market for black cattle and sheep brought in 'immense numbers . . . very few remained unsold', an economic phenomenon still true in the 1820s when the new Market House in the Shambles had been built. At the inauguration of the water-driven corn mill in 1768, the miller Cockburn gave a great entertainment 'to give the impression of an old English banquet', at which a vast dumpling eight feet in diameter, weighing 147 pounds, was set before 200 guests.

Both Shambles and mill, and the new churchyard installed for St Michael's in 1830, (the old one being 'in an excessively crowded state'), were done at the Duke's expense, as were the repairs to St Michael's Church earlier in 1789 and provision of the silver communion service. Sykes' volume 2 displays similar themes: the Duke with Earl Grey founding in 1824 the Mechanics Institute (a useful bridge between a high Tory and a Whig leader demonstrating their investment in a better-educated working class). Seven years later this was upgraded to a new building for the Scientific and Mechanical Institution in Green Batt.

> Upwards of sixty of the members and their friends assembled at the Star inn, at six o'clock, and marched in procession through the principal streets to the site of the building. The procession was preceded by a band of music and the flags of the free shoemakers and butchers, and a tri-coloured union flag. Mr. George Tate, one of the members, read a paper respecting the institution and its projected building, after which the paper, along with a few annual reports, and a catalogue of books then in the library, were deposited in the foundation stone.[15]

George Tate was to expand and to some extent challenge Davison's views, and those of Thomas Bewick, who wrote nostalgically about earlier days of a harmonious rural society, even if he too omitted the dark side of early nineteenth century Alnwick: the grinding toil, long hours, poor diet and low wages for labourers, racial mistrust of newly arrived Scots, and the underclass of criminals, thieves and whores who serviced the inadmissible needs of many of the people Forster shows here. Later, in an 1871 lecture on changes since the eighteenth century, J.A. Wilson, a local solicitor and antiquary, showed himself more critical concerning Alnwick's ancient glories, pointing out how small it had been until the fifteenth century. But he did not run down the Percies, nor did he expose the seamy side. For that he would have had to reproduce posters, which, as a young attorney in 1829, he would have seen displayed around the town.[16]

> Borough Of Alnwick.
> NOTICE,
> WHEREAS several Persons have of late,
> by willfully and maliciously setting Fire
> to the Gorze or Furze growing on the
> Alnwick Moor, destroyed the Herbage
> thereof, and caused other great and grievous
> Damages to the Freemen of this Borough.
> The Chamberlains of the Borough hereby
> give Notice, that they are determined to
> prosecute every Person . . .
> AND be it enacted, that if any Person shall
> unlawfully and maliciously set fire to any
> Stack of Corn, Grain, Pulse, Straw, Hay or
> Wood, every such Offender shall be guilty
> of Felony; and, being convicted thereof,
> shall suffer Death as a Felon. And if any
> Person shall unlawfully and maliciously set
> fire to any Crop of Corn, Grain or Pulse,
> whether standing or cut down, or to any
> part of a Wood, Coppice, or Plantation
> of Trees, or to any Heath, Gorze, Furze,
> or Fern, wheresoever the same may be
> growing; every such Offender shall be
> guilty of Felony; and being convicted
> thereof, shall be liable at the discretion of
> the Court, to be transported beyond the
> Seas for the Term of Seven Years; or to be
> imprisoned for any Term not exceeding
> Two Years, and, if a Male, to be once, twice
> or thrice publicly or privately whipped, (if
> the Court shall so think fit), in addition to
> such imprisonment.
> Alnwick, 23rd Feb., 1829

The furthest that Davison went was to put some weight on the distinction between enlightenment and economic improvement on one hand as against the lack of any industry to compare with the Tyne Valley, apart from mining the poor local coal used for burning lime for export across the Borders. This is how he explains why its population grew more slowly, despite the rapid increase of Northumberland as a whole — 168,000 in 1801, 304,000 by 1851 — which of course came about through the expansion of industries to the South and County Durham. So we are left with a picture of a country/county town, as if it were a small principality, outside the stimulus of growing numbers of the young seeking work in industry, as it was to be out of the direct route of the railways which, in the 1840s and 1850s, (like Kelso in Roxburgh, also with a resident Duke) ensured that it was apt to be a backwater by the end of the nineteenth century.

Tate's sadness at what might have been, like Bewick's memories, ignores both the mindset and the political balance, the dependence of trade on agriculture which, in the long run, determined both. Yet it seemed to its people, and indeed in long retrospect was, a Golden

Age resting between the post-Napoleonic War unrest and the often violent adjustments of the mid and later nineteenth century, heralded as far as Northumberland was concerned by the 1846 repeal of the Corn Laws and the arrival of the new railways.

For the majority of Forster's people — at least the two-thirds of Alnwick's population who could read and write — the years between post-war depression and the troubled 1840s constituted a sort of renaissance, recapturing the Enlightenment era of the later eighteenth century and allowing that inheritance to be handed down to a socially much wider and more numerous population.

If a visitor had ridden over the moors from Hexham, or taken the Great North Road by mail coach from Morpeth, how would he have recognised this place and, without knowing all this about its past, appreciated its distinct identity? The modern tourist may come furnished with a guide; or the recent survey by *Country Life* assessing which is the 'happiest town in England'. (According to the latter, what took Alnwick to first place was not its weather (poor), or even its crime rate (minimal). True, it combined historical buildings with relatively low house prices. But it was the sense of local identity, tangible history, community and harmony of the built environment that put it ahead of numbers two and three, Midhurst in Sussex and Fowey in Cornwall.)

History is important in shaping identity, and at the least, provides the context in which to discover it, but as George Orwell argued, those who hold power usually try to rewrite the past to justify their control of the present; and in the process they manipulate the lives of the dead. For this reason, history as inheritance is a less loaded term than 'tradition' or 'heritage'.

But to frame Forster's portraits properly and in context, it is not enough to show the history of monuments and the cultural environment in which his people grew up, taking with them from childhood the views of their community that they had been taught by parents and school teachers, orally and in print. Whatever we know now about the coincidence of long and short trends, they knew in historical order, sharing Davison's assumptions even if the more articulate were to dispute his pious conclusions.

What matters here is the particularity of the town's community; for if the craft of the historian is to see the world in a grain of sand, it is nevertheless necessary for him occasionally to revert to the grain itself, and emphasise its uniqueness in order to reassess the whole. This means not textbook stuff, the Tudors and Stuarts or twentieth-century World Wars, but the circles of friends or gangs, the church choir, the layout of a favorite pub, the memories of aged relations (Plate 61. 'Morrison's pills', grandmother and child); everything, in short, that was required to know in order to belong, to have a sense of pride and self-assurance. Without understanding that, there can be no real understanding of this community, its associations and what its people believed was its identity.

Through Forster's lens, Alnwick and its inhabitants can be seen in several dimensions, all complementary: the circles of local trade, agriculture and artisan crafts supplying local markets and demand; but also the growing scale of its professionals, ranging from legal and banking services to what passed for high fashion in Dodds' draper's shop which had over 400 clients on its books even before 1820.

Plate 27 [45]. Ald Jack
Kirkup 1831 from memory
November 30 1831, for long a
driver at the White Swan.

Up to the late eighteenth century, its economic links with the North East had been local or regional: even the sheep and cattle drovers crossing the Borders by the ancient 'dry marches' did not anticipate exporting their stock. But by the early nineteenth century, long chains had developed, no longer following the old pattern of timber and fur trading with Muscovy, or fleeces and wool with the Low Countries. These now linked north Britain to the Americas: from which stemmed the sugar and tobacco monopolies centred on Glasgow and Liverpool, and within Britain, the new manufacturing cities and engineering plants joined by turnpikes and canals which continued to prosper even during the 1840s railway boom.

Into this increasingly modern industrial matrix, local chains of production were being assimilated. But they did not disappear: wheelwrights, carters, saddlers and blacksmiths coexisted in a cycle tied to horse transport. Local loyalties and regional traditions ran deeply together, providing a bulwark against an outside world which was still hard fully to understand or predict, as the Napoleonic War era and its sequel had proved. Family connections were more extensive and thickly woven perhaps than they had been even in the seventeenth century, certainly if one examines the town's dynastic families, neither landed men nor landless gentry but retailers and professional people; and these were, of course, Forster's people at work (Chapter 3).

The year 1831, in which the majority of his drawings were done, is a good date to set for the cusp of change, before the Evangelical revival's constraints on popular entertainment took hold, before the consequences of rapid industrialisation spread even to rural-urban areas. In the year Darwin set sail for the Southern oceans, this applies not only to work but thought (Chapter 4), leisure (Chapter 5) and politics and power (Chapter 6).

Where country and county meet is not only an intersection of work or politics. It is likely to be a market place for trading, merchandise, new ideas, or simply frequent gossip. Buckingham, Melton Mowbray, Guildford, Maidstone or Stamford offered similar ways to define their identities which is why carters and coachmen knew best what was acceptable at the inns where they stabled their horses and lay in narrow beds after an evening of beef and ale.[17] Naturally the world of hand labour provided a more distinct identity than what the professionals, insurers, bankers, land agents, or lawyers did, because the latters' knowledge was shared across whole counties and their qualifications or disciplines were common to the whole of England.

Alan Everitt suggested twenty-five years ago that such towns all had 'a core of dominant families', with their staid townhouses, well-furnished in the new, often mass-produced Regency style, with their names above their pews in church. They no longer resembled the better-off farmers whose labourers and craftsmen, housed in farm buildings, were *theirs* (apart from itinerant farriers and blacksmiths), but rather little coteries of drapers, grocers, saddlers, or (less numerous) millers, corn-chandlers, seedsmen, combining in a hierarchy of valued skills still dominated by the sheer expertise of gunsmiths, makers of fishing rods, or the carvers and gilders, mostly Italian, employed at the Castle.

However competitive, such people had to live together bound by a certain respect and by unwritten conventions. They had perforce to trust each other some of the time, pay bills in the end, because the community's density and the comments of others held them to it. These dynasties, even more than those lower down, had reasons to educate their children who would inherit what wealth they had, according to the fundamental laws of kinship, exemplified for example in *Mill on the Floss* (Mrs Glegg). Cohesion signified far more than diffusion (which was the twentieth-century legacy of the First World War) and cohesion lay at the centre of independence and identity.[18]

If asked 'Where do you belong?' the great majority portrayed here would have replied 'Alnwick'. If pressed, 'Northumberland'. They would of course, after the long war, have understood what it was to be English (or Scottish) but not, probably, as a primary element of their identity — that was for the gentry, clerisy, ex-soldiers or schoolmasters. They were definitely not yet proto-Victorians, but inhabited a mental blend of traditionalism, massive increase in knowledge, and some modern technology, where aspiration for improvement had become not just rational but desirable and feasible.

What was not clear yet (but which Tate began to investigate) was the fact that history is not a given passage determining identity, but a reservoir into which different generations and classes may dip, seeking the springs of self knowledge.[19] The history of the crowd was not to be written for another generation, and then in the form of Marxist polemic about capitalism and industrial exploitation: construction of, but not understanding about identity. Yet it was there in embryo and the radical protests of 'an Old Craftsman' against those in power (Chapter 6) recall the Peasant's Revolt slogan: 'When Adam delved and Eve span/ Who was then the gentleman?'

Traditionalists and reformers of the time of course argued the consequences of change, as they discussed the shape of future events in the light of their individual ambition, and as their understanding of the wider world impacted on their relatively stable community. On the basis of a shared sense of who they were and where they came from, they could more easily dispute *where* they were going — which was, in all its dimensions, a political matter. We must therefore look at day-to-day 'neutral' records to try to see how these standpoints ran together, and whether, if at all, Forster's people were a little like us but quaintly dressed, or our equals in a separate dimension, just as quirky, diverse, opinionated, even cantankerous.[20]

Behind all this framing, the 'six characters' have to find not an author but a book in which to express themselves. I hope they no longer float restlessly but can live within the frame, whose strength is not simply to pin them down like butterflies in a Victorian display case, but to emphasise their nearness to each other; which begins, from association in a single place, to constitute a community.

from Memory Oct 4. 1831

CHAPTER 3
WORK OR OCCUPATION

A MODERN TOWN'S BORDER with the country is usually defined by where its suburbs end. Alnwick was only just in the process of creating a suburb, as its new Regency Terraces reached out southwards into fields or the woodland around Swansfield House – the north and east being barred by the Duke's Park. But the town, like all market centres, had had for hundreds of years what most of today's equivalents lack: an intensive relationship with the agricultural region which its tradesmen, markets and artisans served; and from the town's side, where its farmers and labourers looked for their tools, clothes or transport for what they produced.

This was the geography that Cobbett knew, his contemporary sources for *Rural Rides*, directed at a literate, predominantly urban audience; just as this had been the road which Arthur Young had travelled from the 1760s, propagating the gospel of agricultural improvement. Cobbett took the side of the down-trodden labouring class; Young directed his investigations at landowners increasingly attuned to markets and higher returns on corn, root crops or livestock breeding, using Leiceister and East Anglian sires. Under Cobbett's withering prose these were 'tax eaters', inhabiting or actually owning 'rotten boroughs'. Neither could have imagined what is now called 'the countryside', the decorative, idealised open space around the place where most urban people now live.

None of Forster's people was idle: if not physical work (the numerical majority) and retailing, trading, he or she had an occupation, either as one professionally qualified by the standards of the time, or, by virtue of gentlemanly status and sufficient means, enjoying a position which carried with it a certain responsibility for how things in the community were done. The latter implied an element of leadership in society, but not necessarily the authority to carry it out: first because this upper class was no more united in its aims than any other, second because a leader's appeal varied, depending on his individual personality, age, degree of affinity with other groups, and sense of propriety or duty concerning what should actually occur.

Idleness was in any case not a serious alternative, even for the rich, managing their estates or businesses. At any level, indolence attracted censure in the Alnwick broadsheets and mockery from a handful of radicals printing their own ill-disguised critiques and satires of town and rural life. Too much of the Protestant – or rather Presbyterian, Dissenting, and non-conformist – ethos ran through the community, where only the grandest families, Greys or Percies truly lived apart from and above it. Even the Duke inhabited Alnwick's Castle, an integral part of it, though he himself had other lives in London or Paris as well. The criminal fringe, too, did not live apart, unless briefly in the Correction House, and worked equally hard, often dangerously, to earn an illegal living. Only the poorest, the indigent and very old, actually lived apart and they existed within a Poor Law regime dating back to the Elizabethan era.

OPPOSITE *Plate 28 [76]. Ben Nicholson 1831 from memory October 4 1831 a well-known character in Alnwick from 1818.*

Out in the fields, agricultural labourers worked for farmers, themselves usually tenants of the large estates. Around them circles of craftsmen extended from farriers shoeing horses to blacksmiths making and repairing farm machinery; and a separate world of carters, carriers, draymen linked grain harvests, sheep or cattle traders with village, town and regional markets. Others ran small shops in the town, traded or marketed their goods in the streets, or staffed and owned the growing class of larger retailers. Highly skilled leather workers, armourers, cabinet makers, sat at the apex of pyramids at whose base were carpenters and joiners, saddlers, glaziers, plumbers, masons, tilers.

Such profusion of small businesses and single artisans needed and supported a professional class:

Plate 29 [25]. William Baird, Rich merchant in Alnwick, a bachelor.

lawyers, doctors and apothecaries (surgeons had already emerged as a group distinct from mere barbers) while clergy and schoolmasters included many younger sons of the local squires, who were not able to inherit the land and had therefore to choose – if properly educated – between army, church, law or medicine, with a touch of politics according to taste and inclination. Given that some basic education was already provided for the majority (see Chapter 4) the distinction catalogued by Marx and Engels in the mid-century between workers by hand and by brain, was already in danger of becoming out of date.

The 1831 Census set out simple but useful headings: Families in Agriculture, Families in Trade, Manufacturing and Handicrafts (the majority), followed by Occupiers Employing or Not Employing Labourers (39 farmers against 10 others) and Labourers Employed in Agriculture (25). That Alnwick had not been a manufacturing town since the late eighteenth century decline of its tanning and woollen industries, is clear: 11 against 720 employed in retailing and hand-crafts. Then came what the Census-takers called 'Capitalists, Bankers, Professional and other Educated Men (124) and finally, Non-Agricultural Labourers (272) and Servants, 28 male, 313 females.[1]

Not till 1841 did the next Census record names, addresses, place of birth. But early-nineteenth-century directories such as Pigott and Parsons[2] listed the people themselves by name, gentry coming first, then traders, artisans, merchants and all the professional services from libraries to banking. Advertisements, of course, but the best contemporary source for many of Forster's people. But even if these directories set out individuals' claims in the market place of the time or its educational and clerical equivalent, Forster the artist concerned himself more with character, style, reputation, working dress, and relegated what they actually did for a living to the caption.

The interconnected circles of work and occupation linked producers, whether of grain, roots or livestock, with markets in the town, served by traders, clerks and merchants like William Baird (Plate 29), whose operations also involved transport by local cart or heavy long-distance wagon in a vast area stretching from the Scottish Border counties to Cumberland, Durham and North Yorkshire, feeding the industrial heartland around the Tyne and Wear rivers, still dominated by Newcastle but already challenged by Middlesborough. Ten years before the railways revolutionised it, a complex rural-urban, craft-industrial set of markets had already been integrated.

These formed interlocking circles and must be described as such rather than using general concepts such as 'industrialisation' or 'capitalism', which do not lend themselves easily to capture regional or local faces.

AGRICULTURE

Grain, root crops, livestock (sheep, cattle, pigs, and of course fish and poultry) in the hands of farmers who were mostly tenants on twenty-one-year leases, although large entrepreneurs like the Culleys[3] owned their land. Unlike modern tractor drivers whose skill is to handle ever-larger machinery, their workmen were categorised by the tools they used, from plough-men to reaper, ditcher or hedger; in livestock, cowmen, dairymen, shepherd and shearer, together with the woodman and forester, all served by local carters, draymen, waggoners – and of course vets ('cow doctors' to Forster)

(Plate 31) and the blacksmiths who made and mended farm tools and machinery, the farriers, (Plate 30) saddlers and wheelwrights, the lime-burners whose field-dressing was essential until the arrival of South American guano. At the town end, these were matched by millers, skinners, butchers and the array of dealers, merchants and shippers, while humbler street vendors and stall holders – often women – (Plate 7, Old Peg Downison) completed the circle.

Some of this John Langland, the fourteenth century cleric-poet, author of *Piers Plowman*, would have recognised as he looked down on the plain 'thronged with all kinds of people, high and low together, moving busily about their worldly affairs'.[4] But while their rural skills

Plate 30 [55]. Henry Trotter 1832 from memory March 19 1832. Horse farrier Alnwick from 1820.

RIGHT *Plate 31 [71]. Purvis 1826 a cow doctor.*

were much the same and their working clothes similar, he would have been astounded by their light ploughs drawn by horses not oxen, their reaper-binders and steam-driven machinery, their threshers and the quality of their hand-forged sickles, spades and flails.

Even more surprising was the quality of their herds of Cheviot sheep crossed with Leicesters, the weight of their black-horned cattle and vast pigs, illustrated in the agricultural magazines, as well as the powerful cart horses and fine mounts on which even modest men could ride, or gamble on at Alnwick races. To give an idea of the weights involved, the *Courant*, 1 January 1831, recorded 'a fine ox slaughtered at Alnwick, of the short horn or Durham breed, rising four years old. . . . The four quarters weighed 141 stone, loose tallow (for candles) 20 stones . . . fed principally on grass.'

Steam powered the pit pumps, draining off incoming water, allowing miners to win coal, mainly for lime burning and local supply north of Alnwick and beyond to Berwick on Tweed. One hundred and fifty years of steady improvement peaked in the early nineteenth century, despite the bad post-Napoleonic War harvests, a peak in which crop return per acre more than doubled thanks to better seed, crop rotation, and good estate management of fields since enclosure bordered with hedges and newly planted coverts. While labourers differed in reality from the cheerful peasantry drawn by George Morland, they were still better fed, housed, and increasingly literate. For them, as for the farmers who employed them, life was more comfortable and rewarding than at any point since the agricultural boom of the thirteenth century.

The typical agricultural labourer in Northumberland had a British reputation: the 3rd Earl Spencer asked for 'not only a first-rate

ploughman but the sort of fellow you have in Northumberland who can be trusted to overlook the other labourers'.[5]

Yet, like everyone else, they had still to cope each year with the harsh Northumbrian winter, a foot or more of snow for much of January, the bitter north-east wind, and the less frequent onsets of cholera or typhoid. In the severe winter of 1830–1, as Forster put this folio together, the *Newcastle Courant* recorded the Great North Road wholly blocked for much of February by three feet of snow, followed at the end of the month by gales and floods, which forced coach travellers to hibernate for seven days in Haggerston Castle.

If their diet was adequate – as Forster's

LEFT *Plate 32 [65]. J. [John] Bickerton 1831 from memory, October 10. A labourer going home from his work to Alnwick.*

scab, foot and mouth disease (though sick cattle were nursed through it, not slaughtered, being too valuable to lose). Lung diseases hit almost everyone dealing with agriculture and mining dust, not just the miners themselves but lime burners and millers. Some lost fingers, hands or feet in unprotected horse gins or reaper binders. Fishermen in their small cobles out of Craster were lost at sea, while higher up the social scale came debt recovery, banking or insurance failures, peculation, small-town corruption or (still not illegal) misappropriation.

The land agent, now a professional by education and training, or an independent farmer like the Culley brothers, lived as gentry. Yet social division in rural life had hardened despite all these improvements: chances for a cottar or husbandman to break out from his small toft or plot of land had virtually disappeared since the seventeenth century, as had their semi-independence, to be replaced by the habitual term 'AgLab' used in the 1841 Census. What AgLab actually meant is illustrated by Plate 32: John Bickerton walking home from work.

Farming had become a business, supervised by factors who kept proper account books, supplied grain or livestock traders, organised transport, watched closely prices and shipping rates across the country, and operated in markets as far away as East Anglia or the Merse, the ports of London and Leith. Most of what late-eighteenth-century improvers advocated had been achieved: enclosure, crop rotation in larger fields, draining heavy clays, liming and manuring them and bringing in effective machinery to replace hand labour. Only the work of woodmen and hedgers (Plate 9) seemed unchanged. Yet Tom Beasley, the Duke's forester/woodman 'died worth £7,000 (£700,000 in modern terms) – the good old days' (Plate 13).

portraits suggest – they were still prone to rheumatism or tuberculosis, that is, assuming they survived the high rate of child mortality. Labourers were already old at forty-five, not that much better off in physique than the farmers themselves, for all the latter's stone-built houses, surrounded by well-constructed farmyards and buildings, milking parlours, hay barns, biers, stalls and sheds, orchards and protective woods, increasingly the norm since the eighteenth century. Few could hope to live beyond sixty-five and Old Thew in his nineties was such a phenomenon as to rate three portraits in Forster's collection.

Risks were therefore endemic, not just crop failure, insect ravages and blight, but sheep

Plate 33 [36]. *George Henderson 1831 from memory December 7 1831. For many years the miller at the Abbey Mills Alnwick.*

employed the greatest numbers even in the 1900s. Meanwhile, at least until the railways were built, herders and itinerant shepherds (Plate 95, Hector Thompson) would bring the Galloway cattle or Cheviot sheep to Alnwick market along green lanes and drove roads, as they had done for centuries, while at the mill down by the river, the miller ground local corn (Plate 33) and lived well, as the drawing suggests.

Within this well-integrated rural economy, others worked in ways for which the Census did not yet have space – the gamekeeper (Percy Forster's father), Miles Sayer, the Duke's hunts-man (Plate 89) with hound, the hunt whipper-in and earth stopper, Luke Skelley of Washburn Cottage (Plate 63), the river fisherman – though most of the catch in Alnwick's fish market came from small North Sea harbours like Craster, Amble or Alnmouth. Craster kippers were already famous.

Meanwhile the town sucked in everything the country grew, to markets in flesh, hides and skins,[6] fish, poultry, eggs, or butter, vegetables or fruit. Twenty-nine butchers occupied the Shambles, incongruously set in the arches under the newly-built Palladian Assembly Rooms. Forster gives us three of these; one, the butch-er's boy having only a hook for a hand (Plate 34), another evidently prosperous enough to be styled 'Mr' as a gentleman might be (Plate 35), while George Nicholson is given the accolade 'respectable' (Plate 36).

Grain was sold by sample, while the fish market in front of the Town Hall on a Saturday offered salmon, salmon-trout, turbot, skate, haddock, whiting, plaice, sole, herring, lobster and crab. All this, with its smells and rubbish within a cobbled area 60 yards by 40 yards, under the eyes of bread weighers, flesh lookers, ale conners, searchers and scalers of leather,

Thus Alnwick's hinterland formed part of the modern business world, as did East Anglia, often in advance of the rest of rural England. Coal-mining in the Tyne Valley and Durham and the huge volume of North Eastern indus-tries ranging from steel-making to cutlery, glass and china, salt or chemicals, still led the whole country, though ceding ground to the Midlands by the 1830s; but agriculture actually

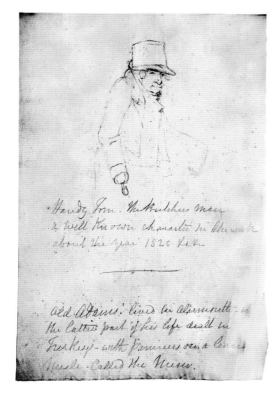

ABOVE LEFT *Plate 34 [75]. Handy Tom [with a hook for a hand] the Butcher's man — well-known character in Alnwick from 1820.*

ABOVE RIGHT *Plate 35 [92]. Mr Clark June 14 1838 with dog and sheep, a butcher Alnwick.*

BELOW LEFT *Plate 36 [78]. George Nicholson 1832 from memory March 19 1832. A respectable butcher in Alnwick.*

BELOW RIGHT *Plate 37 [74]. Ald Adams 1831 from memory December 3 1831, lived in Alnmouth the latter part of his life with panniers and a lean mule called the Miser, dealt in turkeys.*

supervised by two grieves and ultimately the Town Council's Clerk of the Market.

In such disciplined chaos, at its peak in the three major fairs of May, July and October, each vendor's stall had to be set up in a narrow space, handed down from father to son or mother to daughter, supplied with water from the pants or troughs, stemming from the Town Moor. This water might be cleaner than in the 1790s, but even in the 1850s, complaints continued about the stench, the piles of offal, dung and fish guts; at least the stray beasts had since the 1800s been impounded elsewhere. Housewives and servants crammed narrow passages between the stalls and the noise lasted from dawn till dinnertime, while Old Adams, driving his cart in from Alnmouth (Plate 37) brought 'a lean mule called

"the Miser"' with panniers stuffed with turkeys.

This was the town's heart: the fulcrum for the levers of farmers, fishermen, poultry breeders, for deciding the labourer's daily wage, and the hiring of servants, and the rentals or owner's revenues which funded gentry and aristocratic life.

Alnwick was not a self-sufficient extended village like Wooler, Belford or Rothbury, a few miles away: its complex society possessed the same range of occupations as the contemporary mercantile city, albeit in microcosm. It was certainly not a place where a romanticised class of yeoman farmers had recently been hounded into extinction by enclosures enforced by aggressive landowners. On the whole, in north Northumberland, twenty-one-year leases gave

LEFT *Plate 38 [69]. John Liddle October 19 1831 from memory, of Denwick, the hedger and 'lock greaser' in Hulne Park called 'Sly John'.*

RIGHT *Plate 39 [109]. The Hind's wife at Shipley July 22 1835.*

farmers time to establish tenure which, if properly farmed, sons could then inherit – a more modern version of the old Border 'kindly tenure'.

Those who suffered from the long effects of enclosure, on the other hand, were distinguished partly by their very small extent of productive land, and partly by their terms of tenure which exposed them to what benefited the larger farmers, enclosure of common land. The enclosure process was expensive, often more than they could afford, since it had to include fencing, redraining and levelling the old long-rigs and mounds. New hedges, while appreciated as a storm shelter, had to be trimmed regularly. But, restrained by bigger farmers who relied on them as havens for ground game and birds, hedgers like Bob Hudson (hedger to his Grace,

missing, no. 29) or John Liddle of Denwick (Plate 38, who doubled up as local 'lock greaser') came only once in seven years; so that the trees and bushes grew far out, encroaching on arable land, while acreage remained in single figures.

Bickerton is Forster's only choice to demonstrate the post-war transition in human terms, to the landless labourer, hired at will, living probably in a hovel of wood, wattle and daub under a thatched roof, with a window sometimes brought with him, and only a rudimentary chimney. His wife might bring in a little extra money sometimes (like the hind's wife at Shipley, Plate 39) spinning rough yarn, or as a servant in the farmhouse nearby: a hard life, excoriated by Cobbett and the radical William Place, when the yearly costs of a family with three children in 1831 were £31 (£20 for food, £3 for rent, £8 for clothing, but less if there was a plot of land attached and if, like Bickerton, he could carry firewood home for free).

Those who did best in Alnwick's hinterland were the new post-war class of knowledgeable well-to-do tenant farmers, of whom Forster drew four (Plates 40, 41, 42 and no. 77), housed in comfortable stone-built farms, like minor gentry, while the once-celebrated yeoman disappeared. Yet this vast, slow transition did not, as Engels imagined, produce an agrarian proletariat.

In Alnwick's surroundings, like the back gardens on Canongate Hill, there was usually a small plot for a few potatoes and chickens. This gives one explanation why North Northumberland escaped the worst of agrarian depression and discontent in the south. Certainly, before the 1840s, there appears to have been no spur to agricultural trades unions such as Joseph Archer tried to organise in the 1850s. A man tied to the land or livestock cannot easily

Plate 40 [63]. George Hudson April 23 1831. A farmer in Hulne Park. An ill-tempered man.

Plate 41 [64]. Joseph Edmondson October 10 1831. Buried October 19 from memory. A farmer in Hulne Park commonly called Cunning Joe.

Plate 42 [30]. Tom Brosby 1831, from memory December 7 1831, farmer of the pasture before the Castle, commonly called 'Damn you, dog.' With large dog.

walk away, leave crops to rot, or cows painfully unmilked. In any case, he can easily be replaced at the next hiring fair, and see his children forced to emigrate to the industrial towns of Tyneside.

In this economy, Forster's women are not apparently subservient. They evidently work hard but stand in their own right in the market or the weekly fair. But we cannot ask about servants, who were different, given their low status and subjection to a chancier sort of tenure at the six-monthly petty fairs and hirings 'for country and husbandry servants'. Forster did not draw these: the house and parlour maids, the scullery women or childlike servant girls.

CRAFTS AND RETAILING

Independent-minded artisans, traders and their families, not only co-existed with the owners of property and wealth, but had become interdependent with them, there being little risk now (as there had been in and after the Civil War and again in the 1810s) of wages being undercut by Scottish immigrants or civil peace subverted from below. Supervision, defined under the Town Council as proper weight, measure or quality, seems to have worked adequately, requiring no input from the central state. Crime appears to have been at least contained by local constables, while higher up the social scale, grosser forms of fraud were met by instruments worse than the Correction House or Morpeth jail: social denigration or outright disapproval by one's peers.

Some of the town's craftsmen and artisans practised across a wide area of north Northumberland. Itinerants included blacksmiths and wheelwrights at one end, shepherds and shearers at the other, while local carters linked town to village and back. The blacksmith might even be called a small entrepreneur, for

he could probably make, certainly repair a horse gin for threshing corn or draining a mine, as well as hand tools, even saws – though increasingly these and the woodman's axes came from industrial factories on the Tyne.

The ten historic craft guilds survived, under the town's Steward and Bailiff, and the four Chamberlains – in local political ritual at least. But Pigott is a better guide to what actually mattered. His 1829 *Directory* lists in Alnwick (together with Alnmouth and the neighbourhood):

Nobility, gentry and clergy 89 (of whom 58
　　living in the town)
Academics and schoolteachers 19
Attorneys 8
Auctioneers 4
Bakers and flour dealers 9
Blacksmiths 14
Booksellers and stationers 3
Boot and shoemakers 31
Brass founders 2
Brewers 3
Bricklayers and plasterers 3
Butchers 29
Cabinet makers and joiners 12
Carpenters 5
Cartwrights 3
China and glass dealers 3
Chemists and druggists 4
Clog and patten makers 3
Confectioners 5 (3 women)
Coopers 5
Corn merchants 4 (all resident in Alnmouth
　　port)
Corn millers 3
Curriers and leather cutters 4
Dyers 2
Fire and insurance agents 10

Flax dressers 9

Gardeners and seedsmen 6

Grocers and tea dealers 27

Hairdressers 5 (all men)

Innkeepers 3

Iron merchants 2

Iron mongers 4

Linen and woollen drapers 14

Milliners and dressmakers 11 (all women)

Millwrights 2

Nailmakers 3

Painters and glaziers 7

Physicians 4

Rope and twine makers 3

Saddlers 4

Shopkeepers (general and sundries) 18

Skinners 2

Slaters 2

Stone masons 8

Straw hat makers 8 (all women)

Surgeons 4

Tailors 18

Tallow chandlers 6

Tanners 4

Taverns and public houses (of whom 10 women) 40

Timber merchants 2 (and 4 in Alnmouth for shipping)

Tin plate workers 5

Tobacco manufacturers 4

Veterinary surgeons 3

Watch and clock makers 6

Wine and spirits merchants 11

Beyond these came miscellaneous crafts: furriers, stockingers, gunsmiths, gas providers, pawn brokers, carvers and gilders, architects and surveyors, brick and tile makers – and three portrait painters, of whom the best known was already Percy Forster.

The list can be compared to any one of a hundred provincial English or Scottish towns of the period. But what is notable are the surprising numbers of gentry living in the newly smart-ened streets like Bondgate, Percy Terrace, or in Bailiff Gate near the Castle; the proliferation of new professional people in insurance, banking or medicine, and the costly trades and crafts that all these well-to-do middle class patron-ised: watch and clock makers, makers of fishing rods (Alnwick would soon boast not only Hardy's world-famous brand, but its equal in Walker Bampton, only 500 yards apart), coach builders, straw hats, and cabinet makers (as against mere carpenters), tailors and dressmakers and the twenty-seven grocers and tea dealers. Old Brown the Hatter (Plate 43) is captioned 'a bad character who neither believed in God or the Devil!'

LEFT *Plate 43 [13]. Old Brown the Hatter 1825. From memory October 17 1831. A bad character who neither believed in God or the Devil!*

Plate 44 [15]. Tom Wilson, spirit merchant in Alnwick commonly called Winey Wilson.

Disparity between three brewers listed and the forty pubs and taverns which sold beers and spirits can be explained by the fact that most beers were brewed in the cellars and under supervision of the innkeepers themselves, whether male or female, while imported wines and spirits (and smuggled whisky from Scotland) kept eleven shops at work. Winey Wilson the spirit merchant may well have been a local intermediary in the illicit trade (Plate 44). Alnwick was not a teetotal town, for all its non-conformist majority.

Neither was its hierarchy simple. Several of the craft workshops' masters were also retailers, selling out of shops around the market place, up Narrowgate and Clayport, Fenkle Street, and along Bondgate, bounded by Hotspur Tower. Small workshops in little alleys, backstreet closes, might consist of just one workroom with a bedroom over. Yet a retailer like Dodd, whose widow (Plate 45) had richer clients, had a grand façade in Fenkle Street, in complete contrast to the street vendors Tom the leather cutter 'with eels for sale' (Plate 46) or 'Sandy Tom' Wardell (Plate 48), with his barrow full of building sand, who came and went according to demand and the day's catch of fish or eggs and poultry.

Apart from the house servants, who except on Sundays were more or less confined to their masters' or mistresses' houses, most women worked, if not in the market itself, in retail shops. They ran some businesses such as milliners and dress makers (Dolly Wilkin, the butcher's mother, Plate 47), but not drapers shops, still reserved for men like William Teasdale 'a good character' (Plates 49 and 50). They were a major-ity among confectioners, which is not surprising; what is, is that ten of the forty taverns and pubs (but only one of the inns/hotels) were licencees – no fair sex exclusion here. The tavern remained the only regular entertainment outpost for

ABOVE LEFT *Plate 45 [52].*
Mrs Dodds August 9 1831
from the life, a good and
religious woman in Alnwick
[wife of Dodds the draper from
1816—17].

ABOVE RIGHT *Plate 46 [35].*
Tom the Cutter [leather]
1831, from memory July 20
1831. A character in Alnwick
often seen standing with eels
for sale.

BELOW LEFT *Plate 47 [42].*
Dolly Wilkin January 5 1832
[wife or mother of Harry].

BELOW RIGHT *Plate 48 [53].*
Sandy Tom Wardall. A well-
known character in Alnwick
who went about selling sand
from 1815—16.

most working class people where of an evening they could jig, chat, drink or applaud the visiting musicians: which was just as true for villages round like Eglingham whose pub hostess was Molly Todd (Plate 8).

But ale house keepers' small, often dingy tavern rooms with a few tables and chairs, sat on one side of a divide: on the other, were the inns where travellers stayed and stabled their horses, like the White Swan, its Georgian façade dominating Bondgate Within, where those with more money and social status could meet for coffee or dinner, or simply to read the papers and catch up with local news. Each had its Chairman, like Wise Willie at the Queen's Head (Plate 51). Perhaps surprisingly, the Swan was run by a woman. Most of Dodds' 400 clients could be found here at some point in the day, except on Sunday when, of course, they sat in their named pews and went home for lunch cooked by their servant(s). Higher up the social scale, 'lady visitors' took time to go to the Poor House or the Dispensary and even to the stews around Teasdale's yard.

It is not easy, perhaps not appropriate, to try to pin labels of class distinction here. Forster's clarinet player (Plate 79) who worked as a leather

LEFT *Plate 49 [70]. William Teasdale 1831 from memory December 3 1831, draper Alnwick [see also Plate 50].*

RIGHT *Plate 50 [58]. William Teasdale December 3 1831 from memory. Buried <u>today</u> 4 December 1831. Draper, a good character.*

cutter making saddles and bridles, and the exuberant young butcher, would never have been excluded from the White Swan's company, nor would the commercial travellers staying for the night. Indeed the plumber (Plate 52) Henry Wilkin is given the title 'Mr', usually reserved for the middle class.

Better the old distinctions, effectively used by Jane Austen, between gentry and traders; but even that barrier could be crossed in less than a generation by proper education (Chapter 4). The shopkeeper, the small businessman, the grocer Old William Johnson (Plate 54) and the chemist James Wilson (Plate 91) – noted by Forster, who shared the passion, as 'a keen fisherman' – were undeniably middle class; the artisan or crafts-man fitted in between them and the labourer. Those who were not, could not join, whether servants, the poor, and in most cases the very old and infirm.

Retirement, after all, except for those with land, property or investment, did not exist. This alone divided society horizontally in contrast to the vertical categories of agriculture, trade, transport, professional services and landowners like P.J. Selby (Plate 62). 'Middle class' as a precise definition was barely used before the 1820s, working class not till the 1840s by Engels follow-ing Ricardo's 1817 *Principles of Political Economy*.

Fluidity, long a characteristic of the Scottish Borders, existed equally in Northumberland, more like the Low Countries than France or the German states, where with a little education and luck a man – or possibly even a woman – might aspire to join the White Swan's gossip. James Bell, 'commonly called "Nosey Bell" started as a shoe-maker in Newcastle having gone out of Alnwick as a boy with five shillings in his pocket and returned with nearly £6000' (Plate 55) – more than half a million pounds today.

Plate 51 [90]. Wise Willie May 3 1852, Chairman at the Queen's Head.

WIDER MARKETS

Transport underwent a long, slow revolution in the later eighteenth century, fifty years before the railways, once carrying coal trolleys to the keels waiting on the Tyne, branched out in passenger service.[7] Common roads were improved by locals, while the turnpikes, benefiting from proper engineering, like Thomas Telford's improvements to the Great North Road, became in effect the motorways of the time, carrying mail services, people and their luggage piled high on the roof like Indian trains today. Five Alnwick inns with copious stabling provided starting points for twenty-four coach destinations. Alnmouth itself offered berths for shipping, delivering to small ports south from Berwick to Amble or down to North and South Shields on the Tyne, and these networks required staff familiar with horses or sails, coaches and hulls.

Whole circles depended on the system's efficiency. Corn factors such as John Jobson (Plate 101) and timber traders might be supplying demand in Edinburgh, Hull, Ipswich or London, where delivery on time safely could be counted cash and delays in shipment or misleading descriptions of cargoes would be heavily penalised. Thus Billy Smith the corn factor is shown at the Star Inn, reading the latest market reports (Plate 56).

LEFT *Plate 54 [87]. Old William Johnson 1832, grocer Alnwick.*

RIGHT *Plate 55 [8]. James Bell commonly called 'Nosey Bell' and ditto verso: formerly a shoemaker in Newcastle, went out of Alnwick when a boy with five shillings in his pocket and returned with nearly £6,000.*

Shipping costs already mattered to Alnwick: not just for the timber and grain traders but the suppliers of silks and cotton to Dodds the draper, or wine direct from Bordeaux to the port of Newcastle to Leithead and his partner, a mixture of fine and ordinary clarets, and a surprising quantity of brandy. Yet, as Alan Everitt wrote, 'to a greater degree than is sometimes recognised, the domestic world of mid-Victorian England was still the hand-made world of the craftsman'.[8]

If the users ranged from local grocers supplied by carters from neighbouring villages to merchants habituated to long-distance wagons and carriages, each based his estimates and his profit on the largely unrecorded army of stable boys, farriers, wheelwrights, carters, waggoners, and drivers; as did the postmaster, the fire insurance and banking agents, the doctors (each with his own pony and trap) and other medical men; while yet another line of artisans made the barrels and boxes used to hold merchandise: Plate 60, Jack the Cowper of Canongate.

Lists of bulk carriers (rather than passenger coaches), departure times and predicted arrivals could be found in eleven inns, serving thirty-two destinations across the county.[9] Turnpike trusts ran the services to Morpeth and Newcastle, Rothbury and Hexham, while

RIGHT *Plate 56 [107]. Billy Smith corn factor, Alnwick at the Star Inn reading reports of the markets. June 1 1852.*

the road to Alnmouth port was constantly under repair for potholes caused by the heavy-duty wagons drawn by teams of cart horses. Alnwick's new build from the 1800s to the 1840s depended on local supplies of timber and local sandstone, durable and easily cut by masons and delivered to the new door by the master mason's waggon.

Here is the driver Jack Kirkup, supplying the White Swan (Plate 57) and William Burnett the carter 'a large man' as the drawing shows (Plate 58). Yet it is odd that Forster shows none of the horses nor the attendant grooms and stable boys without which personal mobility would have been impossible. Where is the horse? The answer must be that the horse was so taken for granted as to be invisible. A portrait painter might depict his clients on a fine horse, to grace his favour; but not an artisan or grocer, any more than his modern equivalent would show his subject's car or motorbike.

Today in Alnwick it is often hard to guess where the old stables were. Most have been converted as parts of private houses, some have been demolished. William Leithead, the solicitor (Plate 76) had larger space for three horses than all the clerks at their high stools, and his junior partners visited the firm's clients in a pony and trap as a matter of course. Absent too are the slow-moving cart horses whose drays blocked the narrow streets well into the twentieth century. All that remains of a horse culture in any British town now is the local racecourse; yet then, no aspect of rural or urban life was conceivable without the horse, its accoutrements and stables, often better furnished than the hovels of the poor.

The Royal Mail service under the local postmaster's administration (Plate 59, Billy

Carr, followed by Robert Anderson) stopped, predictably, in Bondgate at the White Swan, carrying the royal mail franked with each town's stamp until introduction of the Penny Post in 1840. It left Edinburgh at 5:30pm *en route* to Morpeth, Newcastle, Durham, Darlington, North Allerton, Thirsk, York, Ferry Bridge, Doncaster, Stamford, Huntingdon, Ware and London, and vice versa. Letters from Alnwick took thirteen and a half hours to get to London, ten and a half to Edinburgh – a first class post even by modern standards. A gentleman could catch a coach at 5:30pm and be in Newcastle to dine or attend a learned society lecture by 8:50pm,[10] or he could take the *Defence* or *Union* at 10:30am if he preferred to lunch at his political club.

For the villages in between, packmen with their teams, and peddlers served, as they

had done since the Middle Ages, avoiding the turnpikes and toll houses, as Wordsworth noted in the *The Excursion*. Their survival did not prevent Cobbett from lamenting that town shops drove both them and local markets out of business: 'shops have devoured markets and fairs', just as internet shopping is blamed today for high street shop closures. In fact shops had begun to specialise and order directly from manufacturers.

Vans — less comfortable — provided a passenger service on both routes twice a week, and twenty-nine regular carriers reached out to Alnmouth, Bamburgh, Belford, Rothbury and Embleton. No matter what the passenger or freight — crops, coal, lime or fish — they kept economic circles spinning, as the regular journeys of commercial travellers kept the towns' shops stocked. Some dealers branched out into early modern trades: Jack the Cowper (Plate 60) 'would exchange anything he had with anyone — a good stock of old books,

LEFT *Plate 57 [44]. Ald Jack Kirkup 1831 from memory November 30 1831, for long a driver at the White Swan.*

RIGHT *Plate 58 [47]. William Burnett April 20 1831. Large man, a carter in Alnwick from 1815.*

LEFT *Plate 59 [49]. Billy Carr 1832 from memory April 10 1832. Long postmaster in Alnwick*

RIGHT *Plate 60 [66]. Jack the Cowper 1831 from memory June 1831. A celebrated character in Cannongate [sic] Alnwick who would exchange anything he had with anyone. A good stack of old books, etc.*

etc.' Meanwhile, the Alnwick Gas Company, a joint stock enterprise headed by the Duke in 1824, manufactured oil gas to start the first street lights.

All this made possible the extension and implantation of another long effect of the Enlightenment, evolution of print culture for a mass audience, an essential preliminary to what can now be seen as the evolution of the consumer and the consumer society. Consumer had been a bad word in the sixteenth century, indicating excess, greed and self-indulgence; but consumers had become the general public to which craftsmen, retailers and merchants now appealed, through every medium understood even by the semi-literate.

Handbills, flyers, advertisements covering the whole front page of weekly newspapers, set out stalls for auctioneers, theatres and circuses, impresarios, hunt balls, assemblies and exhibitions, with multiple spaces for patent medicines, dancing instructors, school teachers, even visiting clergy or political meetings. Painters, publishers and engravers, of whom Davison was the leading exponent,[11] using the latest presses, turned out advertising materials in hours. Books, in full or parts for the less well-off, took only days or a few weeks to set the type. They moulded taste at the same time as they met demand, whether for London or Paris fashions, Italian dancing masters (usually English under a foreign name such as le Cher de Fontane, teaching Latin, French, Italian and German, claiming to hold degrees from Florence and Pisa) or pink pills (for whose impact see Plate 61, 'Morrisons Pills') and patent footwear.

Moreover, it brought news of the outside world, in what today we call 'real time', not yet by telegraph but within twenty-four hours, for example of the Durham miners' strike in 1831, as the miners' leaders circulated broad sheets to 'the Public . . .' setting out 'the case from the pitman of the Tyne and Wear', appealing against the owner's regime of wages, terms of the annual bond, hours of work and days guaranteed – aiming, according to the *Courant* in May, for a mere twelve-hour day, while 'many of the pitmen themselves with their wives and children are wandering about the county begging'.

Alnwick in 1831 lacked a newspaper to compare with the Berwick *Advertiser* or Newcastle's two competitors. The *Mercury* lasted only a few months before it failed, and no regular weekly survived until the *Alnwick Gazette* thirty years later. But Davison and other printers coming from the north and south made up for the lack of newsprint with the sheer volume of one-off production, having learned that they could not compete

with papers only hours old. Consumers, in any case, needed great variety and demanded to see coloured fashion prints before buying a dress or hat, advance notice of the theatre's coming programmes, notices of auctions, of livestock, farm implements, furniture or property for sale and to let.

What the Duke bought in Paris, as William IV's emissary, was of course finer and more costly than Alnwick's offerings,[12] just as Newcastle supplied a much wider range of

Plate 61 [113]. Morrison's pills. Grandma and boy.

fabrics, furs or furniture. But a middle class family in the town would expect to have furniture, possibly from the Adam Brothers factory in Edinburgh, not just in oak and elm, but mahogany probably by the 1830s enriched by machine carving. Designs by Gillow of Lancashire influenced local cabinet makers and the Castle employed Florentine carvers and gilders whose work there could be reproduced more simply for the town. Sunderland Glass work (often engraved with its famous bridge) could be found, together with its rustic lustreware, increasing commercial production from the Wedgwood factory, perhaps even dinner sets from Derby and Worcester, auctioned locally.

Whether advertisement fostered demand or new needs inspired supply, is irrelevant. That a consumer society existed earlier is not in doubt:[13] the novelty lies in how it was enhanced and redefined. Taste and fashion ruled and the majority of townspeople could afford it, as Dodd's account books demonstrate, even among skilled working females. Even if they lacked their own newspapers, Alnwick advertisers took spaces month on month in the Newcastle press, announcing Gas Company meetings, life insurance proposals, concerts, pawn brokers. Miss Pringle invited girls to her Alnwick boarding school, where she taught the domestic arts for 26 guineas a term and an extra 2 guineas for boarding during the vacation. Horse breeders had stallions at stud;[14] there were wine sales by the hundred dozen, auctions of turnpike tolls, news of recent bankruptcies. One farmer's stock sale offered carts, a turnip sower, a roller, three pairs of harrows, two iron ploughs, a ribbing plough and 'a thrashing machine of four horsepower, nearly new'.[15]

More than any other force, this collective interaction drew the town into a novel sphere where its specific interests began to merge, just as the styles of pottery in Sunderland crossed the North East. The economic community was on the cusp between local and national identities, a transition evident not only among traders and retailers, but in the professional services offered by those who had qualified by apprenticeship as solicitors, surgeons or pharmacists, or more distantly in the medical or law schools for which Edinburgh was foremost for Northumbrians. In this category should also be included many who did not need then to qualify by examination: clergy (though most of the Established Church were graduates of Oxford or Cambridge), bankers and insurance agents, post masters and excise officers, together with the locally trained inspectors, weighers and conners in the marketplace.

These, whether officials appointed by the Town Council, nominees of Boards as schoolmasters or incumbents of church livings granted by the holders, often university colleges, up to and including gentry and entrepreneurs sitting on the committees which governed much of what went on, provided what must be seen as local leadership. Town officials' duties were of ancient origin, magistrates, militia officers, constabulary,[16] whereas the school governors or the Boards of savings bank and Dispensary came from among the gentry who had set them up.

THE PROFESSIONALS

In a different category, dating back centuries, lie the town's Freemen: a distinction almost without class identification, composed of the descendants and occasional elected members who were entitled to commoners' rights on the Town Moor: a largely self-interested oligarchy, whose powers had over decades vested almost entirely in the Four and Twenty, the Chamberlains and the Clerk of the Courts Robert Robson, leaving an income for each, and a venerable entry ceremony dubbed by *Pigott's Directory* as 'truly singular and ridiculous'.[17]

Most of the official providers can be found in the directories: the Clerk to the Magistrates, the Clerk of the Peace, the Excise Collector, the Grain Inspector, the Librarian and the Postmaster William Carr. Whatever their paper qualifications, if any, their appointments depended on local reputation, political clout and sometimes carefully-distributed cash. Pigott's job description covered only part of their ground: barbers no longer graduated to surgeons, but a solicitor, having completed his seven years' articles, might still act as an advocate, though probably not in Assize Courts, while offering his clients to act as money-broker, estate agent, conveyancer, and insurance provider, if not banking agency.[18]

Equally important, a physician would act for his private patients, yet find time to work and treat the poor in the Dispensary, perform surgery up to and including appendicitis (of course without anaesthetic) and, if needed, visit the Poor House. No surprise then that practitioners schooled in Edinburgh or London academies demarcated their spheres from those of druggists (apothecaries) or dentists, acquiring in the process the status of gentlemen, as against 'the common run of ordinary practitioners'.[19] What the clerics provided from their pulpits and teachers from their desks, these all supplied a sort of leading role for behaviour, albeit in many forms and under many different names.

The extent of education available for the young, its limited follow-up via the Mechanics Institute, and the parts played by church or chapel, and financed by local notables, belongs to the next chapter. Apart from education however, Alnwick's citizens in the first quarter of the nineteenth century encountered steadily improving standards of professional competence and provision, imposing, at the same time, a system to shape behaviour across most aspects of individual life: teaching or medicine, banking or legal advice.

A Dispensary had been established by William Burrell of Broom Park and his friends in 1815, 'to administer advice and medicines to the poor; to promote vaccine inoculation, and to offer aid in cases requiring the greater operations of surgery'. To this was added a fever ward in 1819 to treat typhoid and smallpox, both of which were then rife in the county's southern towns, and extended a decade later in time to cope with the next outbreaks in 1831–2. Two added elements completed the process: patients had to come in 'properly recommended', especially if they were so ill that they could not attend on the two open days a week, and they were required to show due gratitude for their free treatment – how, was not specified.[20]

Regulated and supervised by William Milne and John Leithead, William's father, the Dispensary underwent a sort of crisis soon afterwards, with a short-term appointment of a female nurse: 'the physician to employ some proper person to officiate (male), the Matron having agreed to take charge of the ward in the meantime, free of expense' (October 1833 resolution).

But the problems of appointing a female nurse, twenty years before the Crimean War brought Florence Nightingale and Eliza Seacole to public notice, highlight a significant gap in Forster's cosmology: where was the midwife? None was listed by Pigott and it seems likely that their services, invariably provided at the mother-to-be's house, were part of the unrecognised side of Alnwick or any other town life. Midwives of course doubled up as foster mothers, carers of the elderly sick, still often as breast feeders for orphan babies, paid for what they did during what was euphemistically called 'lying in'; efficient, painful, absolutely necessary, yet out of public sight.

Lawyers like William Leithead (Plate 76) set the same tone in their practices and range of formal knowledge. He already retained a London 'correspondent' firm of solicitors, Crossman and Block, for wealthier clients with metropolitan interests. Yet a trainee completing his seven years' articles could become his partner and a gentleman at one and the same time, in a blending of professional with social status, whatever his origins might be.[21]

Other, humbler trades had not reached the verge of professional qualification – such as estate agents or auctioneers. Bankers and a surprising number of insurance agents had, however, done so by the 1800s and were soon to be joined by postmasters. The Yorkshire Fire and Life Insurance operated in Alnwick from 1827, the Law Life Assurance Company from 1829. The latter set out its prospectus to clients, a roll-call of the new middle class:

'tenants for life, persons in the Army, Navy and Church, the law or public affairs, medical and other professional men, public and other commitments', together with 'tradesmen and all others whose income depends upon their lives or upon the continuance of their health, to make provision for a wife and children or other dependents, of raising money on loans where personal security only can be offered – of saving the eventual payment of doubtful debts to individuals' etc.[22]

A modern twenty-first-century dilemma can be seen in embryo. Davison wrote 'it is a common observation with commercial travellers that their bills are better honoured in Alnwick than in any other town in the kingdom' – quite why, he did not explain.[23] As Jane Austen, a clergyman's daughter, put it caustically via Lady Denham, 'families come after families but, as far as I can learn, it is not one in a hundred of these that have any real property – landed or funded – an income perhaps but no property.'

Meanwhile, the banks dominated the town's monetary affairs: especially the Newcastle (chaired by the local MP Sir Matthew White Ridley), Gibson and Co., and Tweed Bank. Edward Stamp, local agent for the Newcastle Bank (Plate 10), has the deportment proper to client confidence and customer authority – both very necessary after the post-war bank failures. Memories of the South Sea Bubble and the disastrous Darien speculation in Scotland still survived, and until the equally overblown railway mania of the 1840s, the only secure investment lay in government debt. This was indeed the only security traded on the stock exchange before 1822, and out of it governments had funded the long Napoleonic War.

Funds paid interest. Income from Consols established sixty years earlier by Henry Peckham, paid 3 per cent whatever level the national debt reached (a terrifying £750 million by 1815, reduced, thanks to a Sinking Fund which replaced the old practice of redemption). However circuitous the pattern of government borrowing and reinvesting in the early nineteenth century, funds produced a safe if not glamorous return. But, as Lady Denham pointed out, that was not what the upper class meant by property, except insofar as landowners traded between consols and their acres to offset risks to either.

Deals done in London coffee houses, marginal trading between different bonds, often on partial or incorrect information, had repercussions across the North East. Served by bankers and brokers in Newcastle, speculation thrived also in less-secure foreign bonds, new capital-intensive industries, and maritime services from Tyne and Wear ports. The effect was to put increasing stress on a country banking system that was only a generation old.

For depositors who needed quick access to their money, the older network of deposit banks, in the traditions established by Hoares, Childs, Glyns, or in Scotland the Royal Bank, the Bank of Scotland and the Clydesdale provided what may have been the best services in Europe outside of Amsterdam. Yet, overstretched as they became during the war and after 1815, failures abounded, followed for many by ruin, given their investors' unlimited liability, long before Dickens' Merdle and Thackeray's Melmotte brought fraud to a fine art.

Stockbrokers themselves set up in Newcastle only after the 1830s to replace idiosyncratic local traders in paper like Davison,

so that it was the country banks that served the North East in Forster's day. But any sign of panic brought demands for withdrawal and overwhelming liquidity problems, soluble only by collective action (six times in the years 1772 to 1816). The Berwick Bank failed in 1812 and a whole clutch of guarantees, mostly for at least £5,000, was required in 1816 to save the five Newcastle banks. One did fail in 1818, putting the local notes circulating at risk, and after the establishment of joint stock banks, a period of instability set in during the late 1820s.

Central to this, the 1826 Act allowed the Bank of England to set up regional branches, which it did two years later in Newcastle. Backed by the Chancellor of the Exchequer, Lord Goderich, in Lord Liverpool's administration, the bank then attacked the local banks' note issues, and met strong local opposition. What amounted to a feud was not settled for nearly a decade until a new Bank Agent turned to conciliation and compromise, establishing a foundation for better credit and market supervision. This lasted until the next speculative wave, when joint stock banks' folly, fraud and greed led to the crises of 1847 and 1857.

The Bank's activity can be read from a modern standpoint as a stage in the long conflict between local banks and national discipline and supervision; but at the time, the former fiercely defended their independence, for example, in long letters to the *Tyne Mercury*. Amid all the cacophony, local paper note issue was even described by Goderich as 'an interference with the King's prerogative'.

Coming as this did in the wake of 'the late panic' in 1825, country bankers rejected London domination, claiming they functioned better 'as a medium between the debtor and the creditor interest of the county . . . by means of [their] interference, the stagnant capital of the country is made active when and where its activity is required.'[24] They accused the Chancellor of 'exciting public suspicion' against country bank directors, aiming not only to extinguish them but to turn the Bank of England into 'a grand political engine . . . by means of which Lord Goderich and the Treasury may pinch, grind and govern the country as they please'.

Like the joint stock banks, Alnwick's agents, including Edward Stamp, all came under Treasury fire, sharpened by Goderich's description of their note issue as 'worthless rags'. Such paper had been in circulation for thirty years already and the quarrel ranged from gold backing for paper money up to the issue of national control as against local autonomy. Revenge may have tasted sweet, if cold, when the Bank of England itself had to close its doors in the panic of 1866 and raise the bank rate from 2 per cent to 7 per cent overnight.

All this affected the agents in Alnwick, though apparently not the more stable Savings Bank, founded in 1816 by a group very similar in outlook in expertise. Davison's list of the Trustees and Committee of the Alnwick Savings Bank (p. 230), provides a roll call of the mid-Northumberland nobility and gentry – all those lacking an actual title bearing the word 'Esquire'. They aimed to provide 'for merchants, labourers, servants, and the industrious classes in general, a safe and profitable depository' with the advice of a committee including clergy and auditors. It offered insurance 'against adversity or ill-health . . . and an easy, safe, expeditious, and profitable mode of laying up a competency for support in declining years' – insurance under another name, for those who could not afford regular premiums

and had no other prospect to fund retirement and old age.

Such was the leadership provided by professional groups, each conveying their own clearly-articulated view of how their publics should organise their affairs. Some were more successful than others: the Dispensary especially, soon enlarged to meet demand, lasted into the next century, as did the Savings Bank, whose deposits reached £20,000 by 1821. But most people needed a lawyer at some time in their lives, even if they never had money enough to justify a will. Lawyers offered a due process in disputes over land boundaries, lost entitlements, crimes, but they do not appear to have followed doctors' example at the Dispensary – who offered treatment free, though less lavish than their paying patients expected; while the clergy offered precepts, advice, solace, free and on demand. But it was the banks whose activity underpinned the economy of work, who struggled to evolve trustworthy systems and to elaborate sound principles and a reputable local currency.

A sort of bargain had evolved here. Those who could afford it, took risks and made their fortunes, or lost it all in total ruin, having no limited liability (not for another thirty years) like Sir Walter Scott in 1826. Those who could not afford it, if prudent, found security for their cash, some health provision, legal advice, and what spiritual assurance existed. In return, with the assent of the Alnwick community, save perhaps the criminal fringe, the professionals who had laid down the terms enjoyed their status, freedom and recreation undisturbed by rancorous questioning of this entitlement.

The economic consensus between richer and poorer was of course only implicit, and demonstrably one-sided; but the lack of dissent, when compared with agricultural areas of the south, suggest that it functioned, at least in the two decades after 1815. Moreover it compared well with the much more ancient bond between citizenry and Alnwick's local authorities, whose officials' conduct then and well into the mid-century, lent itself to caricature ranging from Eatanswill elections to Dickens' Mr Bumble the Beadle.

Central government at this period provided a national defence (with heavy reliance on the local militia, especially in times of unrest in the early 1820s), a legal and judicial system, a postal service and the revenue-raising from customs and excise collection. The rest lay with the locality, from constabulary to weights and measures inspectors, to bye-law enforcement.[25]

Davison and Tate both listed the official providers and their long history, largely without critical comment. Yet Alnwick's status as a non-Parliamentary borough, (i.e. without its own MP) was to feature centrally – indeed as a test case – in the 1834–5 Municipal Reform Bill (Chapter 6).

Efficient or not – and there is no average picture across England – the Town Council officially managed the place: headed by the Steward and Bailiff, the Clerk of the Courts, the Four Chamberlains, the Clerks of the Courts and of the Market, whose functions dated back long before the Civil War. Seven sets of constables policed the seven wards, ten guilds had their own officials, and what passed for a Parliament, the Four and Twenty, lorded it over the electors, 200-odd hereditary Freemen of the town, a body corporate by description. In parallel, the Vestry of St Michael's Church, another closed, self-appointing group, ran poor relief and other matters barely related to religion, being as open

as the Council to allegations of oligarchy and corruption.

Openings for corruption had always existed, virtually unprovable and insoluble in a matrix of nepotism, favour and long-running feuds. The money to pay for town government came from the rates on property and local taxes such as brewhouses and salt,[26] so that any new

Plate 62 [3]. P.J. Selby Esq. 1834. From memory [local landowner].

or crisis expenditure, for example on poor relief in bad years or epidemics, tended to coincide with local residents' maximum hostility. Even when reform came in the mid-1830s, bringing greater efficiency and less toleration of corruption, the results tended towards less, not more expenditure.[27]

One explanation for continuance of archaic local government until the Reform era is that the risk of disorder was in decline at least till the later 1830s; another is that enforcement of the new 1834 Poor Law benefited local taxpayers, at the expense of the poor themselves; the third, perhaps the most plausible, is that the better off, led by the gentry, the clerics and the professionals, judged more carefully than in the eighteenth century what charitable or educational provision might meet the most urgent and significant demands. Matched on the reverse side by tough law enforcement, a harsher set of game laws, and fear of Morpeth jail, the severe sentences handed down by local magistrates seemed to have brought the official providers on the Town Council into general agreement with the informal leadership of gentry and landowners like the Selbys (Plate 62).

Magistrates (Justices of the Peace) after all, like Savings Bank Trustees, were drawn universally from the local gentry, stipendiaries being restricted to much larger urban areas. Until the mid-1830s, as JPs, the gentry appointed constables who, although in theory subject to unpaid duty like jury service, drew in fact regular pay.

Meanwhile, local oligarchs on the Council, whose seats had become almost hereditary, knew that re-election depended on keeping the rates low. No experts or enforcers 'from above' could remedy this, even if what passed for central government had wished to do so. The new novelists' critiques, from George Eliot or Dickens onwards, had first to expose the poor-house regime in *Nicholas Nickleby* or the school run by Wackford Squeers, Dotheboy's Hall.

Yet just as the central state's initiation of inquiry into gross abuses such as child labour in the mines, or incompetence in the ancient universities, was becoming acceptable as a means to achieve reforms, so was the idea that the spirit of scientific enquiry might remedy the causes of corruption and politicians' embezzlement, irresponsibility, and self-interest, by exposing them to moral strictures and unfavourable comparison with better-managed communities and towns. Alnwick had been one focus of agricultural improvement, and the Evangelical Awakening, neither of which easily tolerated inaction by a small town oligarchy.[28] Its informal leadership knew enough of the outside world not to put up with excessive and inspissated localism.

So a certain idea of contract underlay much of the town's life and the antithesis between treatment of the old and infirm or disabled, as against the 'able-bodied poor' or out-and-out criminals. In the first category, landowners' provision for good servants in old age was usually an estate cottage: for Miles Sayer (Plate 89), the Duke's huntsman, 'many years living in the Park' and for Luke Skelley (Plate 63), the earth-stopper to the Percy Hounds, Washburn Cottage – all proper, if small houses. For the rest, in town, it was the Poor House. But if the implicit bargain held for the law-abiding majority and provided sufficient means of education and advancement for their children, it never included the whole community, nor all aspects of its activities: and two groups lay outside it altogether, the criminal one by intent and the poverty-stricken because they had no choice.

THE UNDERSIDE: CRIME AND POVERTY

Like any comparable town, Alnwick had its underclass, as it would now be described, well-known to the constables and shunned by the better-behaved. It existed as a sort of dark hole or anti-matter: not measurable, rarely described or discussed, and far more opaque in Alnwick's small community than in the hugely expanding city of Newcastle or the industrial towns along the Tyne and Wear.

Yet the line between criminals and ordinary, occasional wrongdoers remained blurred, obscured by public perceptions. 'Bad characters' carried a stigma which made it easier for what then passed for detectives, aided in most cases by paid informers. It worked to some degree, but very roughly. Robert Peel's new police forces started only in 1829 and as late as 1875 Sergeant Hately was beaten to death trying to control a riot at Alnwick's Hiring Fair.

The Chief Constable in 1837 noted twenty-five safe-houses in Newcastle for thieves to frequent and thirty-one thieves in them known to the police, to say nothing of seventy-one brothels with up to four prostitutes each.[29] But apart from press reports of trials, transportation and hangings (in Morpeth Jail, not Alnwick) crime statistics scarcely existed, even in Newcastle. Yet a belief existed that crime had worsened in the immediate post-war years before falling off in the late 1820s. It certainly worsened again in 1839–40, an increase that lasted through the Hungry Forties.

Magistrates relied for the law itself on Blackstone's Commentaries and advice from the Clerk of the Court sitting in front. They rarely gave reasons for their decisions unless journalists picked up something on a notable case. Judging between the letter of the law and its interpretation, between what appeared to be a life-long criminal and a poor man or woman driven to theft by sheer hunger or despair was a matter entirely for the bench — as was the Assize judges' choice of prison, transportation to the colonies or death by the noose.[30]

Serious crimes and transportation to Australia or execution were the province of Newcastle Assizes, and Morpeth Jail with its scaffold in frequent use, attended by many spectators. Alnwick had no jail, only the relatively mild confinement of the Correction House, and no provision for a public hangman.

Plate 63 [91]. Luke Skelley July 27 1835. The Earth Stopper to the Percy Hounds — Washburn Cottage.

Nor is there much record of the under-class, the illegitimate children or the local prostitutes. All that can be gauged comes from criminal reports, mainly in the Newcastle press. Most of the Alnwick cases were for theft or misbehaviour, and those that reached the Assizes did not meet leniency. This could be read, albeit too simply, as the revenge of supe-riors on those who dared to misbehave; more accurately as the actions of the dominant group in defense of their property and privi-lege; but not forgetting the image of civil peace which they put forward as judicial logic.

Alnwick had also been lucky in that it had had no Peterloo (1819), little machine breaking, and no Tolpuddle martyrs (1834), transported for what now seem justifiable protests against agricultural labourer's condi-tions. In October 1830 the *Courant* reported the riots in Sussex 'where the peasantry have taken the law into their own hands . . . and forced farmers to illegal compulsion agree-ments' for higher wages as if it had been the far side of the Channel. Yet its JPs took harshly a crime which today represents financial loss and invasion of privacy though only rarely violence, but which could then threaten a victim's existence — theft of his horse or cart might lead him straight to the Poor House.[31]

Forster ignored all these, apart from one drawing of Lyetty Jackwith his dog (Plate 64), whose occupation he defined as 'poacher', a far more serious crime than it was to be after the mid-nineteenth century, though magistrates were typically slightly less harsh on locals than outside intruders coming usually in midnight gangs. But then the shooting gentry had no compunction about doing what their consta-bles feared or failed to do.

AFFRAY BETWEEN SOME COUNTRY GENTLEMEN AND A LARGE BODY OF POACHERS — For some years past nearly all the moors in Northumberland have been taken possession of by large bodies of poachers from the adjoining counties, who not only carried away immense quantities of game, but even plundered the industrious farmers of the neighbourhood of their sheep, and did wilful damage to their property. The overbearing insolence displayed on these occasions by these lawless intruders so intimidated the peaceable inhabitants, that they might almost be said to have lost their right over, and control of their property. The 12th of August last (the commencement of the shooting season) was again marked by the arrival of large bodies of

RIGHT Plate 64 [27]. Lyetty Jack, September 1838 fond of poaching and shooting, with his dog.

these intruders, upon which the gentlemen and farmers then shooting on the moors determined no longer to be annoyed by them. Accordingly, on the 19th inst., they divided themselves into two parties, and having ascertained that a body of the poachers would commence shooting at a place called Whitelee, near Carter Bar, the first party, consisting of about forty persons, on horseback, set out from Woodburn about 3 in the morning of the 20th, the second party also setting out for another suspected place of rendezvous. On the arrival of the first party at Whitelee, they discovered about twenty poachers ranging the moors, each armed with a gun and attended by a dog. Immediately on being discovered the poachers formed themselves into a military position, on the ascent of a hill, threw off their coats, and presenting their guns, threatened to fire on the first who came near them. — A young gentleman present remonstrated with the poachers on their illegal conduct, but in vain, they declared they would not be taken, and would shoot the first man who approached them. Upon this the gentleman alluded to, rode over a small burn which divided the parties, instantly followed by his friends, and after considerable struggling, in the course of which the young gentleman's horse was felled to the ground, and he himself wounded in the hand, the poachers were completely overpowered, and brought before two magistrates, who committed them to Morpeth gaol under the Game Act. Too much praise cannot be given to the gentlemen, farmers, and those who assisted them on the occasion, who thus spiritedly secured these daring intruders, against whom, it is hoped, the magistrates will direct proper proceedings.[32]

And gentlemen themselves were not above poaching, 'fined for hunting and shooting hares in the snow' (1823). . . . An outrageous few shot their neighbour's pheasants, sometimes for fun, sometimes out of spite, like the famous sportsman Colonel Peter Hawker.[33] It requires some effort to define all this as self-defence. Yet at a time when carrying a pistol or keeping a sword behind the bed caused no surprise even in court, game could be protected by man traps, and gangs of poachers actually shot dead.

A handful of cases (1830–2) where the accused lived in Alnwick show that surprisingly few *habitual* criminals stood trial (which may indicate that transportation actually worked by drafting the worst offenders overseas), but that violence was at all times endemic.

> Newcastle Assizes January 1831:
> - Henry Dixon, aged 46, for stealing various articles of clothing from Snipe House and reselling them to a shop keeper: 2 months hard labour.
> - George Turnbull, larceny of a coat and other clothing, transported for seven years. Ditto, John Fletcher. Their associates, twelve months with hard labour and a private (i.e., not in public) whipping.
> - February 1832: Hugh M'Gormick, an Irishman, theft of a mare from James Arthur of Shipley (nearby). No defence, sentence of death, but recommendation for clemency to be followed by transportation for seven years.
> - Alnwick Spring Assizes, February 1829, taking and slaughter of sheep, death sentence.
> - August 1830, six separate cases of theft, most transported for seven years.

Some cases, however, were mere hooliganism, like the two Alnwick men convicted of 'willfully knocking off part of the battlement at Alnwick Bridge', to wit a statue of the Percy lion, or the two convicted and fined 40 shillings 'for furious driving upon the Alnwick to Eglingham Road' – the money to go half to the informers, half to the Dispensary.

Other cases arose from revenue evasion and smuggling, not so much of French brandy as in southern counties, but Scotch whisky, due to the different rates of excise. Smuggling passed almost as an acceptable occupation except to retailers who obeyed the law: Alnwick publicans protested to Matthew Bell MP (12 June 1830) 'complaining of the facility with which smuggled spirits are introduced from Scotland'. Meanwhile, landowners who had campaigned for harsher game laws throughout the 1820s succeeded when the 1831 Game Act gave their magistrates greater powers to sentence, over and above those under the 1773 Act: fines of £20 for a first offence, £30 for the second, failing payment, hard labour for three to six months, again half to the informer, half to the parish poor to offset the rates.

By the 1850s, Alnwick had its own resident gang of thieves, led by Charles Richardson, earlier suspected of murdering a policeman, who was actually imprisoned for seven years after foisting off the crime of armed robbery on two innocent men in 1867. It is likely that he had taken over from a lesser-known predecessor.

But proving a case in court could be difficult; hence many prosecutions were based on a system which paid out half the fine to the informant.[34] Alnwick's Parish Association for the Prosecution of Felons offered seven guineas reward in 1825 for conviction of a thief who stole a pair of percussion cap gun barrels from George Davison, the publisher's brother. Similar rewards were offered a year later for breaking a grocer's window in Narrowgate, and £5 for taking a draught horse and a silver watch. It often worked, but, as in the later Richardson case, if aided by police corruption, could grievously harm those whose identity was mistaken. It was also cheaper than employing more constables, and more effective than hellfire sermons.

Some local sympathy for, or at least empathy with, local criminals (as opposed to outside intruders) did exist, if one can judge by later events, when Richardson had finally confessed to the armed burglary (to avoid a possible death penalty for murder) and more than half the town's inhabitants, 3,000 people, signed a petition asking for clemency. Remarkably, given the very long sentence imposed in 1867 on those who had been framed for the crime, the judges in the second round handed down only five years, an indication of how attitudes to sentencing had changed in the intervening period.

But while grievous violence (GBH today), usually following drink, was so common as not to attract much press comment, attacks on a man's livelihood or property (including game) were deplored, on the one hand by religious and educational leaders, on the other by the magistrates who were of course often the same people. Crime and criminality were in fact managed in a rather different way from what became the later nineteenth-century norm, once a national police force had been introduced. Only then did it become possible to dream that crime might be abolished or reduced rather than simply managed within the bounds of order.

That boundary could be defined as good behaviour, and possession of appropriate but limited education, savings for old age: it benefited for example Scottish migrants, keen on upward mobility, but not gypsies, tinkers, not even the descendents of the fabled Gypsy King Johnny Faa of nearby Yetholm, who were still regarded as worse than 'the able-bodied poor' who would not work at all. Even old soldiers from the war had to rely on charity when their savings had gone, or use their military training as gamekeepers to outwit armed poachers (Plate 100, Charlie Carr riding shotgun on an ass). John Beeby, who rose from the ranks in 1793 to become Sergeant Major in the Northumberland Light Infantry Militia at Alnwick Depot, was lucky, because of the Duke's intervention, to become a Chelsea pensioner.[35]

The old, the infirm (Plate 17, William Cleghorn called 'the dwarf'), the mentally defective, like Dukey Greenhead (Plate 65) 'a man of weak intellect', oscillated between bare provision from the parish rate, occupancy of the workhouse, or the charity that the social contract required in times of death or disaster; like the 1831 winter, when 'the inhabitants of Alnwick and its vicinity again assisted their poor neighbours . . . by means of a soup kitchen from which at very moderate expense about 1,600 individuals have obtained great comfort and support by a supply of more than 18,000 quarts of very strong soup and, for part of the time, a considerable quantity of bread'.

Again in November that year, when the soup kitchens had to be reopened in the face of a severe early winter and a widespread outbreak of typhoid, the Duke and Duchess added to the usual soup, milk and bread, 'liberally distributed wine, port, and butcher's meat to such poor sick families as require them', while their son, Lord Prudhoe, 'took an active part in planning means for the prevention of contagion and infection'.

Davison described the Poor House itself, as a key to the balance between repelling the able-

Plate 65 [72]. Dukey Greenhead from memory October 4 1831. A man of weak intellect, a well-known character in Alnwick from 1817.

bodied poor in the Union Workhouse and the need to keep alive the old and chronically sick. According to him, the Poor House was a 'fine airy building', modern (1810) with a room for the parish overseer, a kitchen and two sitting rooms for the poor, with a ward-room for their few possessions. 'On the second floor are six bedrooms, an hospital and a dead-house; and in the attic storey are the work rooms.'[36] The yard had a wash house, privies, and a porter's lodge 'and two cells for lunatics', together with a small room for teaching inmates' children.

The door had to be locked at night, as the keeper directed. Work consisted of basic drudgery, teasing out oakum or spinning wool. Costs to the rates had fallen from a peak of £4884 in 1818 to £3238 by 1820. This income supported

Plate 66 [93]. Boy street seller with duck and kippers July 26 1833. Whar's away man, and tether the Duck!

P.F. [Aug. 26. 1833.

permanently 323 out of house, 22 inside. In addition it covered 33 children under five, 46 under fourteen (possibly a measure of local illegitimacy[37] and the extent of the sex trade), and 161 over sixty years of age or permanently disabled.

These were not large numbers in a town of Alnwick's size and the local record suggests that its regime was not unduly harsh by early nineteenth century standards – indeed, kindlier than the universal prescription of the new Poor Law as it developed in the decade after 1834. According to 1829 accounts, the worthy poor had a diet of meat and beer, with provision for clothing 'and other things necessary for their keeping and maintenance . . . (including) £20 for snuff and tobacco for the use of the said paupers'. Yet it was hard to have to separate men and women, often husband and wife . . .

Work patterns in these economic circles suggest the dots of a *pointilliste* painting, like Georges Seurat's vision of the Seine and the picnickers by La Grande Jatte. What looks close up to be a pullulating mass, seems more like an ordered beehive from farther away, its hundreds of cells making up their own geometry. But work alone, or lack of it, does not constitute a community as the following chapters show. What is clear here is that there existed a public retailing and consumer community, fed by a well-developed print culture, and characterised by what a recent author calls the 'civilisation of the crowd'.[38]

Direction from outside of the *pointilles* is another matter, informally grounded and upheld by common consent. An upper class sensibility to shame or disorder, seems to have provided a type of leadership, whether it came from Whigs like Lord Grey or Tories like the Duke – whose peregrinations up from London attracted as much adulation in the local papers as the rarely-seen sovereigns George IV or William IV.

The Duke, Hugh Percy (Plate 97) in particular, from the townspeoples's point of view (rather than advocates of the Reform Bill which he opposed), was seen as patron, spokesman for the defence of ancient rights, a charitable donor to whose father the Tenantry Column near the town centre was erected in 1816–17 'to record forever his Grace's many acts of munificence and generosity'. Most gentry followed his example, remitting a proportion of rents in very bad harvest years, serving on the Boards and Committees: a century of later scepticism should not eliminate the proposition that such gifts represented one side of the implicit bargain between self-evident leaders and the town's community. Pigott's *Directory* listed the gentry first, as if to prove a point: these are your local deities, they live in or beside the town, they appear on the same printed sheet as the professionals and tradesmen who in turn are all jumbled up together – a hierarchic order, but within the same frame.

Education and discussion, thought and scholarly research, together with leisure, sport and politics, are needed to complete the picture of how this society imagined it should properly order itself. One historian of the North East describes it as 'a new refinement of manners . . . a great increase in the consumption of luxuries, an emphasis on education and the provision of public forums, open to paying customers, for the enjoyment of arts and entertainment'.[39] But it is the strength of locality as against the intrusions of the modern central state, that can be detected in the circles of daily work and the early evolution of a consumer sciety.

CHAPTER 4
THE EDUCATED MIND

Sunday morning, summer 1831: service of mourning after the death of King George IV. For perhaps the first time since the death of his predecessor in 1820, the various competing branches of Christian faith in Alnwick stood more or less in line. Tolerance was already permeating English society, in Alnwick as much as London, where 1828 had brought relief for Dissenters, through repeal of the Test and Corporation Acts, and 1829 after nearly 300 years, Catholic Emancipation.

Yet competition between them still ran on in the town, so that not until thirty years later, in his *History*, George Tate (who had been twenty-six at the funeral obsequies, an impressionable young linen draper), could write 'the storms of (religious) political controversy have passed away . . . the various members of society carry on together the practical business of life, without troubling themselves with curious enquiry into the orthodoxy of their neighbours' creeds.'[1]

The long Evangelical Awakening, starting perhaps with John Wesley's critique of the Established Church in the 1750s, reached a sort of climax in the early 1800s, after which Wesleyan Methodism sharply declined. But Dissent in Alnwick had far deeper roots, starting in the Civil War, with the Covenanting Army's occupation of the Castle and the distinguished leadership of a Presbyterian minister, Gilbert Rule, from the pulpit of St Michael's Anglican Church. Charles II's re-institution of Bishops brought Rule's dismissal in 1661 and a decade of persecution; but Dissent survived, partly because of its Presbyterian implantation in the surrounding countryside, partly because of a long-lasting transition in which pulpits moved from instilling fear of God towards emphasis on God's love for mankind.

Respect if not obedience was paid through the early eighteenth century to the Scottish 'synod in England'; by the 1730s established at the Pottergate Meeting House. Under the Reverend George Anderson in the 1820s and 1830s, a congregation of 600 could still attend, to hear him preach the virtues of good education and the Scientific and Mechanical Institute, 'looking beyond the narrow range of sect and piety'.[2] Buoyed up by 'the Great Awakening', linked to the anti-slavery campaign, Methodism, Presbyterianism, and the rest enjoyed an Indian summer.

Even so, the Free Church advocates seceded in 1837, embodying an anti-Wesleyan complaint and their Alnwick brethren set up in the Sion Chapel. Meanwhile, after 1834, the United Presbyterian secession, meeting in Clayport, divided along ancient Covenanting lines between 'burghers' and 'antiburghers' — yet still drew congregations over 500. But while the Scottish connection attracted more than one-fifth of Alnwick's citizens, the Wesleyan implant declined after its 1750s peak and died back, to be sidelined by the Methodist New Connection at the Bethel Chapel, noted for its intellectual freedom and public debates.

Taking account of the Established Church's long-delayed revival of St Mary and St Michael's

OPPOSITE *Plate 67 [94]. Dr Turnbull MD. A celebrated character in Alnwick from the 1820s [see Plate 70].*

itself (now able to seat over 1,200, following the Duke's reconstruction) these descendants of Presbyterian and Anglican persuasions accounted for the great majority of church goers. Quaker numbers faded away, as did the Plymouth brethren. Baptists, Unitarians (Ebenezer Chapel) and Congregationalists completed the list. Roughly 60 per cent of Alnwick's church-goers were non-conformist (according to the 1851 Census, the only one to ask for religious affiliation). Earlier, the Catholic numbers grew, backed by old recusant gentry families like Claverings of Callaly, Beadnells of Lemmington, and the Collingwoods at Lilburn Tower, or Selbys in the town itself, filling the pews of the new Jesuit-run church in Bailiffgate with a regular attendance of fifty.

Belief, as opposed to pious custom and ritual, is impossible to assess, except for a handful of individuals who kept diaries of their souls' progress, and these can never have been typical. We simply cannot know whether the citizenry attended out of deep faith or public compliance. Anglicans had to struggle against the unpopularity of tithes, the competitive hours of chapel services (evenings after work), and an overriding assumption that the religious Establishment represented the central state in disguise. Yet it benefited indirectly from the non-conformist challenge, and from new attitudes towards Catholicism.

One historian of the Church of England, Kitson Clark, used to tell his Cambridge audience that by this time it was impossible that an educated man should actually accept the gospel as laid down from the pulpits – the rest was mere concurrence. Other historians disagree, and it is worth quoting the inaugural meeting of the Berwickshire Naturalists Club in 1831, a private gathering of intellectuals, which ended with the President's paean to the Creator.

Ecstasy and enthusiasm characterised especially the meetings of primitive Methodists at which worshippers frequently fell about, like West Indian 'holy rollers'; and on one occasion in 1829 the Kirk's General Assembly congratulated the Presbyterian minister 'on the measures adopted to check the spirit of heresy in the church'. Popular superstitions, on the other hand, and practices which could be called 'white magic' fell away, leaving behind a detritus of astrology, magnetics and millenarian followers of Joanna Southcott.

But on one subject, education, the preachers' rival cacophonies halted. For each minister, the good neighbourliness of God-fearing congregations could be ensured (as indeed Jesuits had always argued) by induction of children as soon as possible in scripture as well as the other two Rs, reading and writing. This could only be achieved in schools. Yet late-eighteenth-century schooling in Alnwick could not possibly cope with the numbers,[3] and new school buildings were beyond the capacity of church or sects alone to provide. Thus the other side of the social bargain appeared in the consensus that developed steadily from the 1790s: that basic education was a common good, where gentry endowed with wealth and farsightedness could ensure at the same time godliness, good order, and good behaviour. On this, even the radicals could agree: Lovett, like Cobbett, sought 'The Best for all Classes'.

From this point of view, it did not matter too much if the donors really believed in a personal Christian God, though the evidence of passionate devotion to the sense of mission and the hope of redemption is clear enough.[4] Their leadership was to be inscribed on the stone portals above the schools' handsome doors and what was taught, initially at least, apart from a generalised insistence that God existed, proved to be so basic that even the more enragé sects could hardly complain – which left the rest of the week and all Sunday to enforce Calvin's, Wesley's or Anglican dogmas at Sunday schools . . . plus, the unceasing war that allied them all against drunkenness, marital violence and infidelity, and of course the graver sorts of crime. Common ground for a type of social contract complementary to the ethos of work shaped primary and secondary schooling, the keynote being 'useful knowledge'; while similar charitable practice allowed the brighter pupils to aspire afterwards to the Mechanics Institute or even professional qualification.[5]

So long as funding was not a burden on the rates, and so long as the older Borough and Freemen's schools restricted their entry to the children of Freemen families, the radical impact of this confluence of interests could be tolerated by the governing majority.[6] Alnwick had always been a relatively fluid society where social mobility was accepted, even for immigrant Scots, and sometimes positively advocated. George Tate himself, born in 1805, son of a stonemason, ended as President of a learned society, Secretary of the Mechanics Institute and Postmaster by the 1850s.

Such a mercantile, mobile society does not easily fit Marxist modes of analysis. Better Antonio Gramsci's concept of hegemony, according to which more players by the early nineteenth century involved themselves than at any time since the traumatic disputes of the 1640s and, unlike the Civil War protagonists, with far more success. Scottish influence needs also to be remembered, as well as that of North American migrants (Canadian, embodying settler experience, rather than the USA). North East England had no dalit class like India condemned to the most menial tasks, even if its heavy-industrial areas witnessed deep unrest and a sort of war for labour's independence among Durham miners in the early 1830s.

Yet at the same time and associated with access and control over the borough schools, the town's oligarchs and Freemen had ensconced themselves and their children's succession throughout the eighteenth century. What began to break this carapace was on the one hand the new availability of free schooling, and on the other, the rapid growth of professional careers, no longer restricted simply to gentry leadership. Migration from the countryside to the town, and often on towards Newcastle and the south, helped, as did the fact that those characterised as outsiders were now restricted to gypsies, tinkers, etc. This phenomenon eventually set the town's oligarchs in defense of their privileges against an implied alliance between both gentry and a better-educated working class.

Put rather differently, this society's contract was not Rousseau's abstract version, nor Thomas Paine's version with its critique of inequality and the social convention which enshrined wealth, so much as a culture of self-improvement, progress towards civility and a strictly limited return payment of decorum and gratitude, which the already-civilised upper class could accept as both welcome and achievable. Insofar as the work patterns and trading interconnections allowed a market in innovation and consumption to grow up to meet public demand, so a new climate of education had come into existence, on which the Age of Improvement, to borrow Asa Brigg's phrase, was to capitalise.

No need here to point to a 'traditional' set of social understandings. What occurred came about not as a legacy from a lost Golden Age but as a result of early-nineteenth-century post-Enlightenment change spurred by the self-interest of most groups in the community. Unlike the German states, France or Italy, the nobility and gentry could make concessions here, as they were to do on a wider stage with the 1832 Reform Bill, understanding that limited change would be enough to stabilise middle society and allow sufficient upward movement to fulfill Robert Peel's vision and to prevent what some, like the Duke in 1830, feared might bring revolution.

This is not to claim that no dissent existed, that there was no criticism of privilege and wealth, no scorn for elaborate ceremony or claims to ancient lineage. All that existed, but it was contained (though in industrial areas of the South and part of the Midlands only with the aid of the militia and magistrates),[7] appearing in public here only in scurrilous pamphlets and satire. Prosperity, as Adam Smith's readers knew well, could be good for all, provided wages rose enough to stay ahead of prices. Failure to do that led to the bitter miner's strikes; indeed in Durham and on Tyne and Wear, mine owners and factory bosses acted sternly to prevent the supply of better education because that, in turn, encouraged the growth of miners' self-help.

The key questions evidently were: what to teach, who should teach it, and how far could it be taken? Here the tide ran strongly in Presbyterian and non-conformist traditions, reliant on individual thought, bound to a concept of work – useful knowledge being a necessary accompaniment to religious consent. Twenty years before Darwin's *Origins*, the ethos of a clerisy pervaded religion and scientific enquiry – so long as the results did not challenge the orthodoxy of either. Tate himself, antiquary, paleontologist, geologist, who knew, like all members of the Berwickshire Naturalist Club, that Bishop Ussher's 4,000-year religious chronology from the Creation was ridiculous, learned in the 1830s a sort of 'intelligent design.'

What should be called Alnwick's intellectual elite could agree not only on the basic curriculum, half a century before the 1870 Education Act began to take effect, but also on whose *duty* it was to pay for the buildings and teachers who staffed them. The Regency years, seen from that standpoint, were where the anti-slavery campaign, emancipation and political reforms offered three fundamental criticisms of the old order, a contrast very different from later picture of a licentious, ribald, loose-moral era propagated by eminent Victorians and by the Queen herself after 1837.

Behind all this lay the late-Enlightenment conflict between post-Malthusian gloom about mankind's struggle for existence (which found many practical examples in the state of mid-Northumbrian farming in the dire post-war years) and Ricardo's more hopeful principles of political economy. Harriet Martineau, in her short *Illustration of Political Economy* (1830) indeed tried to interpret these scholarly arguments for the middle range of literate people, while asserting, ten years before Engels' *Condition of the Working Class in England*, that there was no inherent conflict between employers and employed.

For much of the Victorian era, despite the appearance of a slowly expanding central government, and perhaps until its final breakdown during the First World War, it seemed that this local state – a balance between many groups, formal and informal, and many interests – could maintain a negotiated hegemony adequate to prevent deep unrest or protest. It was of course negotiated (as Gramsci saw) between interest groups and people of influence, leaving out the working majority except in the sense that they held *negative* power; but like the great municipal corporations of the later nineteenth century, the result appears to have worked.

A body such as the Society for the Promotion of Christian Knowledge (SPCK), denigrated a century later as a propaganda machine, could at that time be seen as an agent in pursuit of literacy, even if its 315-volume branch library was heavily moralistic, like the Parochial Library in St Michael's, catalogued by Davison in 1830. What mattered most was the effect of religious *practice* on the community as a whole, instilling the comfort of custom, the security and mutual trust of fellowship, and the assurance that no believer was actually alone.

Practice, like the wooden piles driven into Venetian islands to support the marvellous city, sustained a sense of commonwealth above and beyond the competing prospectuses on offer. Even burglars could rely on it: Davison noted one case of robbery 'during absence of family attending Divine Service'. Practice also depended on local opinion-makers, forceful families and charismatic preachers, of which education provision was a tangible sign.

LEFT *Plate 68 [54]. Dr Haswell April 30 1831 Alnwick.*

RIGHT *Plate 69 [56]. Dr Foulder April 30 1831 from memory. A celebrated man in his day.*

Though technically 'public' schools (as opposed to fee-paying private academies) the old Grammar School and its preparatory English School whose children started at six years old, were tied, admitting Freemen's children only, thus benefiting a maximum of 300 of the town's 1,000 to 1,200 families. They were funded by seventeenth century tolls on grain, topped up by the Town Council. It was in fact a small, non-compulsory system in each case, staffed by one master, conjoined with the equally small Borough School. The first intrusion on this cosy arrangement came, surprisingly, from the Duchess who instituted a school for girls in 1809, soon to be followed by her Duke who funded his equivalent for boys to mark George III's Golden Jubilee, which opened in 1811.

Ensconced in the Castle grounds, girls learned the useful domestic arts, writing, reading, knitting, sewing, and needlework with a view to learn from Her Grace what Davison called 'early industry and mature propriety'. The Duke's school aimed more ambitiously at 200 boys (half the numbers in Newcastle's Jubilee School serving a city ten times the size, but also funded by the Duke), but did not reach that total till the mid-nineteenth century. Sons of the poor received prizes and retrospective bursaries for those who afterwards 'won their employer's approbation' – a continuing string to hold them to decorous behaviour. But it was no Dotheby's Hall and its long-standing Head Master, Robert Beilby, a relative of the Newcastle glass maker and his partner Thomas Bewick, was well-remembered as kind and humane. So was Percy Forster's own schoolmaster George Barkas (Plate 71) 'an honest man is the noblest work of God . . . I was taught at his school and never knew a better man'.

The system followed Joseph Lancester's 'monitorial system' under which the most able pupils stayed on, often to sixteen years old or more, to teach. This had the dual effect of enhancing their commitment and saving master's fees. But it was not until the early 1840s that geography, history, drawing and vocal music reached the curriculum. Instead, as the 1911 centenary year's speaker put it, 'present day education is not without its dangers . . . there is more in education than spelling books and figures . . . one should not confound the whole-sale and retail dispensing of crude facts with the development of character and intelligence. The great test that pupils have to be prepared for is to face the stern realities of the world.'[8] Matthew Arnold's Rugby would be re-founded on lines similar to these, in the 1840s.

The list was completed by 'several reputable private schools for both sexes', establishments 'for instructing young ladies in the useful and ornamental branches of female education'; the only specifically religious offerings being three Sunday schools for Methodists or Presbyterians 'for teaching the catechism'. Most working class children left school at ten or eleven, invariably to start work, which explains why Plates 72–73 and 84–86 show only younger children at play or others on Sunday afternoons.

It may have been no better than what was offered in Kelso, a comparable Border town with its own Dukes of Roxburgh and Buccleugh; but it was already an improvement on what was generally available in the south of England and it was hardly at all fragmented by religious divisions. Education manifestly fostered a sense of community, rooted in the conservative, self-improving aspects of non-conformity. As George Eliot put it in *Adam Bede*, people who retained the sense of history and custom as guides actually lived in a wider world, held together by a moral code, owing allegiance to ideals based on local loyalties; as opposed to a logically more 'open' but disoriented modern one.[9]

On the other hand, many of the children, girls included, went to school barefooted, mocked by their peers;[10] and girls' futures remained almost wholly preordained, since that was believed to be the way to restrain social evils, greed, misbehaviour, rudeness, or sexual licence.[11] Those who chose not to take what was on offer, or whose parents rejected it, were likely to live outside, perhaps like nomad shepherds,

to acquire a different sort of local culture, based on a different definition of knowledge . . .

What followed school could hardly be called continuing education, even if more than three-quarters of all men were literate by 1830, half to two-thirds of all women.[12] But for the brighter ones (still called 'scholars' in the Census) the Mechanics Institute provided free lectures and access to a small library, unlike the town's subscription library which only the better-off could afford.

The Institute had been founded 'under the auspices of many of the nobility, gentry and

LEFT *Plate 70 [38]. Dr Turnbull 1831 from memory June 7 1831. A doctor of Divinity resided in Alnwick in 1820 or thereabout.*

RIGHT *Plate 71 [61]. George Barkas from memory July 10 1831. An honest man is the noblest work of God. A celebrated schoolmaster in Alnwick. I was taught at his school and never knew a better man than Old Barkas.*

clergy of the town and neighbourhood' according to Sykes' *Local Records*. But 'it must operate to check habits of idleness, and dissipation among the working class in this district, and to render them more intelligent and moral'.[13] No easement there or debate about how what leisure existed should be used (apart from possible free access to museums on Sundays). Like the mutual improvement society the Oddfellows, the Institute enjoined evening classes and early morning study while the SDUT (Society for the Diffusion of Useful Knowledge) published for its students the *Penny Magazine* from 1827.

These precursors of Samuel Smiles would later on be derided as surrogates of middle class orthodoxy, even after the Mechanics Institute began to move from education towards recreation, including a lecture series on architecture and the classical orders accompanied by plans and models. What they provided was on a take-it-or-leave-it basis, with no cash advantage (unlike the Oddfellows' sickness benefit and funeral costs). Yet in 1830, when the Institute had added the word Scientific to its title, it had reached 110 members, a one-third increase on 1829, benefiting from a library five times the size of the faith-based ones, its own reading room being open 8–9 daily and 1–9 on Sunday, and possessing 'some philosophical apparatus' (whatever that may have been).

Land for the 'New and handsome' building in Percy Street came from John Lambert, a local gentleman, other benefactors being the Duke and Lord Grey. On this bi-partisan foundation, algebra, astronomy and chemistry were added

ABOVE *Plate 72 [94]. Child holding a toy, barefoot, December 5 1832. 'Bramble prick.'*

BELOW *Plate 73 [105]. Two boys playing marbles March 21 1840.*

to its range, with weekly lectures on Wednesdays at 8:30pm. The course in Mechanical Philosophy and Electricity, cost 4 shillings in April 1829, and ended with two entitled 'How to avoid the dangers of a thunderstorm' and 'Reflection on the majesty of God displayed in the aweful phenomenon of Electricity'.

For all this, the presiding committee charged £11-10-6 a year payable in advance, (quite a substantial cost), selection being by ballot to exclude undesirables. A pattern is clear, as with the Friendly Societies and the Savings Bank, except that their good conduct rules were rather more explicit. So long as one obeyed the rules and demonstrated benefit, so long the better-off providers' sense of social duty was fulfilled. There could be no question about how their superiority was encapsulated in the various forms of private education available (the Borough schools being appropriate for the town's trades people, and self-employed artisans).

Most gentry families, in any case, employed a tutor or governess, this being typical until the end of the nineteenth century for girls, whereas boys, as Thomas Arnold observed in *Tom Brown's School Days*, were already sent increasingly as a matter of course to 'public' schools such as Rugby or, if destined for the army, to Wellington. That upper-class transition was for novelists to mark, just as satirists noted the erosion of dialect, words and country accents: brass and class becoming brahss and clahss at Eton by the 1850s. For Forster, however, what mattered more was the character of the local schoolmaster (Plate 71) kindly as well as authoritative in contrast to the old Anglican Establishment townees (Plate 74 and 75, 'as strange a couple of ecclesiasts as ever graced the Established Church'). His portrait of children imports an element of domesticity

to the family, almost prefiguring what one modern commentator saw as 'the invention of childhood',[14] but there are too few to judge.

Reading may have seemed a matter of improving the mind with 'useful knowledge', serving as a guide to good behaviour; but the books available in the non-religious libraries show that it was also an adventure and a pleasurable diversion. What else could it be in the age of Jane Austen and her host of imitators, followers of Henry Fielding or Tobias Smollett and the picaresque novelists, or the travellers' accounts illustrated with curious scenes, temples and indigenous tribes, offshoots of the serious anthropologists and geographers, but aimed at a mass audience having real leisure time to enjoy reading, for the first time, as a hobby rather than for instruction.

Popularity represents professionalism of the older print culture: nineteenth-century volumes copiously and better illustrated, with sophisticated tone printing, aquatints coloured by hand, or, in Forster's lifetime, the arrival of full-colour lithographs; books published in cloth bindings, allowing the wealthier the choice of rebinding in leather with or without crests and monograms, or, for poorer clients, published in parts – as were all of Dickens' novels. Bookplates had become commonplace, needing elaboration to dignify the owner: 'this book to be returned to its place'.

The publishers, led by Davison, who became partner of John Catnach in 1806[15] and afterwards one of the leading regional printers of the north of England, used Stanhope's new presses and intaglio machines for his engravings, as well as Gamble's up-to-date paper-making machine; and he supplied stereotype blocks for much of the north. He fed a wider print culture ranging

LEFT *Plate 74 [85]. Thomas Patterson from life February 20 1835. Long Parish Clerk at St. Mary's. Contemporary with James Bamforth, sexton. As strange a couple of ecclesiasts as ever graced the Established Church.*

RIGHT *Plate 75 [23]. James Bamforth from the life, sexton January 15 1833.*

from advertisements to theatre handbills, periodicals and cheap magazines. *The Spectator* or *Edinburgh Review* had spawned competitors throughout the eighteenth century, and by the 1820s, Forster's people could choose between the relatively expensive publications such as the *Gentleman's Magazine* or the cheap *Penny Magazine*. Alnwick itself offered (albeit briefly) the *Alnwick Athenaeum*, a liberal and scientific register of six pages in 1828 (T.H. Bell) and the equally short-lived *Alnwick Quarto* (Bell being in competition with Davison's *Alnwick Review*).

Thomas Bell was a one-man band as the sole surviving copy of the *Athenaeum*, priced 2 pence (no. 1) proves: under various guises, he filled the six pages himself, including an epitaph on the deceased *Quarto*. He opened with a notable claim 'a Periodical Publication may be considered as an intellectual steamboat; public opinion is the lake or sea to be navigated, ingenuity the steam, and patronage the boiler.' Few modern newspaper editors could disagree. His patrons were sundry 'Gentlemen of Alnwick' and in deference to their opinion, he gave a strong puff for the Mechanics Institute. Pompous and verbose Bell may have been, but he epitomised the last stage of Alnwick's renaissance with his essay 'On the Cultivation of a Philosophic Spirit and the Investigation of Scientific Truth'.

Yet the town failed to support a regular newspaper and both the *Athenaeum* and its 1827 predecessor, the *Alnwick Theatrical Observer* (Joseph

Graham) soon died. Mark Smith, another printer-editor, launched the *Northumberland Mirror* in 1837, the first weekly paper edited by William Ferguson and the Reverend William Telford, who doubled up as its main contributors. But that too died quickly. Even in 1852 the *Alnwick Punch*, a satirical magazine of four to ten pages, lasted only a year.

Failure to survive could be explained by the newspaper tax, which put such print beyond most of the public's readers (the *Berwick Advertiser* being 4½ pence in the 1800s, i.e., four hours of a labourer's wage) – except that, after its repeal in the late 1830s, the *Alnwick Mercury* (an eight-page monthly selling over 1,000 copies) offering local reportage, court proceedings, sports, fairs and shows, also folded. After Davison's death it was finally taken over by the successful *Alnwick and County Gazette*, reconstituted in 1858, to become a long-running weekly from 1883 with sales of 6,000.[16] The causes relate to Alnwick itself where, despite the availability of post-chaise or carrier pigeon a decade before the railways came, speculation and inaccurate reporting remained a greater danger than in Newcastle. (Even after his move to London, Catnach headlined in 1818 Napoleon's fictitious escape from St Helena together with his local mistress.)

There was a clear transition in what was actually published across the early nineteenth century, from Catnach's focus on the English classics (*Paradise Lost*, 1793), typography (*Beauties of Natural History*, 1804), local history (*The Hermit of Warkworth*, 1806), and Davison's rather wider range which included playbooks for children, stories and ballads, all with coloured woodcuts, sold by 'peddlers and chapmen'.[17] At a more elevated level, Davison printed Burns' *Poetical Works*, Boswell's *Life of Johnson*, *The Cabinet of Natural History*, and in 1819, Bewick's *Complete Works*: 153 engravings modelled on the French *Histoire Naturelle* (Buffon). Beyond these came texts of ballads, garden design, sheep-breeding, arithmetic, theology, and sermons. Davison was a polymath who built the Theatre in Fenkle Street, put in a manager, and printed its handbills (Plate 82), ran his new print machines in Bondgate, had his own circulating library, a sideline in pharmaceuticals, and a shareholding in the first gas works, giving light to read by.

What is more surprising than the newspaper failure rate, however, is the astonishing variety and ambition of several printers competing for an audience of no more than three and a half thousand literate adults. Space and money existed even for a politically critical *Alnwick Scandalismo* (no editor's name) 'being a critique upon the existing state of society in Alnwick', and an 1829 follow-up under the pseudonym Philip Mentor.

This whole enterprise lay outside the old margins of authority prescribed by the church or chapels and the town's elite. Alnwick's printers and publishers had created a new intellectual market in which a wider and increasingly emancipated crowd could shop unchecked save by the limits of literacy. Reading was in the process of becoming a common good, no longer, as in Russia or Timbuktu the preserve of scholars and the upper class. Even if it were taught only as the way into useful knowledge (for example by Charles Knight's Society for just that), for those who sought it, speculative knowledge followed. Lack of time alone could not prevent this passage, as Tate's list of Alnwick's intellectuals demonstrated. Percy Forster, the gamekeeper's son, had passed this barrier in his teens, as did George Tate himself. As an earlier Master of a Cambridge College put it, 'one part of learning doth convey light on another.'

Some of these vigorous, clashing debates can be related to Cobbett's legacy, the Reform Bill, and the origins of Chartism — and to personal combat between Bell and Davison — but also to the climate of intellectual challenge in which critics attacked not only economic exploitation but social preaching from above, Bell's 'detestation, nay abhorrence' of lectures, for example, given at the Mechanics Institute. Yet by the late 1830s, as Forster closed his project, the balance was shifting to an introverted, much more narrow-minded focus on religious tracts and a rather narrower definition of 'useful knowledge', in which Davison (ever-sensitive to public demand) took the lead.

The years 1800 to 1840 can therefore be seen as a sort of brief intellectual renaissance, open, argumentative, disputatious, irreverent. The so-called mid-nineteenth century Age of Improvement, in that view, worked to downgrade or even extinguish the long post-1770 legacy of the Enlightenment, the flowering of Regency thought being subordinated to Victorian moralism and hard economic logic. But that may not have applied to Forster's generation as they grew older, and certainly not to the freewheeling minds of gentry and the well-to-do who enjoyed and took part in the scholarly culture of learned societies, debates or lectures and exhibitions, even if Henry Collingwood Selby's grandiose project to build his own observatory at Swansfield Park to rival that of the Duke, was never actually completed.

In this society, the educated reader (to use Jane Austen's categorisation of Elizabeth Barrett, in contrast to Mr Darcy's claims of good breeding) bought books for the famiy library, not just the sumptuous coffee table volumes on birds and reptiles, Middle Eastern travel, mysteries of the Orient and India, but novels (a quarter of Davison's list), history (Hume and Gibbon or, in fiction, Scott's novels), science or astronomy. He (rather than she), however, was unlikely to have read Adam Smith or Fergusson, though their volumes may have been on his shelves; even less likely that he dipped into Blackstone's legal tomes or *Gray's Anatomy*, the provinces of real professionals.

Books were available for all tastes, accessible and affordable well beyond the range of earlier gentry habits. It is clear that by the first quarter of the nineteenth century, there existed a reading class and a regional dimension within it — the point being that Alnwick society was probably more advanced than the south, and that its 'habitual readers' (to use Griswold's phrase)[18] retained a sort of regional independence of mind, despite the access to reviewers at national level — provided by the weekly book review in the *Newcastle Courant*.

Without putting too much emphasis on one publisher/printer, Davison's approximately 100 volumes after 1807 included 50 per cent religious works across all the sectarian divides; to which should be added 25 per cent travel, history and science, and a 25 per cent coverage of contemporary novels: not just the great Jane, whose popularity lasted much longer after her death in 1817 in the north than in southern England, but forgotten competitors such as 'the ingenious Miss Hindmarsh', author of *The Cave of Hoonga, a Tongian Tradition and other Poems* (1818). Davison also had a ready-made market in second-hand books, 'several thousand volumes warranted perfect unless otherwise specified'.[19] On 28 January 1829, Mr Busby's auction rooms held a four-day sale of valuable books and engravings, preceded by a viewing 'and should any lady or gentleman be desirous to proceed by private bargain, Mr. B. will attend for that purpose'.

Given all that, there is no reason to disagree with Griswold that 20 per cent of the population in the north (perhaps more than in the south) constituted a *reading public*, with all that that meant for discussion, gossip, argument, diversion, and good company. What is often typified as the Victorian family's evening entertainment had in fact already existed for half a century; William Gardener, master hosier of Leicester, called his 1838 autobiography *Music and Friends*.

Alnwick could not have produced so many notable intellectuals as Newcastle, which is not surprising in a small town. But Edward Mackenzie who had commented on the city's Jubilee schools 'some of the boys in the upper classed display an acuteness and rapidity of thought almost incredible', in 1835 went on to cite Adam Oliver the distinguished Alnwick mathematician 'whose extreme modesty and diffidence prevented him from rising in life, nor did he desire it, as leisure and retirement constituted his happiness'. George Tate was already what is now styled a public intellectual; scholar at the Borough School under George Dixon in the early 1820s, he had by 1840 become a member of the Society of Antiquaries, the Anthropologists Society, Newcastle's Literary and Philosophical Society, the Geological Society of Edinburgh, and an early recruit to the Berwickshire Naturalists Club, later its President.

That he was a linen draper, son of a stone mason, was irrelevant. He was a gifted lecturer and for thirty years Secretary of the Mechanics Institute; and in his gas-lit house he had his own museum/laboratory.[20] Robert Embleton, the surgeon (1806–75), also a student at the Institute,

master of botany, natural history, electricity and galvanism, married an Alnwick wine merchant's daughter and maintained his own herbarium while corresponding with several of Britain's leading botanists. Craster and Alnmouth fishermen brought him odd or unusual specimens, including native corals from Embleton Bay, long extinct; and in 1831 he was one of the original group who set up the Berwickshire Naturalists Club.

Towards the end of his second volume, Tate recited a list of twenty names of intellectuals he had known in Alnwick, several of whom were still alive in 1865 when he completed his *History*. A few had gone south to London, like George Airey, later Astronomer Royal; three were members of the Selby family (Henry Collingwood Selby, who built Swansfield Park, Prideaux, his son the educationalist, and the grandson John, author and illustrator of *British Ornithology*, several volumes 1821–34.)

Among the rest, George Ilderton Benn, the solicitor who founded Alnwick's Literary Society in 1790 which became the model for Newcastle's Lit and Phil; John Carr, Inland Revenue Officer who build Bondgate Hall and wrote an incisive investigation of the whisky-smuggling trade; Thomas Collingwood, physician, an Edinburgh graduate; the Reverend Henry Grey, a notable Presbyterian minister; Isabella Hindmarsh, the poetess of 'melancholic verses'; Henry Ogle and John Common, who invented and built the Alnwick reaping machine in 1802 and perfected it by the 1820s despite public opposition to its effect on labour (which was later copied by the American agriculturalist Cyrus McCormick); John Patterson, another minister and classicist; Robert Weddel antiquary, author of *The History of Berwick*; and John Yelloly MD, from a linen-draper family, physician, scientist and president of

Plate 76 [79]. William Leithead 1831 from memory December 12 1831. An Attorney in Alnwick from the 1820s.

London's Geological Society. To these, between the 1780s and the 1850s, Alnwick's renaissance owed its existence.

Within the learned societies, colleagues circulated manuscripts, essays for discussion, as well as the specimens themselves. The fraternity included in fact all 'educated men' and in due course, their female counterparts, even if these had to be admitted, like the BNC from the beginning, as 'extraordinary members'. Professional rivalries co-existed with scientific collaboration and did not necessarily work to the exclusion of women, such as Annabel Carr, daughter of a Newcastle banker who lectured on mechanics and hydrostatics in the 1820s and published *Conversations on Chemistry* (1807).

Modelling themselves on the Edinburgh Plinian Society (founded by students in 1824), one of whom had become curator at the British Museum's zoological department, nine 'clubbable men [seven doctors and two clergy] with interests in fishing, shooting, fox hunting as well as natural history' set up the Berwickshire Naturalists Society at a meeting under the auspices of George Johnston[21] on 22 September 1831, 'where the gentlemen present . . . agreed to form themselves into a club with the object to investigate the natural history and antiquities of Berwickshire and its vicinage' — the latter defined as including Alnwick on one side and Roxburghshire on the other. All professionals being counted as gentry were eligible to take part in five meetings a year.

Within two years it had twenty-seven members, four of whom were women. Alnwick contributed William Leithead (Plate 76) and W.F. Bow MD; the total soon reached seven clergy, three doctors, six surgeons, ten gentlemen (unspecified), and one academic. The first full meeting in July 1832 was presented with a rare ring ouzel shot by the Reverend Mr Campbell. It already served as a 'rendezvous for the naturalists of the district, where they may cultivate a mutual acquaintance, and talk over their common pursuit . . . where each may nourish his neighbour's zeal; where we may have our careless season . . . in good feeling and humour.'

Beyond natural history, members purposefully opened up the study of local customs, sports, Morris dancing, feud-settling, cockfighting, curious medical phenomena, popular rhymes, sayings and prophesies — an eclectic range of inquiry with time off, on one occasion in 1844, for target practice at sea-birds wheeling around St Abb's Head. In the early days, meetings started after breakfast with observation walks, discussions and an early dinner before listening to the main paper.

But by 1840, numbers were down to twenty-two and the club was nearly dissolved two years later, there having been disputes as to whether to extend its debates to antiquities, and whether to accept 'excursions in the nature of picnics'. Revived, by 1848 it grew to seventy members including bankers and aristocrats such as Lord Hume and the Duke of Northumberland, he being one of three Alnwick members at what was, evidently, the club's southern boundary. Almost impossible to imagine today, it was a serious, thoughtful yet wholly amateur scholarly body, many of them genuine polymaths firing ideas off each other, setting the natural world, its geology and history on a basis of proper scholarship much of which is still relevant today. Thus a new standard was set up to test the assumptions underpinning local identity (Chapter 2) part of Alnwick's renaissance and source of a long erosion of historical myth accompanied by the seeping in of modern scholarly criteria.

It could easily be seen as a distant relative of Birmingham's far more famous Lunar Society, but was actually more closely linked to Newcastle's Literary and Philosophical Society (founded three years after Alnwick's equivalent in 1793), the Society of Antiquaries (1813), and the Northern Counties' Club, whose meetings, however, tended to be less adventurous, centred around lectures and academic papers rather than physical exercise in pursuit of research.

Alnwick had its artistic limits. For a serious exhibition or auction of 'celebrated artists of the Italian, Dutch and Flemish schools', including works attributed to Titian, Guercino, Velasquez,

Rubens, Ruysdael, Poussin, and lesser Old Masters, potential buyers had to take the Great North Road to Newcastle to Mr Scaife, auctioneer in Vail's salesrooms — regional rival to Mr Christie in King Street. But an exhibition of North East contemporary artists in 1828 at the Northern Academy was funded by several local and Northumberland gentry as well as all the northern MPs.[22]

This was what Percy Forster aspired to (following Bewick's famous example) and what he had achieved before his actual move to Newcastle. This may be seen as a sign of the assimilation of one small town into a wider regional style, directly linked to the London art market. But the change did not display any of the nostalgia for a mythical rural culture, rather an extension of or folding in of Alnwick's renaissance to what North Eastern artists such as T.M. Richardson and his son, or J.W. Carmichael exhibited and sold on an annual basis, even when they had become national figures (Carmichael acting as an official war painter during the Crimean War). Indeed, even in the 1820s, John Varley had painted most of the Northumbrian castles in watercolour, which command high prices today, a path followed by George Vincent.

Newcastle's new Academy of Arts, built for the purpose of exhibition and sales, provided a similar meeting place of minds. Whereas Mr Wright of Edinburgh, down for the races in 1829, advertised 'a choice and genuine collection of Gallery and Cabinet paintings', including a Rembrandt self-portrait, immediately after the Academy opened it displayed contemporary work, among that being a life-size version of Canova's Three Graces. North East fashionable taste approved of both Old Masters and the evolving English school, though Constable

Drawn by William Hall.   Engraved by James Kerr

Plate 77. Market Place. Engraving by William Davison 1828 (from Descriptive and Historical View of Alnwick, *1829).*

and Turner arrived later than in the south. It enhanced, rather than diminished regional identity, being in the debatable forefront of the English art market, just as Liverpool, Exeter or Bristol were at the same time.

Such polyphony sets Alnwick within the intellectual machinery of Britain's regional culture, linked directly by learned correspondence not only to Newcastle but to Edinburgh and London, as Davison's manuscript volumes indicate. Alnwick's architecture and its expanding town plan (the word plan being, probably for the first time in its history, appropriate),[23]

its late Georgian façades, Italianate piazza (Plate 77), spacious well-proportioned main halls of local banks or insurance companies, reflects in miniature the Newcastle of Grey Street or Edinburgh's Charlotte Square.

In terms of knowledge and discussion, Alnwick's literate elite had the Newcastle and Berwick papers with news of the Court, House of Lords and Commons debates with speeches almost in full, events in Europe and North America, religious disputes as well as market prices or shipping register news. They could learn what the *Courant* advertisement called 'the delightful art of shorthand' in six one-hour lessons (designed for office clerks) and they could watch in 1829 at second-hand, the executions of Burke and Hare.

Through many levels of reading and conversation, and in the search for betterment, Alnwick folk could relate their town life to like-minded communities such as Kelso and Carlisle, which shared in a similar sort of renaissance. To that extent, though 'provincial' in accent and sometimes dress, they would not have been out of place among their London equivalents, following the example of William Leithead with his London correspondent solicitors and even the Duke himself, at Northumberland House for the season.

Letters took less than two days to London, foreign travel opportunities existed at will, dependent only on money and desire, forty years before Thomas Cook packaged the Grand Tour for a middle-class market. Cecilia Lady Ridley's diaries recorded her journey in 1834 from Boulogne, through France and Germany, to the original Renaissance cities of Italy, with excursions enroute to see the awesome romantic landscape of the Alps. For her contemporaries and gossips, this was the cultural pilgrimage to Mecca – at least until 1914 deleted Germany from the script.[24]

It is not exaggeration to portray a marketplace of the mind, open to anyone on grounds of literacy and proper behaviour: from inns to churches, private drawing rooms (a new term) to the Castle's library where respectable readers could even borrow books. For those with time and money to spare, ideas and prejudices ran together with scholarly speculation, unregulated except by the canons of public decency and order (and not always then); where the ingrained element of caution or restraint on what might be put about in the real, rough marketplace of the crowd, lay not in censorship (yet) but in abridgement for an audience less versed in complex argument.

Was this small world a closed elite? No, if we look at membership of clubs and societies, and their rules for entry. Difficult to access, yes, hedged about by restraints on conformity and respect, of course, but available to anyone of education as George Tate's example shows. Nor was politics banned; indeed, in the modern sense, most subjects were infused with politics.

The local, then, was also global and the global compressed one way or another into local life – as the Alnwick Theatre handbills demonstrate (Chapter 5). There is evidence that this awareness could be common to men and women, along with much stronger evidence about the humanising and civilising of family life, at least when necessity did not force children to leave school at ten years of age. Local linkages, like ligaments, helped: most marriages were made between couples no more than seven miles apart, which created an inextricable web of communication, influence or friendship.[25]

Alnwick's people were also linked to the outside world by shared memory, not just of the far-off past (Chapter 2) but of the first total war against Napoleon, and in some cases, the American War of Independence. Sergeant Beeby was not the only survivor; the unpopular Colonel Lindsay had also served the East India company (Plate 98, 'commonly called the Fox'). Many had relations in what was becoming the British Empire: letters to and from Ontario or the West Indies retain a flavour of local gossip, as if written from Morpeth or Belford.

One lecturer at the Mechanics Institute put forward the concept of an 'Imperial Parliament' while the *Courant's* column 'Multum in Parvo' introduced readers to the latest scientific inventions, such as Humphrey Davy's mine safety lamp or the unwrapping of Egyptian mummies. Newcastle's Society of Antiquaries outdid this, of course; its seventeenth meeting in 1830 was attended by 'foreign dignitaries', to listen to Champalimaud's work on Egyptian hieroglyphs, before turning to the geology of the banks of the Tweed.

Global sensibility helped to shape identity in a community which might respect the achievements of Italy or China, but still suspected its Scottish drovers or 'foreign' gypsies. The foreigner at whom children threw stones might come from France or Wooler . . . he was judged by his appearance, dialect and habits before conversation even began – as Dickens observed in *Little Dorrit*. Even so, foreign words were passing into English use: verandah, coolie . . . while the anti-slavery campaign was educating Alnwick's citizens in what occurred in the West Indies, at a crowded meeting in November 1830, held in the Congregational chapel, before the congregation signed a petition to Lord Grey and his son, Lord Howick MP.

'The view from Alnwick' thus formed a sort of *camera obscura*. At little trouble or expense, the viewer could follow Simon Bolivar's war to liberate South America from Spanish rule (with some fellow-feeling for his Scottish naval commander, Admiral Cochrane, 10th Earl of Dundonald) or the Decembrists' plots against the Tsar of Russia. The mindset that resulted may have been provincial but it was often as complex and diverse in miniature as that of any great English city. Before he became President of the British Association, the Duke, as patron of Cambridge's Philosophical Society, exchanged letters with Sir James Herschel, one of the leading astronomers in Europe, about

providing the university with a celestial telescope made by Canchoix of Paris in 1833, at a delivery charge of 20 guineas; while his sponsorship research into waterproof clothing culminated in 1835, having cost him 15,000 French francs.

Was there then an understanding within and among the literate element in Alnwick's community that linked provision of education with genuinely scholarly activities, individual self-improvement, pleasures of readership, accompanied by proper behaviour, setting more decorous limits to, but not eliminating 'the civilisation of the crowd'? The answer must be yes, though the substance is often hard to document except by pointing to what went on, where and why. As the first Queen Elizabeth pointed out, her religious settlement did not 'seek to pry into men's souls'.

Forster gives little clue as to whether any level of discourse existed between clerisy-gentry, craftsmen or artisans. Clearly the taverns and inns hosted separate clienteles, and much if not most of an evening's drinking centred on local gossip rather than scholarship. Put differently, however, there is indirect evidence that major questions of the day, national as well as local, filtered down, arousing both prejudice and fervour: slavery, political reform, local corruption or inefficiency in the Town Moor administration. A Presbyterian definition of heresy still mattered, as did the imposition of game laws or improvements at the Dispensary.

Alnwick was bound to be an open, contentious place, given the large numbers of travellers and salesmen riding through, and its multiple linkages beyond. How should it have been otherwise in a miniature metropolis? There is a particular openness even about Forster's people, as if their minds were free to argue with the next man, neighbour or foreigner, merchant or gentleman. They do not seem downcast like Millais' peasants or fearful and resentful, as the standard portrayal of the industrial proletariat suggests.

Rousseau's 'social contract' is too legally phrased, too rooted in Roman law to apply. Even the concept of 'negotiated hegemony' seems too abstract, though it allows for and explains the relative absence of enforcement. But Gramsci's work does illustrate the existence of mutual benefit, adaptation time, flexibility, and space for alternative interpretations. To this must be added consent, a central element in constructing any real community.

Neighbourliness, whether at work or in thought, comes about as much by random touch and tacit understanding as by deliberate planning; it concerns governance rather than government, consent mitigating obedience to authority. If there was an early nineteenth century social contract, it had two faces, meeting mass aspirations, while retaining power made acceptable by respect. It also depended, like the ancient Roman Republic, on the provision of spectacle and entertainment (Chapter 5).

Alnwick's well-educated oligarchy presided over but also collaborated with smaller less-endowed oligarchies, for example the guilds of artisans and traders. Like Scottish stone sundials, the result was multi-faceted and polyhedral, in sharp contrast to the Civil War preacher's text: 'desire not to be singular, nor to differ from others, for it is a sign of a naughty spirit which hath caused much evil in the world from the beginning.' It allowed both gentry awareness and artisan literacy to coexist. An element of public spirit provided justification and challenges (very different from the modern evolution of public service, where targets are defined by providers not recipients) to which a duty-bound elite could respond; and with a widely shared pride.[26]

Educated people, as Norman McCord puts it, could therefore deplore an earlier lack of education, or the existence of administrative corruption, in order to seek proper funding, practical regulation, trustworthy local government, and incentives to better behaviour. Disease, disorder, crime, illegitimacy, of course continued, but to a slowly diminishing degree; as William Morris put it, 'men fight and lose the battle, and the thing they fought for comes about in spite of their defeat, and when it comes, it turns out not to be what they meant, and other men have to fight for what they meant under another name.'

The town's elites lived not in separate worlds but physically together within the town; having lives often far outside, and far more fashionable tastes, they still engaged with each other, even if, collectively, they diverged on contentious matters such as reform and the practical implications of their self-interest. Its community was not of course one of Edmund Burke's 'small platoons', an extravagant phrase which took for granted the presence of a common enemy and a shared danger against which to unite . . . and which in this period was reflected only in the Duke's correspondence with his diehard colleague the Prime Minister, Duke of Wellington, in 1830–1 (Chapter 6). If nothing else, the taste for drink, vast dinners, bawdy songs, and what by modern standards were extremely rough sports, provided common ground, whatever the churches and chapels deplored.

The Wee Fisher!

Chapter 5
Sport and Leisure

From a modern perspective, early nineteenth century Alnwick lay at the centre of a small world, a single cog engaged with other minor wheels in a vast and complex mechanism, its importance apparently small. Yet without small cogs, the machine does not work at all. Alnwick had its own ethos. If its pattern of work resembled many other county towns, its range of intellectual activity was surprisingly diverse. What then of its leisure life, its own focus on

play, collective, competitive or solitary at will, where time allowed — for commoners of 1831 did not enjoy much leisure, and only the roughest sports?

Before the idea of holidays for working people even crept into the popular imagination, their entertainment was restricted to occasional public celebrations and feasts, together with Sunday afternoons, religious festivals, Christmas and Easter, perhaps ten days a year altogether. One simple way to distinguish who had leisure and who had only time, is to ask who wore a watch. Even a silver pocket watch cost five shillings and it hung on a fob from the owner's belt (the wristwatch came a century later). Forster is careful to distinguish: some of the bearers are not those one might expect.

Yet at night, or at least after dark, he (not yet she) had the ale house or tavern with their home-brewed malt beers, while his wife cooked supper. Vastly extended after the 1830 Beer Act made licences cheaper (£2) and easier to obtain, in these he could gossip with friends, free of the children, listening or singing to a little night music on the fiddle or flute (Plate 79, James Riley, clarinet, and Plate 80, Ald Tom Coward, violinist), drinking house-brewed ale or perhaps a snort of smuggled whisky enlivened with a pinch of snuff (Plate 81) and a game of skittles. His wife may have been careworn, borne down by too much child-bearing but, outside the Poor House and its sad inmates, she kept her doorstep scrubbed while gossiping to her friends, 'a good clack' in the local idiom.

OPPOSITE *Plate 78 [16].*
Little Jimmy Harrington the
wee fisher!

LEFT *Plate 79 [19]. James*
Riley a celebrated clarinet
player and leather cutter,
Alnwick October 1831, then
from memory December 2
1831.

LEFT *Plate 80 [41]. Ald Tom Coward April 26 1831. A celebrated violin player Alnwick.*

RIGHT *Plate 81 [98]. Snuff taker 'I'll no be the waur o' anither pinch, I'm thinking.'*

All this changed little before Gladstone's 1872 Licensing Act (which was so unpopular that it helped to bring down his government two years later), despite the desperate efforts of the Temperance Societies. Later analysts were to style this 'the civilisation of the crowd', for pub and street had a life which rarely overlapped with the inns and hotels, except that some musicians played in both. Alnwick prided itself on variety: forty-eight taverns and four beer houses, the distinction being between take-home drink and an evening's entertainment (say at the tavern still called the 'Dirty Bottles' from the eighteenth century green glass bottles in its bay window, protected by local superstition and by the mid-nineteenth century patronage of the Richardson gang). Eight of these were run by women and Barbara Wilson managed the distinctly up-market White Swan Hotel for most of the 1820s.

Serious pursuit of study, by those motivated to attend evening classes after a day's work, might mean less or little leisure time. There is no evidence however that, apart from a handful of 'godly men' and their families, this meant that there was no sport, no gossip. The sheer number of drinking places and the volume of what was drunk argue otherwise. There is no evidence either of the crowd's absence at public dinners and entertainments, indeed the reverse:

more invitations, more baking, more brewing to keep pace.

Music in concert form rather than pub players had become both available and affordable. Restricted to cities in the later eighteenth century, it had reached most provincial towns, usually in the form of choral societies at which the non-conformist chapels excelled. Brass bands flourished, helped to higher performance by the introduction of valves for their instruments in the 1820s.

But the word 'civilisation' requires a definition attuned to early nineteenth century customs. On one hand, public hangings or whippings attracted large, vociferous crowds in a ritual barely changed since the sixteenth century; on the other, so did notable sermons or political meetings. The old distinction between the smelly crowd in the theatre pit or watching cruel sports and the quasi-elegant inhabitants of the boxes and galleries remained. What differed from Hogarth's drawings was the viewer's transition, the better seats now being paid for by the town's new middle class and retail shopkeepers.

As the Alnwick Old Theatre handbills demonstrate (Plate 82), that menu had to attract all sorts. Programmes ran all year, providing mostly melodrama, excitement and spectacle rather than high theatre (though that did have a place . . . even if still subject to the Lord Chamberlain's censorship).[1] Attractions ranged from Atkins's and Wombwell's Circus, with its clowns, acrobats and conjurers, to bawdy pantomime and satire.

Alnwick could not rival Newcastle where Billy Purvis in the Tyneside Concert Hall had his own company in the 1820s near the Theatre Royal, preparing the North East for what became the Victorian musical. But Alnwick did provide what Davison the theatre's proprietor

THEATRE, ALNWICK.

Mr DEANS assures the Ladies and Gentlemen of this Place that a

Gentleman of Alnwick

will perform the PART OF PIERRE, in the celebrated Tragedy of VENICE PRESERVED.

This present Thursday Evening, Jan. 2nd. 1817,

Will be acted the admired Tragedy of

Venice Preserved;

Or, a Plot discovered.

Priuli	-	-	-	-	-	-	Mr DEANS
Jaffier	-	-	-	-	-	-	Mr VILLARS
Pierre --	-	-	-		*a Gentleman of Alnwick.*		
Renault -	-	-	-	-	-		Mr DALRYMPLE
Spinoza -	-	-	-	-	-		Mr SMITH
Elliott -	-	-	-	-	-		Mr GARDENER
Redamar	-	-	-	-	-		Mr J. ANDREWES
Executioner	-	-	-	-	-		Mr FILLAN
Duke of Venice -	-	-	-	-	-		Mr DEANS
Belvidera	-	-	-	-	-	-	Mrs DEANS

After the Play the following Entertainments:-

Singing	-	-	-	-	-	-	by Mr ANDREWES.
Recitations	-	-	-	-	-	-	by Mr SMITH.

To conclude with the laughable Farce of

FORTUNE'S FROLIC

Or, the Ploughman made Lord.

Robin Roughhead	-	-	-	-	-	Mr FILLAN
Mr Franks	-	-	-	-	-	Mr DALRYMPLE
Old snacks	-	-	-	-	-	Mr DEANS
Rattle -	-	-	-	-	-	Mr J. ANDREWES
Clown -	-	-	-	-	-	Mr ANDREWES
Countrymen	-	-	-	-	-	Messrs VILLARS and
SMITH						
Margery	-	-	-	-	-	Mrs DEANS
Dolly -	-	-	-	-	-	Mrs FILLAN

THE MAYOR OF NEWCASTLE

called, rather hypocritically, 'general satisfaction to all classes of society, as they are divested of all Buffoonery and conducted with Utmost Decorum' — as exemplified by Morgiana, the musical Hoop Dancer performing the Dance of Death called 'the Animated Skeleton'.

Plate 82. Alnwick Theatre Bill, 2 January 1817.

Turtle Soup
Salmon
Pig
Moor Game

Friccasee Sweetbreads		Turtle-a-la-bran
Orange Jelly		Italian Cheese
Glazed Tongue		Turkey Pout
Potted Lobster		Pickled Macrels
Fricando of Veal		Beef-a-la-mode
Piramid Paste		Jelly
Lemon Pudding		Stew'd Duck
Blancmange		Cold Lobster
Almon Soup*		Gravey Soup**
Potted Beef		Strawberry Cream
Grill'd Chicken		Mock Venison
Jelly		Tartlets
Ragood Pigeons		Moor Game Pye
Pickled Salmon		Potted Veal and Ham
Chickens		Grill'd Ham
Chantilly Pye		Orange Jelly
Friccassee Turtle		Lamb Fry

*Removed for Leveret.

**Removed for Moor Game.

Turtle Soup
Salmon
Sir Loin of Beef
Moor Game

―――――――

G. Angus, Printer, Newcastle

Plate 83. Assize week dinner menu, Newcastle 1816.

In the same way, as Ackerman's widely-selling and still popular coloured engravings show, public sporting taste ranged from steeple chasing (a new 1820s term),[2] to bare knuckle boxing, cock fighting, and even archery — at which well-dressed ladies could play (Leech's cartoon *The Fair Toxophilites c.*1835). To hang such

pictures on the wall gave even a modest home an illusion of gentry association and in the case of boxing, cock-fighting or racing, a memory of wagers lost and won.

Unlike nineteenth-century equivalents, spectator sports attracted all classes; only the quality of the chairs in tight-packed circles separated aristocrats from workers in the cock-fight saloon, both being avid gamblers. One of Leech's most perceptive cartoons shows a hunt meeting, the Duke at the centre on a fine mount, a motley group of hunt members around, and in the foreground, on a bent nag, the local tailor: 'the beauty of 'unting yer Grace is what it brings all classes of people together'.

To attend a ball in the Assembly Rooms required a ticket[3] and proper dress; but no bouncers policed the great dinners or royal anniversaries and ducal celebrations. At the other end of the scale, the children playing in the streets (Plates 73, 84, 86) can be seen simply as ragged urchins, juvenile delinquents holding up traffic, or as Forster drew them, kids making their own entertainment free of the tiresome adult world. Beyond the brief period of child-hood, a world of non-work also existed, not criminal (for that was hard and dangerous) but St Monday, the day set aside for recovery from hangovers, the last day paid for by the pawn broker before the watch's owner had to start again, in order to reclaim it.

COLLECTIVE PLAY

Leaving out the serious, ideological gatherings and the Assembly Room gatherings as being, by definition, for the wealthier or the intel-lectually committed, public entertainment centered on fairs, festivals and regular func-tions such as racing, celebratory dinners, hunt

Plate 84 [96]. Boy and girl
'Well he began to have strains
first, he twick up a muckle great
strain an' <u>hat is</u> on other lug!

meets or gardening exhibitions. The tradition of public celebration goes back to Roman times of course, its grandest exhibition being those of Louis XIV, with the interplay between real power and the 'prerogative of pleasure'. Yet even in the French King's time, Molière satirised in *Le Bourgeois Gentilhomme* the social climate where upper class splendor surrendered its exclusivity to the competitive aspirations of the newly rich middle class.

Some of the grander dinners celebrating great events such as the Duke's appointment as Lord Lieutenant of Ireland in 1829 or, earlier, the end of the Napoleonic War, appear to have been truly epic, and what they lacked in variety was exceeded by the volume of drink and the sheer size of the dumplings and meat pies. For a fine, choicer menu, one needed to be invited to the Fancy Ball Winter Assembly in Newcastle, where the first dance was set off by the High Sheriff, Henry Collingwood's wife, the 'Turkish mode of fancy dress being preferred', which lasted till 3am. The Bill of Fare on Friday in Assize Week in Newcastle 1816 shows what variety could mean (Plate 83). Crown and Court might be disregarded or unknown in the provinces, but the celebrations for Queen Victoria's coronation in June 1838 set a new standard for entertainment, now bounded by restraint.

For the mass audience, even the Duke did not rival his cousin in Sussex, Lord Egremont, who in 1834, according to Greville the diarist, invited 4,000 guests. Six thousand actually attended and the gentry carved for the rest. But as the *Courant* put it on the Duke's birthday in February 1829 'the deputation, after partaking of refreshments provided for them . . . left the Castle much pleased with the urbanity of his Grace and the reception he had given them'. At least they could still walk home downhill via Narrowgate. The following year, on the same occasion, the towns' tradesmen gave a reciprocal lunch for eighty: 'After the health of the King was drunk, all the branches of the illustrious House of Percy were drunk with enthusiasm and followed by appropriate tunes from the band of the Northumberland Regiment.' Then on to the evening dance in the new Assembly Rooms. In 1832, eighty guests again for his Grace's birthday, 'sumptuous entertainment provided by Mr Johnston of the Star Inn', regimental music and a salute of guns in the market place at each toast, accompanied by bells and a huge bonfire.

Such dinners began habitually around 3pm in the 1820s, the time of day gradually shifting later by mid-century. Speeches punctuated them, necessarily because many by the end could take in little more, being as in Hogarth's *Midnight Modern Conversation* (1758) irretrievably drunk. But one feast did precede the fair, on the last Monday in July, for cattle, sheep and horse sales. On the Sunday night all the town officials and most of the trades people wined and dined in the Castle and watched the display of ancient weaponry across the Barbican, while the kids pelted each other with fir cones and crab apples to symbolise the older Border warfare.

The ancient fairs continued, only slightly curtailed by Dissenting propriety and the arrival of new, less public fashions. The Lord of Misrule, abolished during the Civil War, had been reinstated under Charles II but had finally disappeared during the later eighteenth century. The Waits survived, singing on dark winter mornings accompanied by the Northumbrian pipes and fiddles, all dressed in the town's livery, blue coats faced in yellow, silver lace and buttons with the Alnwick crest.

Their most famous piper, James Allen, was finally hanged for theft in 1810, and replaced as chief musician by John Hogg. But that all ended in September 1831 as the Four and Twenty tried to capture 'reform', shutting down aspects of a soon-to-be-forgotten past.

What remained, until 1854, was the induction of new members to the Freeman body, 'leaping the well' (see page 168, note 17). Decline had many causes and moved irregularly according to public taste. It affected in the end even the Shrove Tuesday festivities, with its pancakes in the streets, following Collop Monday's slices of salt meat fried with eggs, so that Tate's comments have an elegiac tone. Yet the rough side of fairs survived well into the twentieth century with tent-booths presenting 'bearded ladies', fortune tellers, near-strippers, and pugilists taking on all comers, while Punch and Judy held the children outside.

Greater decorum finally came about as the result of long Dissenting hectoring, matched by the growth of new fashions for *spectator* sports such as cricket or ballooning where the audience watched increasingly skilled performers from outside. The moralists eventually got rid of cock fighting, as they had done with bear- and bull-baiting earlier,[4] but as late as 1829 the *Courant* could still carry on its front page advertisements for Best and Company's cockpit with huge prizes from £50 to £100 'the birds to weigh in on the Saturday before and draw as usual' (which the Town Council supported and drew fees from the cockpit at Pottergate Tower). Cock fighting together with dog fighting, could still be watched in villages near Alnwick in secret in the 1930s and 1940s.

Boxing was scarcely more civilised than the Alnwick stocks, where criminals could still be pelted with stones, sticks and rotten fruit.

Fifteen rounds with bare knuckles produced hideous and long-lasting injuries. The era of Tom Cribb and Tom Spring and their crowds of supporters and punters was, in retrospect, both brutal and vile, pandering to a taste for blood. But young, less fastidious gentry enthusiastically challenged the professionals, who may have softened or misdirected their blows so as not to create permanent disfigurement. Thus Cuthbert Shafto a landowner near Morpeth fought Tom Skelton in Alnwick in 1821, surviving several rounds. But by the Reform period, gloves were being introduced, as well as more effective discipline by referees.

Football, though no longer so violent as in the eighteenth century, remained street territorial and wild until the council and Utilitarians banned it from the town centre in 1828. Still, for several decades thereafter, each February, the match took place in the Duke's Pasture between married and unmarried Freemen, lasting never less than two hours. Formalised rules and a sense of public decency only then began the long conversion from urban warfare to modern clubs and supporters. Thus cricket could still be a violent game, curved bats turning easily to clubs in an era before overarm bowling established itself. Football remained anarchic, closer to the riotous exchanges between Montagu and Capulet than the disciplined FA-ruled matches of the later nineteenth century.

Other pastimes produced less mayhem: a sort of primitive golf (though Alnmouth had the first real course – it being regarded as a slightly suspect Scottish import in the North East) and for the girls, keppy-ball, a combination of handball and rounders played up against ancient trees in the Castle meadow, followed by songs about lovelorn swains around the evening bonfire.

All day in the corners of the market, cursed by stall holders and passersby, children kicked balls, played marbles and tops, skipped and played hoopla, hunt-the-hare, stealy-clothes (the last touch of Border thieving for coats, caps and knives) and a sort of street cricket without wickets like three point baseball.

By the 1840s most of this unlicensed gaiety had been driven out of the marketplace to more distant playgrounds in the name of improvement and non-conformist prejudice, in favour of 'rational recreation', egged on by the Societies for Lord's Day Observance and for the Suppression of Vice, as Tate sadly recorded. The Duke even offered a properly appointed recreation ground as part of the Town Moor enclosure settlement. Carling remained, on Good Friday and Passion Sunday, with pease steeped, then fried in butter, fermented sugar, pepper and brandy, handed out at the inns like *tapas* to help the drink down. And still, Tate remembered, superstition, old wives' tales, Faeries Green, and dancing revels at the top of Clayport Bank, and after that

> as one that on a lonesome road
> doth walk in fear and dread
> for he knows well some fearful fiend
> doth close behind him tread

The other great spectator sport, horse racing, of course legitimised gambling in a way that Dissent and the SPCK could never check. Indeed by trying, they served to professionalise it, at the hands of itinerant but usually wealthy bookmakers most of whom remained on the course for another hundred years, many being ready to run if losses ran too high . . . Alnwick was no exception: the old course on the Town moor had been removed to the race ground, and prizes in the 1820s ran at £50 and upwards with a three guinea charge for entry. Sir Charles Grey and John Reed acted as stewards, responsible among other matters for handicapping, while Lords Tankerville and Ossulstone presented the prizes. Alnwick's race meetings, like those in Kelso, had long been public spectacles with over twenty regular days a year, attendance being divided by price while enough local nobbling and bribery made even betting problematic.

Gambling could attach to any sport and some which can hardly be called sports such as the Chillingham bet between Lord Tankerville and the Scottish Lord Breadalbane, *c*.1835, that the former should turn out his deer hounds on one of his wild white cattle bulls. The game went badly wrong, the bull turned on Breadalbane 'being a stranger and fair game' till Tankerville ran his horse between them, taking one horn on the side of his left leg. He shot the bull at once and, being unblooded, claimed the bet.[5] But no one in North Northumberland lost as much as the notorious Midlands Squire Osbaldstone, £200,000, followed by bankruptcy and flight from his creditors to France.

However much the classes met, argued, fought or wagered, the community was slowly being polarised by the time of Queen Victoria's accession. Gentry isolation grew steadily in the 1830s, showed itself most obviously in the town's domestic architecture, least perhaps in dress and style of living. But mixing became something which occurred 'on occasion', and the small race course stands and paddock were already fenced off by enclosures.

This being the area of life which was still free for self-assertion, male pride, exemption from toil, ill-disciplined, violent, and disorderly, was the last aspect of Alnwick's renaissance age to submit to formality. In the end, the combination of Calvinist dogma, enlightened education, and legal restraint separated players from spectators, gentry from those without much leisure time, leaving the latter with the pub's warmth, conviviality and booze, the former to deplore working class lack of manners, brutality and lechery — however much they, too, fenced off their private sports, driven by the same desires for gambling, lust or violence. It was a slow, epochal transition, due not just to authority[6] in the legal sense, but to education and the widely-disseminated sense of better behaviour — which was itself the core of a common understanding, that percolated down, yet was constantly modified and curtailed by the need for public acceptance.

COMPETITIVE GAMES

Competitive games are, inevitably, intolerant, even where rules exist. It is doubtful whether the concept of fair play, invented in Thomas Arnold's day and finally endorsed by the educated Victorian elite, even existed when Forster began sketching. Yet such competition contained and sometimes assuaged dangerous feuds and ambitions: the tournament rather than the battle, *á plaisance* not *á l'outrance*. To settle quarrels with fists outside the pub, or by a desperate wager, was probably a better outcome than the sixteenth-century Scottish blood feud or its North Eastern equivalent. Forster portrays one children's verbal feud (Plate 86, 'Pin him Bobby'), which has little to do with the lovable Cratchitts of Dickens' *Christmas Carol*.

Women were not wholly excluded from this aspect of Alnwick's renaissance, but it was already clear what was permissible (no physical harm), outrageous or obscene (no nudity, no public acknowledgement that loose women and whores even existed). At most sports — even rowing — they were merely spectators. Yet they

ABOVE *Plate 85 [106]. Two boys playing hoopla March 21 1840.*

BELOW *Plate 86 [95]. Three children playing for a fight [with a schoolbook on the ground] 'pin him, Bobby'.*

had a certain licence, if only to amuse crowds of men at Feast Day pancake races, or to ensure some degree of elegance at celebration dances. As Leech's cartoon suggests, in private assembly they might compete at archery (croquet came twenty years later); they could demonstrate horsemanship (but only sidesaddle); they could go fishing, often with the family (Plate 107); and they could travel, albeit with companions, to the Continent, sketch,[7] walk and admire the greatest cities of France, Germany and Italy.

The one collective sport open to anyone with even a small patch of land was of course a hobby rather than a sport. Even before Paxton's transformation of Chatsworth, the great landscape gardeners had created pleasure parks for the gentry and the professional world to emulate — provided they could employ gardeners. Gardening became the new craze of the 1820s, following its long history in Italy and France, preceding what became the mid-nineteenth century watercolour fascination with the cottage and its climbing roses still being painted by Helen Allingham at the turn of the next century. Humphrey Repton's 'Red Books' offered a choice open to anyone with, or even without the estates which had attracted the existing English canon of landscape designers from Vanbrugh through Kent to 'Capability' Brown. Davison's description (pp. 264–5) makes the Duke's own pleasure gardens as splendid an example as Alnwick's other monuments, an ever-present challenge for more modest practitioners.

Foundation of the Royal Horticultural Society in 1804 had encouraged British plant explorers, including the Northumbrian Robert Fortune, to explore Sichuan or India for new trees, roses, wisterias. The old walled garden was now replicated in the 1820s Alnwick villas such as Prudhoe Croft and Barndale House. Nurseryman's sales, seedsman's early catalogues, supplied a growing demand somewhere between artistic creation and fanciful nostalgia. In the North East, as in Scotland, the kitchen or fruit garden rivalled or was mixed in with the flower garden as the prospectus headings of early competitions show. Supply of new types of seed could reach Alnwick from Bristol or Liverpool, the Atlantic ports, within months.

Alnwick's Botanical and Horticultural Society however had more complicated origins. It dated back to 1769 and its membership certificate traditionally provided a supply of *Hortensia Arcana*, a sort of gardener's bible, at a cost of one and sixpence. The impression is of a brotherhood, committed to mutual support, based perhaps on Freemasonry, with a surprising degree of secrecy. By the 1820s however, it had become open and competitive: its AGM, held as usual at the White Swan on 12 September 1828, for example, awarded fourteen silver or bronze medals for fruits, flowers and vegetables. Edward Thew, the old farmer's son (Plate 87) ran a local nursery and advertised himself as a seedsman and supplier of linseed oil, clover, rye grass, and fancy seeds — a somewhat eclectic range, and in competition with James Crozer's nursery, which advertised many varieties of turnip seed and bedding plants and his own services: 'he will feel a pleasure in giving his opinion regarding any improvement in the Garden, Pleasure Ground and Planting Departments'. Repton's advertising had penetrated a long way.

Even the tiny toft's occupants in Canongate took part as allotment holders, while the new houses in Percy Terrace already displayed the nineteenth-century pattern of a small plot in front, the real garden at the back. Those with most gardeners usually won, but it was the gardener and not his master who took the credit. At the June meeting 1830 held at the White Swan, one of the Society's first gold medals went to Thomas Cook, gardener to T.W. Beaumont MP. Matthew Brewis of Alnwick, gardener to the Cresswells, won the same for his red-and-white Brompton Stocks and 'the best exotic plant in flower' (Cresswell Versicolor).

The last spectator pastimes (not sports) were of course exhibitions and travel, both appealing almost entirely to the truly leisured class. (Twenty years were to pass before Ruskin realised that excellent reproductions of Renaissance art and architecture could serve as models for British craftsman to copy.) Northumberland lay well within the classic English spectrum and John Varley's delicate watercolours included Bamburgh and Dunstanburgh Castles, a practice which continued to the end of the nineteenth century, extended by the next generation T.M. Richardson and his son.

The art market aimed to be international, as the sales at auction in Alnwick and Newcastle illustrated. Many exhibitions displayed living artists as they did their Old (sometimes dubious) Masters. The monthly *belle assemblée* in Newcastle provided a venue for the dealers to mount exhibitions of portraits by their (invariably eminent) artists. In January 1829 the Duchess sponsored her own: portraits of society ladies from Colnaghi in Cockspur Street. Newcastle of course held the grandest sales, Alexander Allen offering in 1830 Derby porcelain from Robert Bloor's own collection, in his Biggs market rooms.

For the local amateur, one of Percy Forster's Alnwick colleagues, H.T. Watson (Plate 88, with a sketch of nearby Embleton verso) advertised himself as 'drawing master and engraver to the Nobility and the inhabitants of Alnwick'.[8] Such training (apart from that provided by governesses and school teachers) could equip the would-be traveller across the Channel to sketch the Alps, the Rhineland castles or the cathedrals of Tuscany and Venice.

Most travellers kept diaries and on return displayed what Davison called 'things bought in France and Italy' – not so much the Old Master paintings (true, faked, or copies) and marble sculptures formerly acquired by eighteenth century Grand Tour noblemen, but by living artists whose works were becoming art objects created for a post-war market. Visitors who still came under their own steam, and usually

ABOVE *Plate 87 [20]. Edward Thew from memory February 13 1846 [verso a cow and two names]*

BELOW *Plate 88 [7]. Hugh Watson by P.F. [fellow artist and friend] (verso Embleton sketched by Hugh Watson).*

in their own coaches, might stop in Paris to be drawn by Ingres before crossing the old routes over the Alps, even the great St Bernard Pass, where as often as not in the Hospice, the vast beds already held other travellers with whom they had to share the night.

Some went farther, to Egypt in the 1820s. They wrote home of course, assuming with amazing confidence that in the era before postage stamps, letters would arrive. John Hodgson, the historian, entered in his diary for 10 October 1832: 'Mr Swinburne read two interesting letters [from his brother] regarding his interview with the Pascha [sic] of Egypt at Alexandria . . . also about Sidon and Mt. Lebanon', a neat conflation of politics, classical antiquity and Biblical study.

Yet as Charles Dickens remarked in 1852, 'travelling is a very troublesome business'. Even the best Continental hotels often lacked cutlery and clean sheets, to say nothing of hot water, many still with outside privies, having not yet heard of Thomas Crapper's invention of the water closet. Even so, according to most recent accounts, drawn from French police and port archives, 10,000 crossed the Channel after Napoleon was exiled to Elba in 1814.[9] This had doubled by 1820 and again by 1830, though it only reached 250,000 once Thomas Cook began his tours for the middle class.

Month-long voyages remained *de rigeur* until the railways came, the journey to Paris alone taking three to four days. Yet the cases of true extravagance were vanishing: Colonel Thornton's party with many servants, butler, falconers, thirty shotguns and 120 hounds, or Byron's purpose-built coach with its folding beds and miniature library. But this did not mean that display was not essential, even for modest gentry from Northumberland.

PRIVATE SPORT

Essentially individual, being expensive as well as exclusive, private sport barely existed for the majority. Only hunting, as Leech drew it, did, until the later nineteenth century, cross the class barriers, as Surtees' Jorrocks and Mr Sponge demonstrated. Unlike shooting, which was subject to the most brutal and penal legislation reprisals against poachers in Europe, hunting could be *shared* since every man of any means at all had his own horse; but only the gentry had guns or rifles.[10] Pheasants were property, foxes were vermin that everyone could join in to destroy.

Yet behind the cartoonists' view and Surtees' series of sympathetic novels, hunting was also carefully contrived and maintained by compromise between landowners and farmers on one side and the Master and the hunts on the other.[11] Surtees, born in Northumberland in 1803, was himself later a Durham squire, son of a Master of Foxhounds, who teamed up with Ackerman to launch the *New Sporting Magazine* which took over from its parent in 1831. 'An inverted snob rather than a snob', he had his own pack by the 1830s and took part in the change from packs owned by aristocrats to ones run by subscription.

Nevertheless his idol was Lord Lambton in County Durham, who shared his satiric wit and total lack of sentimentality and his accolade for the new railways which ended the long blight of coaching inns, bad food and outrageous prices for ill-made beds. Perhaps his most memorable remark, apposite to the North East as well, is that 'English people in general have no notion of society beyond that of animal gregariousness' — yet all his life he deployed, whether as MFH or hunt follower, the idea of mutuality in a sporting community.

Forster touched on what became a genuinely popular sport with the full run (Plate 89, Miles Sayer, huntsman, and Plate 63, Luke Skelley, earth stopper), diggers, and vastly better-bred hounds. Tom Newton, keeper of the Brizlee Tower (Plate 90) was known as a keen rider to hounds. Northumberland itself was one of the last to change from personal ownership of hunts, being dominated by the Percies' vast estates. But the future lay with subscription packs, in the new fashion drawing coverts well after dawn.

The problem, from the tenant farmer's point of view, was that the riders at that time preferred to push through the hedges rather than jump and that, being many, no one but the MFH could be blamed for galloping hooves' damages. So the MFH had to appease them to ensure that they, in turn, did not shoot the foxes. As a result, farmers too could join in the pack and ride, while both sides took against the man-traps and spring guns laid down by game-keepers to protect pheasants from poachers. Farmers would agree not to destroy too many litters and the MFHs like Lord Lambton would pay their claims for lost poultry and damage, while avoiding the need to import French foxes or 'bagmen', which prevailed in the South and the Midlands.

How many Alnwick people took part is obscure, though George Eliot's character Squire Hamley, more yeoman than gent, may have been based on the generations of local farmers who grew up under the contemporary practice. The *Courant* and its rival carried the hunting fixture lists, and the annual advertisements in the Duke's name, informing all the local gentry where the Percy hunt's borders actually applied; boundaries not being fixed until the late nineteenth century despite the legal adjudication by Lord Ellenborough defining trespass.

ABOVE *Plate 89 [32]. Miles Sayer, April 13 1831, from memory. Huntsman [whipper in] to his Grace the Duke of Northumberland about the year 1800. He lived in the Park many years after this date. With hound.*

BELOW *Plate 90 [34]. Tom Newton April 23 1831, Keeper of the Brizley Tower Hulne Park and his dog, Doctor. A keen fox hunter, etc.*

GAME

It is requested that Gentlemen will refrain from shooting on the following places, within the manors and estates of the Duke of Northumberland, they being strictly preserved, viz:

Plate 91 [67]. James Wilson a chemist in Alnwick, a keen fisher in the years 1814–15 etc.

The Kielder District; Hulne Park; West Park; Bilton; and White House Lands; with the rides and woods in the vicinity of Alnwick Castle; Aydon forest; and the grounds near the Black-Lough. The woods in Acklington and Cawledge Parks. And that part of Rothbury South Forest, which lies west of the Hexham and Alnmouth Turnpike Road.

All the other parts of his Grace's Estates, excepting Prudhoe, Newburn, Tynemouth, and the southern part of New Bernley, which is preserved till the 1st of October, being open for the season.

– Alnwick Castle, July 27, 1821.

Since one local MFH was not able to hunt his pack in November 1839, the Duke wrote to his friend David Robertson, 'I have great pleasure in allowing you to hunt my coverts as far south as the River Coquet.'[12] Robertson thanked him, noting 'the general wish to sport in the county and to share it with those in it'. Other packs around Alnwick consisted of Matthew White Ridley's Gallwood and the Alnwick Hounds; and 'the rights and privileges of fox hunters', it seems, had an etiquette of their own. The quarrel with Lord Fitzwilliam over who would follow the Gallwood's own MFH (to which Robertson brought his hounds four days a week), was finally resolved through the Duke's intermediation at the end of that season.

The cost of hunting, especially with far-off packs, put off many, yet the subscription had to be set low enough so as not to exclude the tradesmen whose membership now really mattered. Northumberland packs were much cheaper than in the Shires where a four-day-a-week man might pay £2,000 to fund his dozen horses and fifty couple of hounds. Hunt touring, hiring horses at the destination, was becoming fashionable; the cost of a groom being £6 a month and £16 for two horses, according to Surtees. Even so, Nimrod (pseudonym for Charles James Appleby, whom his rival Surtees satirised as 'pomponius ego') recorded as late as 1851 a meet where riders included a chimney sweep, a tailor, a tanner, and a genuine pauper.[13] A good earth stopper might cost £4 a month to keep. Even Ralph Lambton gave up his personal stake after a bad fall in 1838 and a new generation of professional Masters emerged. (Sir Matthew White Ridley's bid for his pack lost out to a higher one from the Quorn.) John Warde sold the Craven pack for £2,000 in 1825: in Northumberland it would have fetched much less. Only the Duke managed to invite guests on a non-subscription basis till the 1930s.

Though not exactly a mass participatory sport, hunting provided plenty of spectacle, starting with the meet and its assembly of coaches, traps or barouches. But it was not, in the modern sense, a parade: the gentry, despite their white cord breeches, often turned out worst dressed and not many scarlet coats were worn. Hunting parsons rode as many days as they could, but women were relatively few and invariably went side-saddle. It remained, for all this period, a very popular and reciprocal element in the rural hinterland.

Fishing, though subject to the poaching and trespass laws, appears from Forster's drawings (Plate 91, James Wilson the chemist, and Plate 107) to have been both a family and a private sport, with equipment little different from the rods and reels of the 1920s. But fish poaching, though illegal, never aroused the passions and legal retribution that taking game did. The Aln

From the life June 18. 1842

ABOVE *Plate 92 [108].*
William Carleton from the life
June 18 1842. Fishing. A good
likeness.

BELOW *Plate 93 [97].*
Fisherman's gossip [n.d.].

was well policed by water bailiffs and the abundance of North Sea fish, available in the legal open market, made an illegal trade unprofitable, so that fishing retained its quiet private side of personal sport, undeterred.

Shooting aroused quite different furies. The solitary pursuit illustrated by Ackerman, where the gun was accompanied only by a pointer and a loader, had already given way to driven birds, high over the lines of guns, whose proficiency instantly stood out so that competition flourished. Few would ever rival the record bags set by Lord Ripon, who was a truly obsessive shot, though he barely held his own at snipe against Lord Tankerville, reputedly the best in England. Alnwick Castle Archives have very pungent notes about bad shooters, including the Duke of Cumberland.[14]

In due course, the Franco-German fashion took over, requiring well-kept coverts, keepers and hordes of beaters to flush out the birds. Breeding pheasants became essential (though not necessarily grouse or partridge), creating endless conflicts with local hunts. But in the hilly country, more suited to walking up than driving, and in the Cheviots themselves, the focus was on partridges and grouse or black game; while on lakes and rivers eight-and four-bore guns could be mounted in small boats, producing single-shot bags of up to 100 water birds. Retrievers took the place of pointers and setters, though the dogs in Forster's portraits still look remarkably loosely-bred, far from modern show dogs.

Poaching's history is too well known, together with the landowners' reprisals, to retell except to say that Alnwick had its own poaching culture (Plate 64, Lyetty Jack) linked to the real criminal fringe on whose double market they relied to dispose of snared rabbits and hares,

game birds netted or stifled by bread pellets soaked in rum. Landowners' rights (essentially to private property) had been legally codified in 1671 and for nearly two centuries overrode farmers' and small holders' hopes to invoke mere trespass law against them.

What really mattered, however, was the prohibition on *sale* apart from that of rabbits, woodcock and snipe, which meant that any market was wholly illegal. Fines at £5 per head of game were unpayable by labourers and to run the black market, men joined gangs, which being armed, engaged in often murderous battles with keepers: on the Duke's land in August 1833 an actual affray with shooting took place between a body of country gentlemen and a poaching gang (see page 77).[15]

Thirty-two new game laws were passed in George III's reign, and something like a poaching war developed, mainly engaged at night, to be met with savage repression handed down by magistrates who were usually the landowners, but under another name. Prison, whipping and transportation flourished, as did the double market which supplied London and provincial cities, and the same people as diners. Keepers themselves often provided the supply chain.[16] Gangs and affrays produced in Parliament the Ellenborough Act 1803 so that men could even be hanged. But the trade continued, drawing in a hardened criminality, not remedied by MPs of the pre-Reform House of Commons, in spite of evidence in the lean years after 1815 that many rural families existed on the edge of starvation.

Informers only exacerbated this trade, while rural police often became part of the corrupt system, and murder grew frequent. Man traps were only finally declared illegal in 1827.[17] Yet at another level, gentlemen poachers escaped

*Plate 94 [116]. Young man
with dog riding home, 1834.*

Plate 95 [31]. Hector
Thompson, April 23 1831,
shepherd to the late Duke of
Northumberland. This portrait
was drawn from memory about
17 or 18 years after his death.
With collie.

April 23. 1831.

completely.[18] Captain Peter Hawker shot game at his own pleasure over his hated neighbour's land and woods, and set it out unashamedly in his *Shooting Diaries*, while the 1829 *Courant* advertised excursions by steam sailor to the Farne Islands on 'shooting and pleasure trips'. Since it proved impossible to stifle the market when gentry could get away with outrageous maneouvres, and since juries were becoming unwilling to convict even during the 1820s, the Act of 1831 legitimised what by then accounted for one-sixth of all criminal offenses. Yet poaching continued as a profitable market for many years to come, even if Forster's Lyetty Jack had become an amusement rather than a dangerous outcast.

Something paradoxical remains in this hunting/shooting dichotomy, not unrelated to an un-Reformed Parliament, reluctant to change any of the property laws, and a self-interested magistracy, eager to preserve privacy and private sport. But why one sport could evolve its own roughly compromise solution and the other create only vicious and violent opposition between dissimilar powers was not entirely clear: all that can be said is that, as with agricultural riots and political dissent, the war was worse in the South of England and the Midlands, so that excesses stand out more sharply. One answer may lie in the market itself: fox furs mattered only to London furriers, while game birds graced every well-to-do table, and indeed every meal including breakfast, down to the 1900s under another King, Edward VII.

FASHION AND TASTE

Post-war fashion excesses are usually created by long-frustrated demand, a sense of delayed relief, and the urgent need of satisfaction, the

Regency being no exception. But compared to the Flappers' delights of the early 1920s and the A-line of the 1940s, it lasted longer, into the early 1830s in the North East. After the longer-lasting stable fashions in vogue since the 1770s, variety of choice may indicate one of the earlier stages of retail therapy.

Caught between the Continental styles in vogue in Edinburgh on one side and similar influences filtering through from London on the other, amplified by the southern 'season', the North East had already developed its own tastes, as it had done in architecture and landscape, painting and sculpture with its own regional types of materials and provision of warm clothes in a cold climate. But what the elite collected (and indeed what ordinary folk bought to give some brightness to mean rooms) showed original regional variations, amounting in some cases to genuine independence: Sunderland glassware, Mauchline snuff boxes. The Adam brothers manufactury of furniture in Edinburgh shaped taste well into the nineteenth century.

The Duke's Castle changed from a medieval ruin to neo-classical then Gothic mansion over forty years. The town too changed, in an explosion of late-Georgian façades, graced by slated not tiled roofs, while by the 1830s piped water and indoor toilets changed most middle-class houses' layouts. The dining tables of quite ordinary people had silver-plated cutlery or even silver, the best beds had linen sheets, soon to be superseded by Egyptian cotton; plain chairs were now upholstered in what modern interior decorators used to call 'Regency stripe'.

Men went better dressed and, except among shepherds, the age-old smock had disappeared (Plate 95). Most wore similar clothes, apart from actual regimental uniforms, and the fisherman's oil skins (Plate 11). But fashion and taste are most easily measured by what women wore, and wherever dressmakers, milliners, drapers, shoe makers and makers of straw bonnets sourced their window stocks. Fashion plates, coloured engravings permeated, initially from Paris in the 1800s, but were soon copied increasingly by London manufacturers and retailers and in due course by their provincial equivalents. Newcastle mounted an exhibition in May 1829 of European Empresses and Princesses, together with Female Nobility, 800 in all, in case the North East should feel left out; while in Alnwick itself that September, 'Mrs Temple' returned from London 'with an elegant and fashionable assessment of French millinery, dresses, pelisses, mantillas, and every other requisite for the season'. (That is, for those who could not accompany the nobility to London.)

A remarkable index of Alnwick's taste and its link to global fashion can be found at the start of peace, in the customer books of John Dodds, set out for probate valuation. He was a linen draper and died in 1818. In over 400 separate accounts[19] we can see which families shopped there and what their incomes allowed them to buy. Everyone — traders, professional families, the well-to-do Esquires — is listed by name including Percy Forster's brother in Canongate, and the names give an insight into the different social ranks of extended families: John Leithead, the solicitor, William Leithead cabinetmaker; the printer Davison and his relations, one a gunsmith another a chemist. Some entrants on the list even came from the Poor House, and group headings include the Dispensary, Miss Pringle's Boarding School, Castle Gardeners, and the Duchess' School.

(My great-great grandfather William's account for 1818 came to £3-8-6.) Meanwhile the Duke, Charles Bosanquet Esquire, Lady Georgiana Grey and the Honourable Lord Howick and his father the Earl are all mixed in together.

This most unusual list demonstrated not what later commentators style 'folk variety', but a thriving market of tastes and customs. Forster's people were all better off than in their parent's day, not just because they were richer, but because their lives were more varied, open to outside influence, models and delights. The war's end seems to have freed popular culture from long-regimented choice, given greater affordability as retailers grew up into early mass production. Call it prosperity or affluence, post-war leisure and the urge to compete reshaped the class structure and gave impetus to the increments of reform.[20]

For a time, the disapprovers, mostly in the Dissenting tradition, found themselves on the margin of this consumer culture. A radical might argue, like Harriet Martineau, that all this effervescence diverted female emancipation; a conservative, that this is what the lower middle class and trading families truly wanted, after years of envy, to emulate the well-to-do elite, even if they had to become milliners or dressmakers themselves to afford it.

Other luxury traders extended the fashion machine. Trade advertisements show Isabella Young offering 'Leghorn hats', Thomas Finlayson, hairdresser, attended at his clients' houses 'in the first style of fashion . . . ornamental hair of every description (wigs) manufactured with the greatest dispatch'.

Fashion of course accompanied refinement of manners and thought. To Victorian minds, 'Regency' had an incurably raffish tinge, given the memory of outright aristocratic immorality,

so that John Murray, Byron's publisher, burned his obscene private diaries after his death, and the memoirs of Harriette Wilson, the greatest courtesan of the day, successively mistress to many of the nobility and unsuccessfully courted by the Duke of Wellington, were suppressed. But this was definitely not how it appeared in 1831. Manners were still regulated by status, from salon to servant's hall. There the numbers of servants and the grades which defined them, from butler to chambermaid, differentiated the grand houses from those of the gentry, the professional middle class from the tradesman – who still had two or three servants, leaving his wife free to assist in the shop.

Servant supply in the North East relied on Scottish migrants absorbed into the Alnwick community in the 1820s and 1830s, and recruited at the annual hiring fair. The façade of manners conveyed obsequiousness upstairs, discipline below. The levels were plain to contemporary commentators like William Kitchener, whose *Cook's Oracle* (1822) set his subject at the core of most affluent households. Dignity supported the French chef at 80 guineas a year, a housekeeper at 24 guineas, or a nursery maid at 7 guineas. On the shady side, each had his or her perks, to sell off empty bottles, candle ends, while their seniors bribed the local trade suppliers for slices of best fillet or well-hung partridges.

Upstairs, although the women retired after dinner, as Frank Harris observed even in the 1880s (to avoid the smell of farts and men's use of the sideboard chamber pot), drunkenness had become less acceptable, presaging what was to come about under the new Queen Victoria. Only old fashioned farmhouses accepted the traditional maxim 'where I dines, I sleeps' i.e., on the floor, habitual in Hogarth's day. Wine now preoccupied the upper class, shipped from Bordeaux to Newcastle; many developed a yen for punch and only the lower classes, as ever, drank beer.

DOMESTIC BLISS

1831 provides a rough halfway point in a long irregular transition of the Alnwick crowd, governed by the currents of better manners and improved literacy which had already transformed the lives of those in business and trade or artisan workshops. It is hard to imagine Mary Wollstonecraft writing her *A Vindication of the Rights of Women* (1792) or even Jane Austen defending Elizabeth Bennett's educated status against Mr Darcy's breeding, if they had been publishing in the early eighteenth century.

Changing attitudes to women and children had begun to erode male dominance even among labourers and, twenty years in advance of Victorian family morality, Forster illustrates it in the dress and bearing of his women and the development of childhood as an epoch in its own right: leisure, pleasure, fun. But little of this extended to the down-side among lower domestic servants, whose long hours, cramped quarters, sheer drudgery and restriction as to bearing children, appalled novelists of the 1840s. Nevertheless, for the majority, the era of 'domestic bliss' might at least be seen on the horizon. Radical commentators, notably Friedrich Engels in *The Conditions of the Working Class in England* (1845) had in focus the insufferable squalor of new industrial cities, not ancient county towns. Early social investigators concentrated on where abuses appeared most obvious, for example in the Tyne Valley, overflowing with Scots and Irish immigrants, or Newcastle, with its seventy-five thieves'

kitchens and brothels known to the early police.

Alnwick, although it had its stinking slums, never succumbed to such horrors and there are consequently no records of the transition in relations between men and women which Dickens exemplified at its worst in the contrast between Bill Sykes' thieving and Nancy's dogged devotion. Meanwhile, child labour in the local Alnwick pits seems to have disappeared once their seams were finally worked out. Instead, one has to apply the preoccupations of George Eliot or Elizabeth Gaskell using *Cranford* and *Middlemarch* as a compensating set of observations. Skeletal facts about illness, childbirth (and its all-too-frequent result, death) and marriage, blend with assumptions about domesticity and acceptable female roles. By comparison, in early industrial cities, the concept of a respectable working class barely existed before the 1850s, when prosperity slowly began to filter down.

Percy Forster portrays his sister as an equal (Plate 96), his mother as a benign family repository (Plate 6). Yet he shows only two couples and very few working class younger women. He takes for granted what much later generations recalled with nostalgia, that if both parents worked to earn enough — even if the mother worked as a dressmaker at home — grandparents brought up the children;[21] and what in twentieth-century households still operated, the man handed over his wage to his wife, to be given beer money for himself. This was a highly complex financial and physical negotiation which the popular song of 1823 'Home Sweet Home' barely acknowledged.

So intimacy has to be seen through the domesticity of households, whose family had some leisure after dusk, in houses not just

*Plate 96 [6]. Charlotte Forster
sister to the artist Percy Forster,
Hulne Park Alnwick, April
26, 1833.*

hovels or pubs, where privacy actually existed, where wine and beer were bought in, where convention flourished and stories were told or read out loud, where the new middle class icon might be a Broadwood square piano (actually rectangular, with its flat frame and pedals below) shipped to Newcastle, £40 for the best version, brass line-inlaid and in rosewood in 1828, £25 for the cheaper mahogany version).

The Victorian family evening has remained a stereotype for 150 years, yet the Victorians themselves often looked back with nostalgia to a supposed Golden Age of the late-eighteenth and early-nineteenth centuries as if it were an antidote to the ever-present boredom of relations' gossipy reminiscences. This had already become a topic for novelists, from Jane Austen to Elizabeth Gaskell, commenting on how families actually lived together . . .

Nevertheless, an independent, self-driven working class did already exist in Alnwick by 1831, respectable in their families' own eyes, which did not exclude the pub, racing or moderate gambling. Working class wives, as Peter Laslett observed, frequently held the status of manager and partner, with room for affection as well as work, despite bringing up four or five children. Such families might see the Mechanics Institute on a take-it-or-leave-it basis; but their dress in the pub or street mattered to them, which is why many shopped at Dodds. So did the wife whose role of homework such as dressmaking or shop work was always acceptable, but the attraction

of outside labour (apart from farm workers) less and less. This vigorous independence thus avoided middle class prescription, whether from proprietors or pulpit, and limited what outsiders like Engels believed to be bourgeois hegemony.

Power *not* to conform existed at most levels, but especially in sport, leisure and indeed style of life.[22] It did not destroy what was also held in common, however: privacy, domesticity, even love and affection, but it did constrain the power of the community's leaders to dictate how the community would evolve, harnessing change through a mixture of negotiation and convention, at least until in the later nineteenth century separate differentiations and a truly mass culture emerged.

One family pleasure seems clear enough, especially in a town surrounded by good farming and fat livestock on three sides, a rich North Sea on the other. Eel vendors, herring and crab dealers vied with the eighteen butchers under the Assembly Rooms to supply demand not just for the great feasts, but for daily household cooking, with masses of meat and fish, a diet which continued to astonish visiting Europeans by its grossness and limited variety of cuisine – to which the English could and did reply that their staples were so much better than what France's thin beasts offered that they had no need for fancy sauces and puffed up decoration.[23] In terms of quantity, Mrs Beeton turns out to have been a recorder of existing habits rather than an innovator . . .

Hugh Percy, From Memory on July 19 1824

CHAPTER 6
THE BALANCE OF POWER

IF ASKED IN THE EARLY 1820s, what were the epicentres of Alnwick's political disputes, virtually all of Forster's people, including the Duke, would have replied: the quarrels over the Town Moor (Aydon Forest's 3,400 acres), together with the last stages of common land enclosure. Asked ten years later, however, the reply would have been very different: based on the 1832 Reform Bill and focussing on the battle to extract the old borough from Municipal Reform 1833–5.

Alnwick stood aside from reform in the early 1830s, lacking an MP of its own[1] compared to the nearby 'rotten borough' of Morpeth, which had two, watching the epic battle between Lord Grey's administration and the Diehard Peers in London – even though Grey and the 3rd Duke lived only 7 miles apart, one in the Castle, the other at Howick Hall. Reform meetings in the town did not disguise the fact that, although numbers of professional people, traders and retailers would become voters, Alnwick's balance of power was not immediately affected. Like many other county towns (and as historians have argued since), the immediate results of the Bill were fewer in terms of voters and less redistributive than the radicals had hoped for.

In any case, extension of the franchise did not substantially alter the political balance of power for its inhabitants. Lacking the industrial proletariat of Tyne and Wear, or the class antagonisms prevalent in the Durham mines 40–50 miles to the south, without the municipal drive for representation from the newly great cities of the Midlands, and the underground quasi-revolutionary outbursts of the rural southern counties, Alnwick's inherent stability survived the turbulent years 1816–30, however unjustly (by later standards), power was distributed.

Yet like a *pays* in contemporary France, local politics engaged every interest directly or indirectly, in particular those of the 250-odd Freemen whose rights to quarry stone, mine coal or limestone (essential for dressing the fields before the advent of Chilean guano in the 1850s), prospect for minerals, or benefit from essential grazing rights, dated from antiquity and had been verified by the Court of Appeal in the first great legal case concerning rights on the Moor 1756–62.

During the century and a half of Percy withdrawal after the Civil War, local authority vested in the Freemen as a whole, the ten merchant/trading guilds, and the largely self-elected Common Council – the Four and Twenty and the Chamberlains. These and the interconnected Anglican Vestry had maintained a self-perpetuating oligarchy no less closed and corrupt than the eighteenth-century norm. In this sense, a local state had come into being in which the array of powers had been established in ways allowing the town to function, make compromises and resolve even intransigent disputes.

It was not of course democratic but it worked adequately, and it escaped the front line of criticism by public radicals such as Thomas Paine and William Cobbett in the later eighteenth and early nineteenth centuries. However inefficient by later standards, it maintained order, water supply, street lighting, some schools,

OPPOSITE *Plate 97 [60]. Hugh 3rd Duke of Northumberland, July 19 1824 from memory. Likeness very good [1817–47 in a later hand].*

workhouse, and law enforcement — more or less, depending on the political pressures that operated at each level in this small society.

National government barely touched these people's lives, except in the defence of the realm, official religion, and the enactment of laws, which were mostly aimed to safeguard the privileges of the gentry and the rights of property, including game. But once the Smithson Duke and his Percy wife took up residence in the Castle, rebuilt and renovated it and enclosed the park, the balance of power shifted, apparently irrevocably.

The town's oligarchy had known how to use their established power, but they now found themselves confronted by an energetic, politically successful and far-sighted man whose status came not only from his vast estates of 160,000 acres, but his role as Lord Lieutenant of Ireland and his place in the London political hierarchy. Although not foremost in agricultural improvement, unlike the Cully brothers, he could employ agents and factors who were, who surveyed upwards of 300 tenant farmers most of whom were keen to learn, in order to profit from their nineteen- or twenty-one-year leases; just as he hired Lancelot Brown to create an idyllic landscape surround and officials well-qualified to manage it.

Against this, the town's local leaders soon appeared short-sighted, self-satisfied, and ill-prepared for change. If it had ever existed, their Golden Age had ended, and by the 1830s the last decade of Alnwick's intellectual renaissance, they seemed to be an outdated impediment to the process of enlightenment. Unlike in France, where highly diverse forms of town government survived until the 1900s, English and Scottish equivalents developed in a way broadly similar to each other, as the racecourse crowds at Alnwick

and Kelso could have confirmed. The North East was not a place apart but, like East Anglia or Yorkshire, in the vanguard of improvement, one consequence being that the local state was often opened up to more fundamental sorts of criticism than had been acceptable in Hogarth's time.

An England only half the size of France had developed better shipping services, canals and turnpike roads, as was demonstrated during the Napoleonic War, and to a great extent a common customary framework as to how things should be decided and done locally. Differences which medieval travellers had noted either side of the Scottish border had almost vanished, even if living 5 miles away still defined a 'foreigner'. The marriage range had widened and the North East dialect was no longer, as in Brittany or Languedoc, nearly a separate language. Alnwick was not a political island.

A chapter on politics must therefore question the distribution and exercise of power, which goes beyond the old, habitual wisdom that property and size of estate equated with power. Not all the possessors exercised it, and certainly not all in the same way. But whatever the source, what mattered was how it was exercised and what its limits were. *Negative* power, subsisting in the common people and the crowd, put limits on the landed aristocracy and gentry, in ways quite different from the monarchy of France, the tsars of Russia or the Hapsburg Empire. But the limits of tolerance varied in each small society, being ill-defined and subject to often drastic revision, as the contrast between rural riots in southern England and the relative northern peace demonstrated.

In Alnwick the elites, those who determined how and what should be done, were also aware of these limits and the often-fine margin of tolerance underneath. Many of the improvements adopted in the 1820s, in banks' provision of credit or savings security had, as a significant by-product, the incorporation of tradesmen, retailers and consumers into a society ready for limited reform which could, in the opinions of those who held real power, be trusted to use it responsibly. The crowd may or may not have been civilised but its feelings and passions remained part of the power equation, even after the long Victorian period of more placid politics began, once it had passed 1848, 'the year of revolutions'.

The wearisome, drawn-out battle over the Town Moor gives one insight into the balance of power. The transition from medieval common land to private property had already gone far, with massive enclosures across Britain increasing since the seventeenth century; seen on one side by improvers as essential to modern agricultural practice, by radicals and romantics as the loss of a benign ancient co-existence and popular rights. But that was not how Alnwick's whole population saw it. Only the 250 Freemen could enjoy commoners' rights, a form of property embodying the right of a man to do what he willed with his own. Just as the Four and Twenty and the Chamberlains in the Common Council had set themselves over and above the body of Freemen, these rights, together with Freemen's children's schooling paid for from local tolls, taxes and the Moor's revenues, were what set the Freemen apart from the ordinary population.

Disputes had started in the late 1690s over corn tolls, followed by enclosure, building development in the town and the dues to be paid to the Percy heirs at Petworth on farmers' deaths or sales of land. The new Earl and his Countess had sued for their interpretation of the ancient statutes, starting in Chancery in 1756. Early de Vesci charters and 600 years of customary usage, however, justified the Common Council's stance, for the Percies did not at this point own much property in the town itself, nor land in the 16,000 acre parish, before enclosure. But as George Tate put it 'to the new Baron, a keen shrewd businessman, an independent corporation close to his Castle would seem an intolerable nuisance which must be abated, if not entirely put down.'[2] In the end, in return for keeping the existing system for a generation, the Council conceded the legal basis of most of their public rights to the Lord of the Manor. Yet after the apparent settlement in 1762, a war of attrition continued over the next twenty years.[3]

It was, as Tate wrote, 'a hollow peace' in which the new Duke could prevent Council from improving and benefiting from the Moor. True, they had retained borough status and Freeman's privileges; the Duke did not rule the town. But the Castle had won 'soil and royalties' in return for a mere thirty-year lease over coal pits, limestone and other quarries.

At that point, the Moor amounted to 3,380 acres. By 1820 it had only 2,610, 'a shameful waste, languishing in a miserable state of neglect . . . a wilderness of whins and heath . . . black, dreary and repulsive.'[4] For Davison, as for Tate later on, the blame lay with the Four and Twenty and the Chamberlains who had seized control of rents from those farms which were let. This loss to the body of Freemen was to have been tested at a second lawsuit in 1782 when the Freemen sought proper legal standing and some voice in the Council elections. Much haggling between the Council officials and the town wrecked that proposal, and by the time of the next settlement five years later (at a legal cost of £1,000) the Freemen had been set irrevocably against the Four and Twenty and the Chamberlains. Yet their 1815 committee of enquiry foundered when confronted by the ruling group's hostility. A bill of complaint then ran for another ten years (shades of *Jarndyce versus Jarndyce*), the Freemen having to pay their own costs while the Four and Twenty used Town Moor revenues to settle theirs.

It seemed as if the body of Freemen had forever lost their rights and in 1828 Davison looked to the Duke instead, 'whose philanthropic and beneficent views might restore tranquility and improvement or division of the Moor'. Given the Duke's patronage in the town, Davison's account was fair enough and highly critical of the Council administration. With another forty years' retrospect, and after the final enclosure in 1851, Tate argued that the Freemen had lost not only because the majority discovered that enclosure meant *less* revenue for their own members but that, lacking power to shape the Four and Twenty's oligarchic rule, they could not recapture their former influence.

Enclosure, turning common land into private property, had been a national issue for over a century, leading to sporadic violence and demolition of dykes on the Moor. But by the early nineteenth century its coal pits were worn out and lime could be burned more easily and cheaply 20 miles to the north. Nevertheless, a second ten-year campaign began in 1815 (in which, despite its radical leanings, the Duke took no apparent part). Radical pamphlets, ballads and letters under the name of 'An Old Craftsman' set out propositions which could have been written by Tom Paine. 'It is an immutable truth that all political power resides in and

arises from the people' — so far had the Freemen's argument gone, in favour of a new Constitution to replace the hypothetical one lost in 1782.

Such language could have been recognised all over England after the Napoleonic War but it is rare to find it coming from a basically conservative body. Yet fires were lit on the Moor, prompting rewards for the arrest of arsonists, together with illegal assemblies where the Freemen seem to have won some popular, if limited, support. It seemed at the time to many of the town's elite as if Alnwick was slipping towards the unrest and popular movements in the South. E.J. Hobsbawm's verdict on the Captain Swing riots could be applied: 'The average riotous parish had gone from double to four times as many shoemakers as the average tranquil one', so far had the perceptions of craftsmen in rural areas progressed.[5] But Alnwick's relative prosperity and the small farmers' resistance to new farm machinery worked against any physical expression of discontent. By the end, unsurprisingly, they failed; partly because the Council had actually performed better than it had done in the late-eighteenth century. Two Freemen were imprisoned and not released until their debts of £230/6 were paid by public subscription.

Meanwhile, exploitation of the Moor continued, not by the Duke who had little interest now in its smaller revenues, but by the Corporation, which treated it as a cash cow. Improvement of the land ceased, despite some of Forster's farmers like Edward Thew attempting it even while the Napoleonic War lasted. In 1829, the Common Council offered the Duke in settlement one-sixteenth of the Moor; but his advisers held out for one-third. Later that year, the Castle's demand was reduced to one-fifth but accompanied by conditions unacceptable to the Common Council, because it asked them for more money to pay for enclosure. So things stood until after the removal of Alnwick from the Municipal Reform Bill.

Even in 1840, the dispute simmered on, though the Duke now required only one-tenth plus expenses. Detailed valuations produced deadlock: the Freemen declined £15,295 for what was to be lost, the Castle offered between £8,000 and £9,000, making the latter in 1841 their last offer. The Duke himself obviously wished to put an end to it. Yet that too failed, even over the compromise sum of £11,000. In a penultimate agreement the Castle offered a recreation ground for the town's use, but the Freemen's ten guilds instead reverted to municipal reform, so long as it included salaries for their own aldermen . . .

In the year of revolution, 1848, the Four and Twenty themselves split and the Castle shrewdly exploited the divisions. With the support of 234 Freemen and their widows, and a valuation by Thomas Bell, a Newcastle auctioneer, the Duke won his division of the Moor at last. All that remained was to decide on who should manage the recreation ground (the local Health Board, not as was traditional the churchwardens and overseers). Riots followed in the Common Council, which maintained its privileges against the Freemen until 1851.

In the end, nothing much changed on either side throughout the ninety-year struggle. The Castle held on to minerals and freestone, lime and clay for bricks; the Common Council its revenues; while the Freemen remained divided between a small radical reforming minority and the substantial majority who preferred their benefits in cash and kind to the hope of better government. Tate concluded, on a high Victorian tone, 'the history of the Corporation,

viewed as a whole in the last 110 years, speaks unfavourably of a privileged class in the midst of a community; the moral effect is bad, exciting jealousy and envy on one side and self-conceit on the other (officials, not the Castle) and creating disunion and contention.'[6] He lamented the waste of entrepreneurial talent and the lack of funds that might have helped the town to become commercially powerful and economically independent. But Alnwick's renaissance had already ended before the competing interests ground themselves into a sort of peace.

Rights and revenues had eventually been settled, concessions made to buy off further trouble. Alnwick's people had to live together, save face, keep in with the local landowners, corn factors and retailers who in the end, with clergy intervention, determined how the community would behave. Meanwhile, the Duke's solicitors, Thorp and Dickson, began to oversee on his behalf many of the functions of the local state: rents and tithes, turnpikes, fairs, shipwrecks, road improvement, preservation of antiquities, in addition to enclosures, policing, magistrates, and 'the plague of mischievous boys'.[7]

Even Council began to keep proper minutes and more open account books, concerning itself more effectively with town improvement, drainage or footpaths across the Moor. Edward Thew was one who was given permission 'to take waste or superfluous water running over or out of the trough or reservoir – and to use the privilege in a reasonable manner so as not to interfere with or obstruct ye supply of water in ye trough for the use of ye Public, nor to perforate ye Trough to insert pipes therein'.[8]

Reform indeed, though the corporation had been enfeebled and the chance of self-government lost. But old corruption survived: fifteen pages of the accounts book were excised as late as 1844 'by direction of the Common Council . . . being private not official'.

Part of what was lost during these local struggles was in fact won by the majority of English town corporations whose new voters were enfranchised by the great Reform Act of 1832. Yet radicalism had existed openly in Alnwick (witness the Old Craftsmen letters and *Quarto*) before being in due course transmuted into the wider reform movement. Why then was Alnwick left out, winning neither its own MP like comparable county towns, nor full municipal status?

The vivid circulation of pamphlets and short-lived periodicals (Chapter 4) suggests that the national level debates during Lord Liverpool's long administration did affect the town, especially among those Freemen who demanded change, the professionals (now legally classified as gentlemen) and the trading and retailing middle class. Indeed genuine, carefully formulated radicalism may have been more prevalent in the Borders than the south-west or the Midlands, due in part to the quality of education at least partly inherited from the Presbyterian implantation.

Two tendencies can be detected, whose ramifications affected the town after 1815: the propertied classes' fears of organised crime and disorder, only too evident in southern England from the Captain Swing riots, leading to repression and transportation of 'felons'; and what became known in south-west Scotland as the 'Radical War', which affected mainly the Glasgow region, but whose ripples reached the south-eastern Borders. Cobbett's *Political Register*, disseminated by coach and sold by shopkeepers on commission, capitalised on the former, while in Scotland Major John Cartwright argued for voting reforms and annual parliaments. Such advocacy coincided with the agricultural depression as it had fed on rumours of secret societies filled with demobilised and often unemployed soldiers in the bad years 1815–20.

Although few executions occurred in the North East during the Home Secretary Lord Sidmouth's tenure, with his infamous Six Acts, in whose name agricultural depression in East Anglia led to emigration, riots and machine-smashing across all the southern counties and the Midlands, rumours of sedition remained widespread in the early and later 1820s. In fact, revolt was confined to the hopeless cases such as the handloom weavers, and the unforgiving severity of the government's response was not matched in Northumberland, already under the influence of Lord Grey and the reformist Whigs.

Authorities somewhat farther south, nevertheless held fast against the Tyne seamen's strike in 1825 and those of the Durham miners culminating in 1831. No actual conflict occurred, perhaps because it was sometimes radical gentry like John Grey whose celebrated letter of protest *The Times* published in 1816, and later liberals, who acted as conciliators. Workers' leaders on Tyneside themselves demonstrated patriotic loyalty to the existing institutions so as not to upset the wider public opinion they hoped to win over;[9] and 'tactical good behaviour' often brought surprising gains in working conditions.

But the yeomanry and militia had no problem in attracting recruits from often-fearful gentry families concerned at the wide readership in coffeehouses and taverns of highly critical handbills and pamphlets, spurred on by the national newspapers to questioning the old hierarchy by the farcical circumstances surrounding King George IV's divorce. 'The people of these kingdoms have been an inquisitive, prying, doubting, and reading people,' according to an 1824 treatise on the British press; and former army officers like Colonel Lindsay, 'commonly called the Fox' (Plate 98), resented such intrusions. 'Near the Abbey Mill there is a gate/And to enter in who dare?/Unless he be prepared to meet his fate/For Alnwick is guarded by a bear.'

With his direct knowledge as ambassador of what the French crowd might do when enraged, the Duke (Plate 97) saw himself as a key adviser, maintaining close contact with the new Prime Minister the Duke of Wellington who took office in January 1828, and advising him on ministerial appointments. 'With a leader such as yourself and such a colleague as Mr Peel, I have the most sanguine expectations. Measures, however, not men is what I look to.[10] Two years later, he offered Peel 'a safe seat, without trouble or expense.'

Peel replied, writing as Home Secretary in November 1830, 'I have to request, should any apprehension exist in Your Grace's mind as to the security of the arms of the Northumberland regiment of militia, that you will give immediate direction for removing the locks and bayonets of the muskets with the exception of those of the permanent staff, from the [Alnwick] depot to the Ordnance Depot of Tynemouth.'[11]

This is probably a better measure of upper class awareness of danger than counting the numbers of incendiary pamphlets. The fall of Wellington's Cabinet and the installation of Lord Grey and his Whigs in November 1830 naturally led to more correspondence, with Sir William Gordon, about the double need for weapons' security and unity to maintain the Constitution against disturbances.

Plate 98 [62]. Colonel Lindsay [n.d.] lived in Alnwick. Commonly called the Fox. Very rich. Near the Abbey Mill there is a gate/And to enter in — who dare?/Unless he be prepared to meet his fate/For A. is guarded by a bear.

A more philosophical defence of the old order came from John Hodgson, a Northumberland squire and later an MP, of a more idealistic bent, in a eulogy on the 'good labourer'. 'A parliament is to be guided only by men born to be eloquent and ambitious to rule and to give law; let us have at once a board of talent to examine every child that is born to decide on its talents. Make one set ministers of state, another peers of the realm, a third commoners, a fourth lawyers, priests and physicians, and put all the feebly endowed both in mind and body into inferior stations in various grades.' A foretaste of the Eugenics Society or a school inspector of 1900? Yet Hodgson dined with the Greys and Sir Matthew White Ridley . . .

It would be difficult to measure radicalism before 1831–2 from the elections that Percy Forster witnessed (Plate 99 probably shows T.W. Beaumont in the Beaumont and Howick election May 1831). In 1826, in the Northumberland county election, political squibs were printed by Davison or Bell, and scurrilous but anonymous verses or pseudo-ballads multiplied.[12] In the contest between T.W. Beaumont, Matthew Bell and Liddell, the latter even cried 'no Popery'. In turn, one of the libellous sheets suggested he was impotent or gay.

> Breeches for ever
> Liddell your nether garments never doff
> For if your sex is doubtful, as your speeches
> The girls would at your vain pretensions scoff
> And scorn the empty promise of your breeches[13]

Voting lasted two weeks. The Poll book shows nearly 2,400 voters across north Northumberland (Tindale, Castle, Coquetdale and Morpeth). Liddell and Bell won by only a narrow margin. Alnwick voters numbered 179.

In a post-mortem the next year, vicious propaganda continued, revisiting the old libels, and the huge expense of a contested election (because of which Lord Howick, Grey's eldest son, withdrew before the end).[14]

What is hidden by the plain totals is that, as the proponents of reform focussed their attacks on the old order, its narrow power base and its corruption, with the extended vote as the only recourse to shift an entrenched Parliament, the Tory side refined their plans for the future, without essentially shifting the balance of power. But the wider context of elections such as this, their cataclysmic cost and the existence of a more humane conservatism, split them, liberal Tories versus the Diehards. This worked to the advantage of Grey's administration, but similar motives and beliefs also separated radicals into reforming Whigs versus backward-looking idealists who feared the advent of industry and a free market, accompanied by the Malthusian nightmare of over-population, the decline of custom and tradition.[15]

Peel, a far-sighted member of the national political elite, understood these divisions, fearing that Tory repression would alienate the public permanently – beer, gambling and cruel sports being the crowd's safety valve. His arguments about efficiency and modernity had to wait, however, while Evangelical moral panic and Whig attempts to reform working class behaviour were delayed till the 1850s. It is too easy to say that Grey was a man of his time who saw himself as an aristocrat both by position and by nature, with a predilection for older institutions; but he did see that the Reform Bill mattered more than a series of lesser strikes against particular abuses. Like Hodgson, he understood the fear of propertied men: 1831–2 was to be the final concession, 'which would

Beaumont and Howick Election May 9 - 1831

Plate 99 [4]. Beaumont and Howick election, May 9, 1831 [probably Beaumont himself].

afford sure ground of resistance to further innovation', to admit to the vote only those with a substantial stake in property, even if they still as yet lacked a share in its power.

The Alnwick authorities showed no great interest in being involved. Little pressure existed for the town to seek its own Member and local self-interest undermined any conclusive debate. The Bill's novelty may have been exciting but the crisis exploded far away in London and any generalised disaffection failed to coalesce in the key years 1831–2. As with Chartism a decade later, reform's embrace proved far too widely based for real radicalism of the Cartwright variety: religious influence combined with the Temperance movement, but was restricted, being underpinned by genuine respect for legal means, while at the new militia depot, established since 1824, a retinue of old soldiers such as Charlie (Plate 100) had respect for the Duke's authority, even if he himself had doubts about their capacity if confronted by a mob.

The climax of the Reform Bill is too well-known to describe here. Readily available Whig and Tory papers in Newcastle or Berwick arrived only hours after printing the latest London news, in which King William IV finally accepted Grey's demand to create enough peers to force it through the recalcitrant House of Lords, and to override the Diehard opponents. Exciting news, on both sides, but Alnwick stayed largely on the sidelines, apart from hosting meetings.

Generally Northumberland was Tory, Durham Whig, its Earl, more than Grey, being an outstanding radical who went on two years later to campaign for a follow-up to the Bill, with secret ballot, triennial elections and a vote for every householder. Yet the electoral outturn exposes a sort of fragmentation, whose origin dated much further back. As McCord put it 'any

solidarity among these ruling minorities did not prevent the occurrence of bitterly-fought county elections in which rival factions spent very large sums of money.'[16]

Evidence of actual class warfare is thin, unlike the cases of Tyne and Wear or the Durham pits. Beaumont and Lord Howick stood for the Bill, Bell and the Duke against, from its inception in March 1831. Two and a half thousand people across the county, including '60 of the nobility' signed a petition in favour, and by April, aggressive crowds were asking Northumberland MPs to throw Bell out of the country. But as the *Courant* reported on 30 April, Bell had the Duke on his side 'and numerous private friends and, if staunch, will not easily be beaten.' From the other side, the *Chronicle* reported that, at the

RIGHT *Plate 100 [28]. Charlie Carr, done 1831, from memory June 18 1831. An old soldier who in his latter time rode on an ass to look after the game on Alnwick Moor.*

Duke's annual birthday party in Alnwick, few had drunk to the King, but many to Lord Grey.

At the general election of 1832, Newcastle's two seats went to Ridley and Hodgson, but Beaumont and Lord Howick took the county's North, and Bell was ejected as an MP. Reform meetings drew the crowds from autumn 1831, assembling at Morpeth in October with the High Sheriff in the chair, just as the House of Lords rejected the Bill for the first time. The National Political Union sustained the campaign through the winter and on 3 March 1832 the *Courant* praised Grey, whose career had never linked him to the 'recreant Whigs in Truckling to the Lord of Alnwick Castle . . .' An angry assembly at Alnwick Town Hall two months later applauded Grey's resignation, which was aimed at forcing the King's hand, and resolved 'to persevere in the Reform measure, even to the stopping of supplies' – whatever that might mean.

Meanwhile the Duke helped to consolidate the Diehards, prepared to resist even the King if he acceded to Grey's request to create enough peers to ensure the bill's passage through the upper House. Tate judged him, in retrospect, as 'having more of the courtly formality of a petty German prince than the social freedom of an Anglo-Norman nobleman. His treatment of the town cannot be eulogised as enlightened or liberal.' There followed a list of his reactionary activities – but nevertheless 'this Duke was an amiable man, benevolent and generous in his nature; his charities were profuse and he evinced kindness of heart and a wish to lessen the miseries of poverty.'[17] Only a generation and a thousand miles separated him from the hero of Giuseppe di Lampedusa's *Leopard* in Sicily.

At home, he and Grey had at least to co-exist; on the parliamentary stage they fought more outrageously than at any time since the Civil War, over the profound issues of the Constitution or, rather, the state and the British people. They needed and received the oxygen of public acclaim from pamphlets and the press; and the election result, in that bitterly cold winter, finally forced the King's hand.

The Diehards of course survived, to lament the loss of the supposed Golden Age, like the Earl of Winchilsea at the Bill's third and final reading, who:

> Suffered a pain of mind deeper than he could express, in thinking that he had lived to witness the hour of the downfall of his country. That night would close the first act of the fatal and bloody tragedy. It would close the existence of that house as one branch of the legislature, for its independence, which was its brightest ornament, had fallen, and without that independence it might be considered as having ceased to exist. Those who might live to witness the last act of the tragedy would have to tell of the downfall of the Monarchy, in which case he trusted that the daring and wicked spirits with whom the revolution commenced, might awaken to a sense of the ruin they had wrought. He prayed to the Almighty, whose providence had been extended over this country, that those who had brought down this judgment upon the land, might be cast off, and that those who survived might live to see the insulted laws of their country most amply vindicated. This country had arrived at a degree of prosperity, above that of all other nations that ever existed, under that constitution which was now to be sacrificed at the shrine of ambition.[18]

Grey responded in a less dramatic but greatly applauded speech:

> He believed the measure would restore the institutions of the country, to avoid the destruction of which he had felt it his duty to introduce it, to meet that necessity which he did not create. He was not unwilling to receive the triumph which had been achieved . . . He did not believe that the measure would be productive of any such dangers as those anticipated. He trusted the expectations of noble Lords would be disappointed, and that those who had for the last two years been engaged in agitation would see the necessity of returning to peace and order – of laying aside all angry feeling, so injurious to the best interests of the country – and that the measure, instead of being revolutionary, would, in the true sense of the word, be conservative of the best principles of the constitution. (Great Cheering. The noble earl resumed his seat, evidently much exhausted.)

As the waves of rhetoric subsided, the reformers got their Act and the Diehards did not die. As Lampedusa had remarked, 'things must change so that they can remain the same', and so it seemed for a time. Alnwick benefited from an increase in voters: the 1841 Poll Book suggests that numbers rose by 30 per cent. Afterwards, Hodgson reflected in his diary 'either it will be the proof of the supporters of the glorious rights and privileges of Old England, or else it will be on the other hand proof of the spirit of the noisy theoretical demagogues who now infest the land and if so it will be another blow to the pillars that support, I again say, the glorious and sacred constitution of this unprecedented country.'

The great historian Thomas Babington Macaulay went much further and in public: 'the vast mass of people, being poor and envious of the rich, were a rabble, to control whose envy the intelligent classes, the rich and the "middling rich" should combine'.

But in Scotland, next door, Henry Cockburn the Whig Solicitor General noted 'to be sure it is like liberty given to slaves. We are to be brought out of the house of bondage, out of the land of Egypt.'[19] There, the electorate had been multiplied sixteen times, incorporating the middle class in small and medium-sized towns, together with tenant farmers and small owner-occupiers in their rural hinterland (£10 households and copy-holders, £50 long – leaseholders). It seemed rather less radical in Alnwick, for Grey's government had intended to include only the urban middle class and trades people who could be trusted to retain traditional – that is, landed and propertied – authority. Property remained crucial and the newly-enfranchised cities scarcely entrenched on the balance of power in rural England.

Alnwick did not get a seat in the Commons, like Tynemouth and North Shields, or like the County which received two additional MPs; and the ballot stayed open in much of its parish so that party nominees and 'faggot voters' proliferated. If it *had* been given its own MP, the next decade's history suggest it would, like Morpeth, have lapsed into rotten borough status, though not on the eighteenth-century scale. In fact, it is doubtful if the town wanted representation. It was politically a self-sufficient place, inward-looking, with its own quarrels still festering; and it gained some compensation from the fact that the North Northumberland county MP election was held there.

Yet *The Times* was not wrong to declare in February 1833 'let the government resign or not, the march of affairs will continue and defy all opposition; no sooner is one innovation accomplished than a fresh inroad is proposed, as if increase in appetite had grown by what it fed on.'[20] Lord Derby too, far-sighted and sensitive to popular opinion, described his moderate Tory principles (which he called his Knowsley Creed) in a speech as Rector of Glasgow University in 1834:

> . . . the machine must move forward for good or evil – for it cannot be stopped; like the fire it may purify, if properly kindled by a skilful hand, but if it should be impetuously and recklessly accelerated, destruction and overwhelming wreck must be the inevitable consequences.

He and his party were, of course overtaken by the politically more astute Robert Peel, with the Tamworth Manifesto, and it was Peel who became Prime Minister briefly at the end of that year.

Like a long-delayed earthquake shock, the sequence began again with municipal reform, and this time Alnwick found itself directly and intimately concerned. Just as legitimation of a market in dead game allowed active traders to begin to undermine the whole Game Laws apparatus, so the Poor Law and local government were opened up to public inquiry – and of course to press disputation. Peel put it succinctly: 'Others will outbid you, not now, but at no remote period – they will offer votes and power to two millions of men who will quote your precedent . . . and will carry your principles to their legitimate and natural consequences.'[21] Peel himself was to destroy the foundation of agricultural property/power with his repeal of the Corn Laws in 1846.

While the old high Tory groups began to lose ground at the centre, however, they held on to their local influence; while the Whig romantics whose concept of liberty cited Saxon custom before Norman rule, gave way to modern liberals; and the Victorian political calm, to the surprise of both, laid them aside, to be reinvented from the left and right a generation later.

As a political community, Alnwick remained ill-suited to reform – so the long Town Moor dispute with its essentially venal self-interested alliances suggested. In what followed with municipal reform, however, Alnwick became the cockpit of a much wider, more spectacular quarrel during which the Duke and the Common Council teamed up together on the principle that an enemy's enemy is a friend.

Being a very local society, it was natural enough that before the growth of the modern state in Britain, reformers would envisage municipal reform as the natural correlation to the great Reform Act. The new voters may, in passing, have widened their natural perspective; but for most of them, the greater part of their concerns and indeed their lives were shaped and regulated by local matters, from their education and their children's upbringing to their employment and pleasures, right on to the hands of the Burial Board.

Given its population size and civic importance in the North East, Alnwick naturally appeared in the Municipal Reform Bill's schedule B in March 1835. It was to receive a higher degree of self-government, while the old oligarchy, the

Four and Twenty and the Common Council were abolished in favour of community suffrage, its own magistracy, and a corporate government of mayor, alderman and councillors — in effect a microcosm of what Birmingham, Liverpool or Manchester had already become.

The inquiry started earlier, on 29 October 1833 after the appointment of the national Commission, chaired by the elegantly styled Fortunatus Dwarris and his team of Commissioners under the old King's warrant. From the start, the Common Council opposed it, the Town Clerk John Lindsay even disputing the royal edict, to the delight of the spectators. But after this show of disrespect, the Chamberlains agreed to give evidence, having no other choice. Dwarris was a skilful investigator, a Whig appointment, operating in public in the Town Hall, and he rapidly laid bare where local self-interest lay, extracting from their own witness a description of the corporation's self-interested functions, while exposing how little it actually did and how much its funds relied on revenues from the Moor.[22] The Freemen, not the public, benefited directly through their schools from which non-Freemen were excluded.

George Dunne, the Freemen's main witness, took the offensive and denied any need for change, 'Alnwick not being a place of Trade or Commerce', and having no MP; but he had to admit that its accounts had only been opened after the lawsuit of 1818. Dissatisfaction, he claimed, came from non-Freemen who did not share the spoils. Thomas Williams, speaking for the Duke, declared that the park would lose forever its rural character and become 'municipal', together with the Castle itself — 'a very great loss to his Grace's property', as one of the evidently Tory commissioners, Sir Charles Wetherall put it.

Schedule B nevertheless lumped the town in the same category as Berwick, Newcastle and Morpeth, some indication of the range of reform present in the North East in the early nineteenth century, with the rider that 'a thorough reform must be effected before they become . . . useful and efficient instruments of local government'. Only then did the Freemen wake up to the implications, although the Duke's solicitors were already preparing their case against it.

Put bluntly, the 247 Freemen (only 25 of whom had ever campaigned for reform) did not intend to surrender their privileges and revenues in order to be swamped by the imposition of a new body of approximately 1,000 people to share their revenues and privileges. Neither did the Duke intend his Alnwick estate and the park to be assigned to the new municipality, to be taxed at will by a local authority over which he had little control. As Wetherall had noted two years earlier, 'this place was rather a Feudal Barony than what is called a Municipal Corporation' and the Duke would lose twice, from the existence of a further 750 Freemen exempted from the tolls, and from the fourfold increase in those 'claiming to dig up his clay and eat up his pasturage — a flagrant injustice'.

The old quarrel thus surfaced in a novel form. But what was a 'feudal barony' in 1835? The Duke gave tolls to endow the schools and his munificence could be said (as Tate admitted) to fulfill his part to keep the political balance between rich and poor. 'Feudal barony', four years before the nobility of England assembled to re-enact the medieval Eglington Tournament (only to see it rained off, rusting their brand-new armour) can be seen in high-Tory terms as a compliment not a criticism.

Paradoxically, this Bill brought the two adversaries together in defense of their property, subsuming the conflict between an old order and a new one. It appeared rational enough at the time, but, as Tate argued thirty years later, it was deeply reactionary. Worse, it was short-sighted, as the small minority of reformist Freemen appreciated. The public was not consulted, either by Commissioners or Council and it is possible that a majority of them did not greatly care.

Despite this odd alliance after fifty years of hostilities between oligarchs, landowners and the merchants and small farmers dependent on them, the old guard did not win easily, even after a whipped-up public clamour, petitions to both houses of Parliament, and the employment of an expensive range of lawyers, pleading that Alnwick be struck out of the Bill. Naturally enough, given the Duke's influence in the Lords, the still-lively disaffection of the Diehards, and the majority's evident sympathy against the threat to his position as landowner, the storm centred on the House of Lords.

The Commons accepted a very different set of arguments. Why should Alnwick not enjoy the benefits of reformed and less corrupt government, like 178 other corporations and towns of similar size and economic importance? When the Lords' amendments came back to the lower House, they were rejected and Alnwick reinserted in the Bill. At this point, much of the accumulated resentment at what Grey's government had done combined (in the Eglington mode) with what might be called retrospective nostalgia. The Duke put all his power and prestige into the struggle and it became clear that the entire Bill was likely to be lost, for it was not conceivable that the King would repeat his promise to flood that House with peers.

The Home Office gave way and Alnwick ('the little Jonah') walked the plank to save the Bill from foundering. Apart from the twenty-five opposition Freemen, the majority agreed on a vote of thanks to the Duke on his return in the autumn, with a notable feast paid for out of Town Moor revenues, and then presented a silver tea set to Lindsay, the Clerk[23] who had fought it from the start.

The victors had been appalled at the likely elimination of their cosy oligarchy, as if they had been peers facing up to Lloyd George and Asquith's reform of that House in 1911. Afterwards, they could renew their old hostilities over the Town Moor. But within twenty years, the town paid a very high price, as it sank into a century of stagnation and minimal growth. Tate's population tables showed a steady rise at every nineteenth century census, 1801, 1811, 1821, and 1831, roughly the period of the town's renaissance; but thereafter, very slow expansion, the balance of live births being offset by emigration. All one can say is that, although it remained an oligarchy, the national process of reform worked in the end to reduce the public corruption which had grown up through bribing the electors.

What Elizabeth Gaskell's Cranford experienced, when the railways came, she described as 'disturbance'. Alnwick was not disturbed, because in the late 1830s the Duke ensured that the later stage of the London–York–Durham–Edinburgh line went, not through his demesne, but near to Alnmouth on the coast. True, the land was flatter there and the line cheaper to build, but it also ignored the Great North Road's route[24]; adding many miles to the route to Edinburgh. Its absence can be read partly as political fiat (the Duke against the railway presenters) partly as a response to the sentiments expressed by George Eliot in *Middlemarch* that it would cause the loss of jobs, the end of stability and rural peace, and the abolition of old technologies in a craftsmen's town.

Much later, as stagnation set in, and as evangelical non-conformity turned to piety rather than liberty for the majority, the Town Council voted unanimously to petition both houses of Parliament 'praying for insertion in the Railway Bill now before Parliament for the amalgamation of the York and Newcastle with the Newcastle and Berwick Railway Company, of the same clause which exists in the original Newcastle and Berwick Bill, which requires the company to make and open a branch railway to Alnwick within twelve months, from the main line, under penalty of having the right to take tolls on the main line suspended till such branch line be opened'.[25]

Too late; and the line eventually built – with its sequel in the 1880s from Alnwick to Wooler, snaking on among the Lammermuir Hills to join up eventually with Edinburgh — never carried more than local traffic before its bridges were swept away in the great floods of 1947. It brought few jobs to the town, not much prosperity, and barely changed the pattern of Alnwick life. What did improve, steadily until the great depression of the 1870s, was Northumbrian agriculture, so that the town remained locked into its early-nineteenth-century pattern of economic relationships — a craft town whose most notable exports were the split-cane fishing rods and Hardy reels.

Transport proved crucial, as it did in France where coming of the railways made whole new towns out of villages and dismantled or condemned others to provincial obscurity.[26]

It was not just the Duke's prerogative at fault: in the Great North Road dispute five years earlier, Sir John Dalrymple had written that 'the Duke of Northumberland . . . has been made to believe (by competitors) that our plan is to take the mail off by Alnwick . . . were he in possession of a copy of the Bankers' Petition, he would at once see that this is unfounded . . .' What mattered was his support 'as a friend in place of a foe.'[27]

How to explain the dissonance between the lively professional trading and artisan aspects of the town's life, its vigorous intellectual climate, and the range of pleasures available not only to a predominantly agricultural class but artisans and tradesmen, on one hand, and the deeply conservative, inward-looking stagnation of its political balance of power?

When a prosperous pre-Victorian future was available, why did the local elites, speaking for its inhabitants, not take it up? In some aspects of course they did, by way of banking, education and public health. But these were in fact legacies of the Enlightenment and the improvements made *before* 1830. Even to ask the question ignores the impediment of local quarrels, older traditions, and the obstacles of entrenched local elites, extremely powerful in a small community, where to break out of the past required education or migration to the new industrial cities.

History told from above can explain why, in the mid- and late-nineteenth century, prosperity allowed local self-interest, once it had been stabilised in the 1830s, to be transmuted into a *national* vision of improvement, remoulding, from the top, the crowd in its own, usually evangelical image. At the same time, however narrow, reform had begun to undermine rule by the oligarchy, first the Freemen, then the town Council, eventually (with the 1870s agricultural depression) the rural gentry and nobility.

But if history is told from below, it suggests that Alnwick's people were not deeply embittered, as later Marxist analysis required, nor ambitious for an as-yet ill-developed free consumer market. Most seem to have been content: Forster's people do not appear angry, frustrated or subversive, not even the poacher Lyetty Jack. Grumpy perhaps, worn-out certainly some of them, but there is no evidence in the drawings or the documentation of the sort of rural misery which inspired poverty-stricken labourers' assemblies in the south and which, in the 1843–8 depression, brought about the full regimentation of the new Poor Law and its harsh regime for the 'able-bodied poor'.[28]

They got through the worst of bad harvests and winters or outbreaks of cholera and typhus, out of dogged persistence and were eased, often quite significantly, by the charity of gentry and nobility. Having no alternative in their lifetimes, except among the youngest men, their children being bound to the same work as theirs, they could, whether literate or not, congratulate their locality on being better than Tyneside, Northumberland on its superiority to Yorkshire, and if they ever considered it, on England's precedence in Europe.

Seen in this way, the town probably appeared self-satisfied, perhaps a little dissolute, and to the local clergy unredeemed though not unredeemable. If they had the chance, its people improved themselves, accepted charitable schooling and medicine, though not necessarily as graciously as the providers required. What follows in Chapter 7 suggests that they formed a closely woven sort of fabric, many-coloured, designed, if at all, chaotically, responsive to political rhetoric but suspicious of all politicians and political parties. Not good material for the Chartists after 1838, nor for Engels and Marx in *The Condition of the Working Class* in 1848, not even for the high-minded early Socialists who all looked elsewhere, leaving county towns out of their analytical cosmology.

Perhaps Forster's people's politics reveal, not the crowd (civilised or not) but a community under pressure at a crucial point between the dangerously violent early nineteenth century and the placid era of self-improvement to come with Britain's apogee, freed largely from dearth, and as yet unchallenged by Germany and the United States. Clearly defined in time, named and dated, they also stand almost outside time, like a vivid display of butterflies and moths, but not pinned down, as if in flight, yet still unclassified, free to roam the viewer's mind.

The frame shown here, then, has two separate functions: as an aperture into the past, like a *camera obscura*, giving partial view but in vivid detail, where the long-dead reach out directly to us; and as an enclosure or setting for a definable, particular group of people in their home-town, their time, and their relations with each other.

From Memory March 20th 1832.

Chapter 7
Alnwick's Real Community

This portrait of a vigorous community, its tightly knit, usually good-natured character, a microcosm of what the local state meant in early-nineteenth-century Britain, might be counted as an exercise in nostalgia, particularly from the standpoint of the era of a centralised modern state; even more if we look at how the first quarter of the nineteenth century was, in comparison with our own time, self-evidently also cruel, rough, pain-filled, unfair, especially towards women. But Alnwick was not an ideal community as that tended to be set out by political philosophers, heirs to the Enlightenment; neither were its people bound by the sort of social contract envisaged on one side by Jean-Jacques Rousseau and on the other by Edmund Burke.

For all the contemporary belief that rational inquiry in the hands of educated men of property would produce remedies for local needs and grievances — a basically Whig standpoint — Alnwick was too factious, too diverse, its character (if it could be said to have possessed such a universal attribute) closer to the cynical yet progressive conservatism of Robert Peel.

Dominated on three sides by a Duke whose position was national rather than local, and a landowning gentry and a merchant oligarchy whose various elements were often at feud with each other, Alnwick's balance of power shifted little between 1750 and 1850 — to the town's long-term detriment. Yet this was unusual in Britain, and achieved only through the political-legal strife set out in Chapter 6. Its history up to the 1840s, and its lively cultural springs, would suggest that dissent or outright contrarian activity only just remained under control.

How then was modernity held back? Not by repression, as might have occurred in Continental Europe, against whose ruling elites, Burke had formulated his concept of 'little platoons'. But that — with its vision of a higher harmony — does not explain how the vociferous tendencies within were contained. Something else is required to explain how people actually lived together, sorted out disputes and calmed down quarrels with no more authority than what was provided by market conners and locally recruited constables; and why the underdogs — or in modern parlance the underclass — apart from actual criminals, conformed.

One frequently used way is to cite the supposed British virtue of compromise, without which it might indeed have been a Hobbesian nightmare 'nasty, brutish and short'. They had after all no choice but to live together in the same place, to work, think, or play there, or else to emigrate. If the latter, where? They knew enough about the mining and industrial belt 20–40 miles south, and had daily experience of what emigrant Scots had been only too glad to leave behind in Glasgow and Lanark before reaching Alnwick. To cross the Atlantic meant, in effect, banishment, even if they did succeed in founding a new life in Canada or the United States.

A more modern explanation might focus on the way in which local government, in so far

OPPOSITE *Plate 101 [59]. John Jobson, once a large corn faactor in Alnwick, known as Duddy Willie from memory March 20 1832.*

as it existed, worked through the co-option of interests to form a sort of local state, employed and employer being held together by the growing network of banks, financial institutions and professional people. But that is to predate the evolution of the modern managerial state in the First World War by eighty years, and leave aside the great municipal successes of the later nineteenth century. In any case, the central state cannot at this period be compared to that of a county town. But it shares elements of what Benoît Mandelbrot called 'fractals' – that is, the properties of similarity down to a very small level.

Yet elements of what made Britain's later twentieth-century transitions possible can be traced back at least a century: tolerance, borne out of a primitive understanding of the science of brittle fracture – if a coach spring bends too far, it breaks; the better forged it is, the further it will bend. Knowledge (often from Continental experience) of what was 'too far', and how intelligent design might limit risks, how listening carefully and testing might reduce the chances of revolt; in short, a focus not simply on what was said by those in authority, but on what was heard from below.

Awareness of the consequences of early-nineteenth-century breakdown, from poverty, cholera, bad harvest or bank failure, was, naturally, unevenly distributed among the population, the labourer prone to every risk being wholly exposed to the first three, from which the gentry and middling ranks could perhaps take flight, but who in turn remained vulnerable to the latter in ways that people of no property whatever could hardly imagine.

A path of acceptability could be envisaged, hedged against storms by unspoken rules, indicating what was expected and acceptable; rules developed over centuries, enhanced by the Civil War's Presbyterian legacy.[1] These, until the 1834 Poor Law began to impose central state practice via the hands of parish Guardians, included charitable provisions for the poorest and those most in need, a basic education, together with provision of at least some sort of work for the able-bodied. Not exactly a social contract, but a framework of mind congenial to the various Christian branches (mutual obligations between rich and poor being enshrined in both Old and New Testaments – and in the eastern religions about which at least the educated had been aware since Napoleon's invasion of Egypt), unlikely to be repudiated by the indigent or ill-fed crowd; who in any case could benefit positively from the Dispensary, the Mechanics Institute, or the new schools and better housing of the 1800s.

At a time of very low income tax, payments towards the easing of poverty by the better off came usually in cash or kind, soup kitchens, etc., by direct donation or subscription, quite separate from local tolls and rates. In one sense, this looked back to historic memory and also to a timeless tradition ensconced in religious custom and family duty. It did not, in any obvious sense, follow from the cold realism of Benthamite 'improvement' or Enlightenment thinking but, in the historical sense, from hundreds of years of discussion about how best to fill the gaps left after the Reformation and the despoliation of the monasteries.

Charitable obligations certainly confirmed a sense of identity, akin to the fellowship of guilds, trades and professions, which were on other matters intrinsically competitive and often quarrelsome. It rested on the double-headed virtue of example: to one's peers and to the community at large. It is noticeable that landowners who reduced or remitted rents in times of bad harvest normally issued a short proclamation of their munificence in the press, in the Newcastle papers if not in Alnwick itself. Charitable provision did not divide Whigs and Tories, except in so far as it led on to the much more disputed question of how to sort out and prevent the problems recurring.

In return, the providers, who included most gentry and aristocracy but also professional men and many tradesmen, expected a return, if only to bolster their self-righteousness; gratitude expressed for what the Dispensary provided, the Mechanics Institute's opportunities, by tangible evidence such as the Tenantry Column, which recorded the Duke's remissions of rent in 1816–17. 'This column is created, dedicated, and inscribed, by a grateful and United Tenantry.'

Such an implicit bargain was later to be depicted much more directly in hundreds of Victorian paintings of charitable giving, in which the recipients are always smiling and cleanly dressed (i.e. pre-dressed as a presumed result of the donation). Indeed the existence of such a social contract, as a powerful if mythic element of British identity and a particularly English way of addressing the eternal question of social order and its relations with the natural world, contrasted with the *de haut en bas* assumptions of French, German or Spanish societies. It found its way in due course across the whole late-nineteenth-century British Empire. It differed entirely from the legal-fiscal connection between tolls and parish rates or tithes, all of which were regular impositions to maintain the Established Church and its vicar, constabulary, roads and pavements.

It is easy to assert the hegemony of the upper class, its official as well as its effective informal authority, and the support given by the beneficiaries of the Reform Bill, the practical,

Plate 102. Tenantry Column. Engraving by William Davison 1828 (from Descriptive and Historical View of Alnwick*, 1829).*

well-qualified middle class, mobile and open to ideas about change, over the common people and the labouring crowd. Yet one has only to look at the different ways of life of a hedger, a shepherd, a shoemaker (a trade notoriously radical at this time), a butcher's apprentice, to see how complex overall consent was, how hard to achieve.

But the underlying purpose of this implicit, unwritten social contract was, inevitably, proper behaviour: public order, private respectability. The crowd retained freedom to live a large part of life outside prescriptive rules, even, for some of the time, from legal constraints: witness 'St Monday' (the day off which compensated for Saturday work), violent sports, strong drink, and the debatable areas of the marriage or other bed. This element of independent life[2] actually grew after the 1820s, as public hangings, transportation and legal reprisals in civil society diminished.

It was as if, having learned from political violence's consequences during and after the Napoleonic War, what Engels was to describe as working and capitalistic classes had agreed, at least in urban-rural areas, to certain mutual limitations on aggressive behaviour. Legal process often reduced the value put on stolen goods in criminal charges so that the death penalty occurred less often, while Alnwick magistrates themselves, though drawn mainly from their own estates, whom one might suppose to have encouraged heavy sentences for property offences, seem in fact to have taken some account of local circumstances and distinguished between the criminal class and the hard-put, poverty-stricken underclass.[3]

The extent of outright conflict should not be minimised. At times, the Town Moor dispute witnessed outbreaks of arson and livestock theft, with very severe penalties for both, but nothing of the naked violence of pit warfare in County Durham – whatever the Duke's fears about access to yeomanry muskets in 1830. Conflict never took hold according to Marxist categories, as the lawsuits and machinations described in Chapter 6 indicate. The attempt to include Alnwick in the Municipal Reform Bill failed because two old rivals, the Duke and the town's Freemen, agreed it should not succeed. Opponents in one quarrel might be allies in another and the growth in containment over the first quarter of the nineteenth century ensured that muskets and swords would not be used on the local population as they had been at Peterloo.

Like all communities, Alnwick had its age-cohorts with very different experience of what the town's history was, and how the outside world worked, differences in what they hoped for and might expect about the future or, to put it in Burke's terms, how they imagined the interests of past, present and future to be; whether, if they could, they read the papers in the coffee-house or the pub, in the circulating library or the privacy of their own studies; whether their world-view stretched to Tweed and Tyne, to London, Paris or even New York.

The solitary shepherd in his bothy up on the Moor could hardly share the opinions of a female milliner or a male innkeeper, but he could, as they did, *gossip* wherever people met; and the role of local gossip, like local shopping, as a *lingua franca* holding people together, should never be underestimated.

Obviously, the depth of this social contract and the volume of reciprocity it generated varied over time, but the fact that it seems to have intensified in crises indicates its continued residual value. Even if waves of zeal were followed by troughs of indifference and feelings that nothing much would ever change, it left a sort of openness in Alnwick's polity. Looking back from 1868, Tate might regret that the renaissance time had ended even as Davison was publishing his *History*, citing the loss of municipal status and the main-line railway or its population stagnation. But it was not riven, as many Continental towns were, by violent disturbance, or revolution even in the 1840s.

Tate admitted that there was little in the state of Alnwick that was not eventually remediable. Indeed he praised Algernon Percy, later 4th Duke, who died in 1865, because he carried out much more active and charitable work than his father and lived more in the Castle, improving many aspects of life as a result, while remaining open to discussion about what improvement was, and how it might be implemented on his vast estates.[4] In short, the Duke was judged to demonstrate in person Burke's depiction of the aristocracy as 'the Corinthian capital of polished society'.

Such ideas fit the formulation of the post-Marxist theorist Antonio Gramsci, whose descriptions of contested or negotiated hegemony still apply to actual societies which are more cross-class in composition than class-structured, of mixed occupations, and tastes, but with a coherent sense of identity.[5] Class is as much an attitude of mind as it is breeding and heredity, education or wealth; Alnwick's shoppers and novel-readers already displayed elements of embourgeoisement, fashion being the greatest of all equalisers, at least in aspiration.

Meanwhile the elites could accommodate to the idea of negotiated political hegemony; 'the upper orders in the English countryside held to an ideal of social harmony in which older conceptions of paternalism and deference were reinterpreted within a (Victorian) framework that drew a sharp distinction between the worthy and unworthy poor'.[6] Alnwick's example, however, argues that the reinterpretation took place at least fifteen years earlier than Queen Victoria's reign, but without being publicly admitted, to be rationalised later by the Victorian social reformers. Even Gramsci fell for the notion that hegemony was negotiated primarily from above rather than below; whereas, in Forster's world it came about from within.

Once the age of open satire ended in the late-eighteenth century, the print trade became the animating factor in the making of contemporary history, not controlling it but facilitating

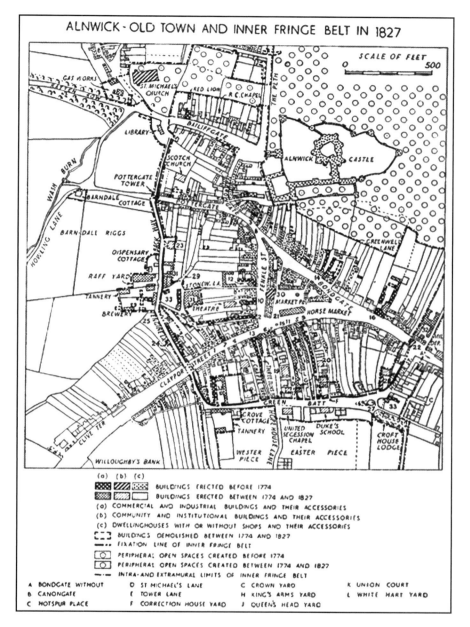

its arrival and actual use. This history, in George Orwell's usage, became a common contribution by all those with power to take part in its evolution. The fact that basic education and addressing basic needs arising from misfortune, proved more effective than the aims of haphazard formal charity suggests that the good intentions of those above were determined not

Plate 103. Map of the Town, 1827, showing the buildings before and after 1774. (Plate 11 from M.R.G. Conzen, Alnwick: A Study in Town-Plan Analysis (1960)).

Plate 104 [86]. John Fairnam, May 28 1838. Went among farmers, very eccentric and would never work. In his later years, lived near Gateshead.

Toryism, the medievalism of Sir Kenelm Digby and the foresight of Disraeli in the early 1840s can be traced here in sharp contrast with dogmatic 'improvers' and dominies' prescriptions. Private philanthropy — properly named — resolved needs which the local and central states only addressed later on.[7]

But in what ways can Alnwick be described as a community at the end of the first quarter of the nineteenth century? Its 3,000 adults lived in the same place, even if the encircling walls had long been demolished, and the cobbled streets extended south and east in waves of late-Regency villas and houses with gardens all round.

Buildings connect to streets, which shape and reshape the town and the way people use them to go to work, to shop, to drink and gossip at the pub or tavern. Alnwick's street pattern barely altered from its medieval design to the 1820s (see map, page 149), yet its alleys and wynds were modified, rebuilt or subdivided into one-room tenements to cope with population growth. The street shapes its neighbourhood, its transport, its networks of intrigue, the throng of its populace, as houses shape what neighbours do with and to each other.

Its people had imbibed from family legend, school and later reading, or tales told in the pub, a rough, usable history of what the town meant. They worked almost entirely within an interdependent mercantile economy based on agriculture and craft skills; many of them had been through the same sort of school curriculum, with its powerful religious connotations, read the same papers, frequented the only theatre, and taken part in the same sports and pastimes, even if for the majority the latter attracted them as spectacles rather than as participants.

Whatever branch of Christianity they proposed, Bible and pulpit promoted moral

just by personal whim but by their understanding of what were generally accepted demands.

It is possible that the elites in Alnwick accepted the fundamental virtue of the common people and their representative patriotism, before 'the nation' even existed. 'Young England's' romantic

rules and hence a sort of cohesion, even among those few who did not attend on Sundays, and the many who disregarded what they heard, (participation does not imply conformity).

These are the foundations of the sense of community. Within that, political or age differentiation counts less. To leave and abandon 'home' presented huge difficulties, not so much of mundane transport but attitudes of mind. The process that drove emigration was far less than in the impoverished Scottish Borders of the 1690s, the Highlands after Culloden and the nineteenth century Clearances. If Northumberland people went overseas, it was to places already known, such as Ontario,[8] where new land was available free. Great cities had less attraction for the poor unless they needed work; London might appear more dangerous than Newcastle, where Foster himself ended up; but then he was well-to-do, having become middle class and locally eminent.

Portraits of a town's society are not rare – witness the portraits emanating from Blandford Forum and Poole, centres of late-eighteenth-century merchant-led intellectual activity, coinciding with the visits of George III to improve his health; but most tend to focus on their outward appearance, like Regency Bath or mid-eighteenth-century Edinburgh. Some tend to idealise, especially when their origins lie in a communitarian philosophy like Philadelphia or New Lanark. Very few attempt to show the warp and weft, the rivalries and tensions, the criminal class and polite society together in the same streets. Hogarth's savage cartoons focussed on the former, the dissolute and the destitute,[9] or the way that even gentry, if impoverished, fell through an open drain to join the lower orders.

New Lanark disintegrated; Saltaire, Port Sunlight, and Philadelphia developed in ways

their founders had not expected. Eden, however enduring as a myth, in reality mutates. In his poem 'The Hands of Others', James Stockinger wrote 'for each of us lives in and through an immense movement of the hands of other people . . . it is in and through the hands of other people/that the commonwealth of nature is appropriated/and accommodated to the needs and pleasures/of our separate individual lives . . .'

Plate 105 [10]. Robert Spearman of Warton, commonly called 'The Giant'.

Enforced mutual dependence and fear or dislike of outsiders may ring-fence a community, but however argumentative or eclectic its composition, tolerance has to outweigh intolerance if it is to survive. It must embody aims in common, a social order which is both acceptable and adjustable, a balance between the wealthy elite, the middle orders and the crowd. This is what Percy Forster's drawings suggest, and the evidence either side of 1831 confirms it. Alnwick *was* a community despite its obvious barriers between the respectable and the outsiders, the elites and the common people, in which a measure of trust between groups did exist, where exclusion was limited to the indigent and servile and where grounds existed for reciprocity based on a fundamentally moral balance between individual choice and the values endorsed by the community.

But that does not make it a 'traditional' society. Its people may have defined themselves within the context of a known past but that did not alone determine their aspirations. Nor does tradition imply conservatism, only the process by which the present acknowledges and accepts the past. Age groups span far too long a period, even when the mortality rate averaged only forty-eight; and while some feared change and modernity, others self-evidently aspired to both. There is no reason to suppose that the young automatically adopted their parents' views or lifestyles, even if they followed in the same trade or farmed the same land.

We should not be deceived by the apparent slowness of early-nineteenth-century change. For them, 'future shock', to use Alvin Toffler's phrase, was just as frightening then as it is now in the twenty-first century. They only started from further down the ladder, as all previous generations had over centuries. The fractures of 1832 and 1835 exposed just how far the town

had come since the Napoleonic War, how far ideas about improvement and progress had penetrated since Arthur Young had first visited Northumberland in the 1760s.

Two major explanations suggest themselves. First, there was no implacable barrier between the town and the country (even in Victorian industrial cities, that frontier was porous, allowing families to move between, rely on relatives, or even plant allotments); second, the long pre-industrial culture mutated through print and retailing and survived — and arguably still does, in Alnwick today, behind the tourist façades (it certainly did in the mid-twentieth century). This, despite the various impacts of mid-nineteenth-century renewed religious controversy, Britain's imperial aspirations, and the socially corrosive World Wars.

Another might be the fallible nature of authority when set against popular demand and customary behaviour. Extensions of the town described by Conzen[10] took place not quite spontaneously but without much evidence of planning by the Town Hall; the foundation, growth and curriculum regulation of schools or the Mechanics Institute occurred haphazardly, at the instigation of individuals — or lack of it. Alnwick signally lacked a central or genuinely hegemonic authority which could get things done without negotiation. Even the Duke could rarely do so, or the Town Moor dispute could not have lasted nearly a century.

When things did happen, they came about through a variety of desires and motives, leading to a rended-down, residual wisdom of what in the end must be called a collective — however venal, narrow and self-perpetuating. There never had been a Golden Age, of course, and the sense of identity which had grown up and reached a sort of climax in the 1820s and 1830s was not unique; but it was distinct and can perhaps be set in context.

Identity is hard to define even for a single mature individual. For a collective, one can begin by conflating history (as understood by its inhabitants), place, time and what people did and how they looked. Since it is the interaction of people which creates community, no one is exactly like another; there is no precondition, no platonic ideal. But without it, the locality would be truly Hobbesian, brutal and solitary. Some historians of the 1830s and 1840s such as J.M. Kemble argued, following Burke, that the English character based itself on freedom deriving from Anglo-Saxon, pre-Norman laws — a position defended against James I by Lord Justice Coke in the 1600s — rather than democracy and the rights of man. Possession of land, a stake in society, laid the foundation for late Victorian theorists such as Stubbs and J.R. Green.[11]

Most of Forster's people would have been familiar with Walter Scott's historical novels and absorbed through them a similar concept of Englishness that did not deny Scottishness but assumed that the Celtic peoples had been subordinated to a higher class of humanity; which was to be one road to the study of physiognomy and race. What mattered most, however, in Forster's time in Alnwick, was not racial theory (hardly even born until the 1840s) or a social contract explanation, but a wider sense of Britishness derived from the recent war years, just as Amédée Thiery's *History of the Gauls* (1828) did on the other side of the Channel.

Forster may never have read Samuel Taylor Coleridge's book *On the Constitution of Church and State* (1830) but he must at least have been aware of the arguments opening up which led to the work by the Arnolds, Thomas and Matthew, F.D. Maurice and the Christian Socialists about the proper

Plate 106 [39]. Harry Wilkin from the life, a plumber Alnwick, a celebrated character.

ordering of society between people of successive generations and the nation-state; and the antithesis between permanence and stability or progression — 'two poles of the same magnet' — the channels of argument that supported 'the free and permeative life and energy of the Nation'.[12]

What mattered to Coleridge, and after him the Arnolds, was that the Anglican brand of religion, being the nation's church, incorporated the essentials of tolerance and included even discord, qualities which necessarily underpinned a small community such as Alnwick. A little later, Thomas Arnold described it as 'the bringing together reasonable and moderate men to meet with us and unite with us.'[13]

The language might vary according to the source: the Durham Report of 1839 into

Canada's future used 'Anglo-Saxon' to signify Englishness, self-critical, liberal whether in the Empire or at home; and what have been called the 'Romantic economists' have been identified by their use of organic metaphors to describe society's links, to incorporate imagination and sensibility into their logic, and to recognise the role of language, culture and identity in describing how the world worked.[14]

Arnold put it best: 'Is it too much to ask of good men that they should consent to unite themselves to other good men, without requiring them to subscribe to their own opinion or to conform to their own ceremonies?'[15] So might Langland have heard it in 'the plain full of people' which introduces *Piers Plowman* in 1362. If nothing else, the debate over Catholic emancipation 1828–9, filling whole pages of the Newcastle papers, would have brought home the nature of Forster's community and the essence of its diverse identity.

It was not simply groups of like-minded people that made it (today's ethnic, gay, gender, or disabled communities), nor was it in any way millenarian. It had no such rules as a monastic community; it had none of the nostalgic force of a mythic past, as still might be found in Romania or Russia. The key is that it incorporated differences rather than defining by difference.

The fundamental elements of community do not require a resort to improbable sharings of taste, interest or religion. Nor does community depend on numbers: it might be a small village or part of a huge city. But it has two faces, the community of inclination and shared interest on one hand, that of geography, economy and politics on the other. The latter rests on identity of place and the identification of inhabitants with that, in association with others and in acceptance of what the place offers and what are the outcomes of

association – rules written or unwritten, a basic mutual respect, the need for a certain commitment to prevent erosion of the idea itself.

It is this inter-connectedness which underlines the ethos described in *Middlemarch* or *Bleak House*: the pervasive sense of proximity, social habits and accepted rules, the sheer density of relations between citizens (to use the revolutionary legacy-word in place of 'people'). And it is this which has very largely been lost in the modern Western world where it is normal for 'people' to be in touch but rarely connected. Perhaps its last echo in English literature was Robert Tressell's *Ragged-Trousered Philanthropists*, completed in 1910.

Home is where you live, not where you were born, and home is by itself insufficient to create a community. Identity is partly what you create, not entirely what is created for you. What community offers is a sense of belonging, a greater ease than elsewhere despite its jealousies, feuds, competition, and conflicting desires. Community gives means to contain argument, settle disputes, decide who is inside, who is 'foreign'. It determines over a long cycle what a town's values are. It provides a protected zone by defining itself as distinct from the less-known, potentially hostile world outside. It is not about rights but helps define what is right. It resists above all the loneliness of the existential nightmare.

That, in turn, may be the deepest explanation of why the artist began to put this collective portrait together, only two years after Catholic Emancipation became English law.[16] Percy Forster, I argue, could not have compiled his folio of drawings unless he understood the community of which they were all a part.

Plate 107 [103]. Forster family fishing/picnic at Warkhaugh. 'Kettle of fish.'

To revert to the first chapter and the artist himself, about whom we know relatively little except his place in Alnwick's community, his profession as a portrait painter and his later, distinguished career in oils, exhibiting across the North East and the Borders. On that question, for lack of documentation, we cannot say more. But *why* did he put together this collection, so precisely annotated; why did he choose the hundred to bind up in such a folio but never exhibit, except to George Tate, the town's historian?

That he was part of a lively community, many of whom he knew well enough to sketch them 'from memory' (because few if any actually posed in the way that portrait painters expect) is obvious, and one can sketch in words what that community may have represented. But was his choice a matter of personal whim, arbitrary pleasure, or part of an undeclared argument? No letters exist to prove the point. One cannot exclude whim and pleasurable habit. But the collection suggests more than that: it might be a humane response to the Census' dry, authoritarian requirements; it might be a way to define what the town and its environs represented. It might simply have been collated for his family's pleasure, whom we can see (Plate 107) on their fishing expedition to the river Coquet – an extension of his own and their experience over time, a sort of history of the place across the generations from seven-year-olds to Old Thew aged ninety-three (Plate 12).

The layout and the notation suggest *intent*, the creation of a community portrait, the hundred being representative of the whole, seen not as history or dull recorded numbers, but as a lively society, whose individuals are, in a private sense, equals in front of his pencil. Why else focus on 'local characters' so often? Whose judgment was that, his or the community? He constructed this collective

Plate 108 [18]. Lieut Hall, lived in 1820s. Fond memory brings the light of other days around me. October 1831. With his dog and long cane. From memory.

portrait, but not in the old established way, putting the patron and his wife centre stage with their children around and servants in the background, in the mode set in England from Holbein and Van Dyke to Gainsborough.

Nor are they curiosities, a series of miserable or degenerate folk, apt to be categorised by the new advocates of nineteenth-century physiognomy and racial science. They are those whom one met in the street or at the butcher's, in the tavern, frequenting the markets, washing clothes, sporting a new waistcoat and a silver watch chain. Each one retains his or her identity and could survive just as well without the caption; but the caption, written in Forster's own hand, ties them into the community as if each was a well-cut piece to fit a jigsaw in the mind. By constructing Alnwick's folk in this way, Forster also says a great deal about himself.[17]

One other question remains. In the Old Testament Valley of Dry Bones, the prophet asked rhetorically, can these bones live? Historians have been trying to bring the past personally alive for centuries, usually from the top down, starting from kings and queens, then generals, admirals, bishops — all those for whom documentary evidence or epitaphs or memorials survive;[18] and in the British Isles until today, their accumulated enquiries have fostered a habit of biography, which Continental writers consider to be almost a British national characteristic.

Oral history, one possible avenue, has become a craft branch of history in its own right, allowing us to record the actual voices and words of people who lived fairly recently, but it is a dynamic which contains all the misunderstandings, misconceptions and plain lies that the voice is prone to. In some rare cases, the survival of artefacts and

writings allows us to see ordinary folk as a group; witness the servant-portraits at Erdig, the inquisition into Montaillou's heretics. By Forster's time, Royal Commissions of Inquiry were exposing the horrors of child labour in the coal mines, with printed transcriptions of the pitiful evidence they gave: 'it is very sair'. Egyptian tomb paintings, however idealised, gave early treasure-hunters a marvellous but usually formulaic portrait not only of Pharaohs' lives but those of their nobles', and even ordinary folk.

The high point of belief — and illusion — that the past could be uncovered 'as it actually was' (*wie es eigentlich gewesen war*) is normally associated with the later-nineteenth-century German school of historians, in particular Leopold von Ranke. Ranke today may be an Ozymandias figure, a heroic ruin in the desert, but his search remains a tantalising possibility for all the subdivisions and often blind alleys into which history has since been fragmented. Among all its originators, from Romantics like William Morris, to determinists such as Karl Marx, it remains the spur to analysis because, to put it in a different way, it describes the pursuit of truth.

But we know that there is an innate distinction between whether a portrayal represents an actual being independent of us, or something which *purports* to be that *to us*. There is no such thing as an ordered result; there is no frame nor prior design to the jigsaw, only endless argument about which approach is to be chosen, which templates to apply, which denominations and categories to use — in a word, the original census problem, where the question asked determines the result. Indeed it can be argued that the novel is the best way to appreciate community. *Middlemarch* or *Cranford* express general truths, however fictional they are, if only because of what we see as *credible* reactions to change.

We cannot entirely recreate the past because there is never enough evidence, even when we take account of architecture or the scientific knowledge they possessed, even if their societies and communities were open and left sufficient written records. But can long-dead people be portrayed so that we can connect to them? In the tomb of an Egyptian noble, Ramose in the Valley of the Kings, one wall contains two marvellously carved stone portraits, one of an elegant woman who might have stood in for Greta Garbo, another of a pert but equally beautiful girl who could be Brigitte Bardot in her youth.

Starting perhaps with the Nilotic burial portraits of the 2nd century BC, sixty generations of painters have tried to convey the essence of the sitter (or the corpse) in a way which would resonate not only with his/her children and the friends to be impressed, but with their progeny across time, if not forever. Occasionally (and the parallel may be with the Nilotic shrouds) there is enough to call the result a community. The same answer might be written of the massed life-size soldiery guarding the tomb of the first Chinese Emperor at Xian, each face a copy of a living human, differentiated forever in the armed crowd.

The question then becomes: can painting or drawing supplement or even supersede the use of fallible words to describe what a person really was? Can it deliver a real person, face to face, looking at you ready to address you by name? Supplement is perhaps a better word than supersede. One could cite the portraits of Rembrandt or Ingres, or the insights of Degas or Picasso into what individuals actually amounted to. Each period of art has, arguably for all human time, made possible later generations' understanding of their predecessors.

In this sense, Percy Forster's battered volume stands in a very long line of evidence, not of the peaks to which the human hand can reach, but about how people, largely unaware of the artist's presence and therefore free of the contagion first described by the anthropologist Margaret Meade, in which the observer conditions the behaviour of the observed, were actually *visible*: their demeanour, their clothes and shoes, their physiognomy, their position in a definable community.

Forster drew them as he thought they were, he shows us our ancestors as a civilised crowd, with whom we have to live, if we are to understand their legacy and ourselves, without the multiple overlays fused on to the original by later analysts seeking general principles, behaviour patterns, and statistical categories. They do not inhabit a parallel universe. They are as close to being real as may be. Pirandello's six characters find their author in the end.[19]

Societies today, preoccupied with and often bemused by the world of databases, statistical monitoring of pre-defined groups (not actual communities), watched over by a political class (not simply politicians and administrators) may seem remote from the actual community of place, work, thought and pleasure. The value of Forster's work lies not only in remembrance of things past, nor even in the knowledge that things were different then (which is too often the source of belief that the past was somehow innocent, its passing a grievous loss), but in the continuity it offers, and the distinction between mere legacy and actual knowledge. We have to accept them as he saw and drew them, if we seek to discover what we think they were.

*Plate 109 [14]. William
Netherston, a well-known
character in Alnwick, 1830
[folded and cut].*

APPENDIX A:
SOURCES AND BIBLIOGRAPHY

I. Archives
- Alnwick Castle includes Poll Books for 1826 and 1831, Census for Alnwick 1831 and documents on the Royal Commission inquiry into Municipal Reform 1834–5.
- Alnwick Freemen, minute books and accounts.
- Hobart Art Gallery, Tasmania: John Dempsey's sketch portfolio 1820s.
- Newcastle on Tyne Central Public Library: files of the *Journal* and the *Courant* 1828–31.
- Newcastle University, Robinson Library.
- Northumberland County Record Office: includes Hodgson, Davison and Donkin papers, Lady Ridley's Diary and documents relating to enclosure in the early nineteenth century.

2. Alnwick papers and reviews
- *Athenaeum* and *Quarto* (Bell, late 1820s)
- *Review* and *Mercury* (Davison)
- *Scandalismo* (no name)
- *Theatrical Observer* (Graham)
  All short-lived; surviving copies in the County Record Office.

3. Local histories
Davison, William *Descriptive and Historical View of Alnwick* (1822, revised 1829)

Hodgson, John *History of Northumberland*, 3 vols. (1832)

Mackenzie, Edward *History and Topographical Descriptive View of Northumberland* (2nd edition, 1825)

Pigott's Directory, 1822 and 1828.

Tate, George *History of Alnwick*, 2 vols. (1866)

4. General and North Eastern
Attick, R.D. *The English Common Reader 1800–1900* (1963)

Briggs, Asa *A Social History of England* (1983)

Briggs, Asa *The Age of Improvement* (1959)

Cobbett, William *Rural Ride*, modern reissue (1967)

Conzen, M.R.G. *Alnwick: A Study in Town-Plan Analysis* (1960)

Emsley, C. *Crime and Society in England 1750–1900* (1994)

Everitt, Alan *Landscape and Community in England* (1985)

Gibson, W. *Church, State and Society 1760–1850* (1994)

Golby, J.M. & Purdue, A.W. *The Civilisation of the Crowd: Popular Culture 1750–1900* (1984)

Halsey, A.H. *Change in British Society* (1978)

Harrison, J.F.C. *Early Victorian Britain 1832–51* (1979)

Hall, Marshall *Artists of Northumbria* (2005)

Kay, John *A Series of Original Portraits and Etchings*, introduction by Alan Bell (2007)

Kitson, Clarke G. *The Making of Victorian England* (1962)

McCord, Norman *North-East England 1760–1960* (1979)

Mingay, G.E. *Land and Society in England 1750–1880* (1994)

Morris, R.J. *Class, Power and Social Structure in British 19th Century Towns* (1986)

Murphy, J. *Church, State and Schools in Britain 1806–1970* (1971)

Pearl, Sharona *Physiognomy in 19th Century Britain* (2009)

Pooley, C.G. & Whyte, I.D. (eds) *Migrants, Emigrants and Immigrants* (1991)

Reader, W.J. *Professional Men in 19th Century England* (1986)

Royle, E. *Modern Britain: A Social History 1750–1990*, 2nd edition (1997)

Stone, Laurence *An Open Elite: England 1540–1880* (1984)

Thompson, F.M.L. *Land and Society in England in the 19th Century* (1963)

Thompson, F.M.L. (ed.) *Cambridge Social History of Britain 1750–1950*, 3 vols. (1990) Contains many very useful essays and still a standard work.

Uglow, Jennie *Nature's Engraver: A Life of Thomas Bewick* (2006)

Watts, M.R. *The Dissenters, vol. 2, 1791–1859* (1995)

Young, Arthur *A Six Month's Tour through the North of England*, vol. 2 (2nd edition 1771)

Plate 110 [57]. Dr Foulder April 30 1831 from memory. A celebrated man in his day.

APPENDIX B:
List of Illustrations as set out with Forster's handwritten annotations in the original folio

Frontispiece: Percy Forster, n.d. late 1820s. He wears the still-fashionable Regency wing collar with cravat high. Although the son of a gamekeeper, he has evidently established fashionable status by his late twenties.

1. John Thew, 1830, aged 91, a farmer under the Duke of Northumberland and one of his oldest tenants. Mr Thew's ancestors have rented land under the Percy family for upwards of 500 years, and he is now the last of the race! [Gilfin Farm Denwick 1810].

2. Female standing [member of Forster's family, probably his sister Mary].

3. P.J. Selby Esq. 1834. From memory [local landowner].

4. Beaumont and Howick election, May 9, 1831 [probably Beaumont himself].

5. [Self-portrait of Forster: see Frontispiece.]

6. Charlotte Forster sister to the artist Percy Forster, Hulne Park Alnwick, April 26, 1833 [see also no. 99].

7. Hugh Watson by P.F. [fellow artist and friend] (verso Embleton sketched by Hugh Watson).

8. James Bell commonly called 'Nosey Bell' and ditto verso: formerly a shoemaker in Newcastle, went out of Alnwick when a boy with five shillings in his pocket and returned with nearly £6,000.

9. [as above]

10. Robert Spearman of Warton, commonly called 'the Giant' [two versions].

11. [as above]

12. William Cleghorn, a native of Alnwick. From the life. Now living April 9 1852. 'He died in the early 1860s' [note in George Tate's handwriting].

13. Old Brown the Hatter 1825. From memory October 17 1831. A bad character who neither believed in God or the Devil!

14. William Netherston, a well-known character in Alnwick, 1830 [folded and cut].

15. Tom Wilson, spirit merchant in Alnwick commonly called Winey Wilson.

16. Little Jimmy Harrington the wee fisher!

17. John Wallace, weather-wise Jack, aged 70, for many years sexton at St. Mary's Alnwick. The same verso.

18. Lieut Hall, lived in 1820s. Fond memory brings the light of other days around me. October 1831. With his dog and long cane. From memory.

19. James Riley a celebrated clarinet player and leather cutter, Alnwick October1831, then from memory December 2 1831.

20. Edward Thew from memory February 13 1846 [verso a cow and two names].

21. James Bamforth sexton [with keys] ditto verso.

22. [as above]

23. James Bamforth from the life, sexton January 15 1833.

24. Old Sally Bamforth the sexton's wife, both very odd characters from Yorkshire. Additional note: 'originally from Yorkshire resided many years at the corner of Fenkle Street and Narrowgate Street'.

25. William Baird, Rich merchant in Alnwick, a bachelor.

26. Old Thew, aged 93, Denwick [verso the same

'good' 1832]. Additional note 'nose end red/ eyebrows grey/wig bay/cheeks in colour with the nose/coat grey with mettle [*sic*] buttons/ topcoat drab/hazel ring'.

27. Lyetty Jack, September 1838 fond of poaching and shooting, with his dog.

28. Charlie Carr, done 1831, from memory June 18 1831. An old soldier who in his latter time rode on an ass to look after the game on Alnwick Moor.

29. Bob Hudson a hedger to his Grace the Duke of Northumberland [missing].

30. Tom Brosby 1831, from memory December 7 1831, farmer of the pasture before the Castle, commonly called 'Damn you, dog.' With large dog.

31. Hector Thompson, April 23 1831, shepherd to the late Duke of Northumberland. This portrait was drawn from memory about 17 or 18 years after his death. With collie.

32. Miles Sayer, April 13 1831, from memory. Huntsman [whipper in] to his Grace the Duke of Northumberland about the year 1800. He lived in the Park many years after this date. With hound.

33. Tom Beasley, July 17 1831, from memory. For long, woodman to his Grace the Duke of Northumberland, died worth £7,000. <u>The Good old times!</u>

34. Tom Newton April 23 1831, Keeper of the Brizlee Tower Hulne Park and his dog, Doctor. A keen fox hunter, etc.

35. Tom the Cutter [leather] 1831, from memory July 20 1831. A character in Alnwick often seen standing with eels for sale.

36. George Henderson 1831 from memory December 7 1831. For many years the miller at the Abbey Mills Alnwick.

37. Mr Henry Wilkin January 4 1833 [see also no. 39].

38. Dr Turnbull 1831 from memory June 7 1831. A doctor of Divinity, resided in Alnwick in 1820 or thereabout [as a younger man, see also no. 84].

39. Harry Wilkin from the life, a plumber from Alnwick, a celebrated character [verso, ditto].

40. [as above]

41. Ald Tom Coward April 26 1831. A celebrated violin player Alnwick.

42. Dolly Wilkin January 5 1832 [wife or mother of Harry].

43. Church Keys of St. Mary's.

44. Ald Jack Kirkup 1831 from memory November 30 1831, for long a driver at the White Swan.

45. [as above]

46. Old Peg Downison aged 81, from the life. Very deaf. For many years went round the country in the neighbourhood of Alnwick selling oranges, nuts, gooseberries in the season, etc.

47. William Burnett April 20 1831. Large man, a carter in Alnwick from 1815.

48. [as above]

49. Billy Carr 1832 from memory April 10 1832. Long postmaster in Alnwick.

50. John Jobson from memory March 22 1832 'Duddy Willie' once a large corn factor in Alnwick [see also no. 59].

51. [Missing from before 1900, i.e. no secondary annotation.]
52. Mrs Dodds August 9 1831 from the life, a good and religious woman in Alnwick [wife of Dodds the draper from 1816–17].
53. Sandy Tom Wardall [n.d.]. A well-known character in Alnwick who went about selling sand from 1815–16.
54. Dr Haswell April 30 1831 Alnwick.
55. Henry Trotter 1832 from memory March 19 1832. Horse farrier Alnwick from 1820.
56. Dr Foulder April 30 1831 from memory. A celebrated man in his day.
57. [as above]
58. William Teasdale December 3 1831 from memory. Buried today 4 December 1831. Draper, a good character.
59. John Jobson, once a large corn factor in Alnwick, known as Duddy Willie [see no. 50] from memory March 20 1832.
60. Hugh 3rd Duke of Northumberland, July 19 1824 from memory. Likeness very good [1817–47 in a later hand].
61. George Barkas from memory July 10 1831. An honest man is the noblest work of God. A celebrated schoolmaster in Alnwick. I was taught at his school and never knew a better man than Old Barkas.
62. Colonel Lindsay [n.d.] lived in Alnwick. Commonly called the Fox. Very rich. Near the Abbey Mill there is a gate/And to enter in – who dare?/Unless he be prepared to meet his fate/For A. is guarded by a bear.
63. George Hudson April 23 1831. A farmer in Hulne Park. An ill-tempered man.
64. Joseph Edmondson October 10 1831. Buried October 19, from memory. A farmer in Hulne Park commonly called Cunning Joe.
65. J. [John] Bickerton 1831 from memory, October 10. A labourer going home from his work to Alnwick.
66. Jack the Cowper 1831 from memory June 1831. A celebrated character in Cannongate [sic] Alnwick who would exchange anything he had with anyone. A good stack of old books, etc.
67. James Wilson a chemist in Alnwick, a keen fisher in the years 1814–15 etc.
68. Edward Allen July 27 1831 from the life! A native of Alnwick a celebrated singer and ventriloquist, sleight of hand, etc.
69. John Liddle October 19 1831 from memory of Denwick the hedger and 'lock greaser' in Hulne Park called 'Sly John'.
70. William Teasdale 1831 from memory December 3 1831, draper Alnwick [see also no. 58].
71. Purvis 1826 a cow doctor.
72. Dukey Greenhead from memory October 4 1831. A man of weak intellect, a well-known character in Alnwick from 1817.
73. Ald Molly Todd 1831 from memory October 14 1831. Long hostess at Coal Eglingham.
74. Ald Adams 1831 from memory December 3 1831, lived in Alnmouth the latter part of his life with panniers and a lean mule called the Miser, dealt in turkeys.
75. Handy Tom [with a hook for a hand] the Butcher's man – well-known character in Alnwick from 1820.
76. Ben Nicholson 1831 from memory October 4 1831 a well-known character in Alnwick from 1818.
77. Tom Grey farmer at Longhoughton missing.

78. George Nicholson 1832 from memory March 19 1832. A respectable butcher in Alnwick.
79. William Leithead 1831 from memory December 12 1831. An Attorney in Alnwick from the 1820s.
80. Wise Willie from memory 1832. A well-known character in Alnwick. Woodman.
81. [Missing from before 1900.]
82. Edward Stamp March 14 1840. Banker.
83. Jackie Thew aged 97. July 10 1835.
84. Dr Turnbull [n.d.]. A celebrated character in Alnwick from the 1820s [as an old man, see no. 38].
85. Thomas Patterson from life February 20 1835. Long Parish Clerk at St. Mary's. Contemporary with James Bamforth, sexton. A strange a couple of ecclesiasts as ever graced the Established Church.
86. John Fairnam, May 28 1838. Went among farmers, very eccentric and would never work. In his later years, lived near Gateshead.
87. Old William Johnson 1832, grocer Alnwick.
88. My mother aged 88 January 31 1840, lived Hope Terrace Alnwick.
89. Robin Patterson August 12 1832, Fisherman Newton by the Sea. Note: verso oilskin cap/ blue jacket/canvas trousers/sea-burnt boots.
90. Wise Willie May 3 1852, Chairman at the Queen's Head.
91. Luke Skelley July 27 1835. The Earth Stopper to the Percy Hounds – Washburn Cottage.
92. Clark June 14 1838 with dog and sheep, a butcher Alnwick.
93. Boy street seller with duck and kippers July 26 1833. Whar's away man, and tether the Duck!
94. Child holding a toy, barefoot, December 5 1832. Bramble prick.

95. Three children playing for a fight [with a schoolbook on the ground] 'Pin him, Bobby'.
96. Boy and girl. 'Well he began to have strains first, he twick up a muckle great strain an' hat is on other lug!'
97. [Cock of the Wood] Fisherman's gossip [n.d.].
98. Snuff taker. 'I'll no be the waur o' anither pinch, I'm thinking.'
99. Charlotte Forster [see no. 6] in middle age.
100. Grinding wheel, Hulne Park.
101. Turkeys.
102. Hound with stick in its mouth.
103. Forster family fishing/picnic at Warkhaugh. 'Kettle of fish.'
104. One year old cow. Alnwick Fair May 12 1838.
105. Two boys playing marbles March 21 1840.
106. Two boys playing hoopla March 21 1840.
107. Billy Smith corn factor, Alnwick at the Star Inn reading reports of the markets. June 1 1852.
108. William Carleton from the life June 18 1842. Fishing. A good likeness.
109. The Hind's wife at Shipley July 22 1835.
110. Evening.
111. Wolf a pup of mine 1830.
112. Tom – my favourite terrier.
113. Morrison's pills. Grandma and boy.
114. Cheese press.
115. Herring fleet Dunstanburgh. August 18 1852.
116. Young man with dog riding home, 1834
117. Ald Rogers nursery-man at Chatton [missing].

NOTES

CHAPTER ONE:
PERCY FORSTER AND ALNWICK'S PEOPLE

1   Earlier records do not exist but in 1808, John Forster's half year wages were £12-10, his board wages £8-6-6 (Castle Archives AC.N.V.3/3). Joseph was not christened till he was nearly seven, together with Charles.

2   Percy Forster FRSA, 1801 to after 1856. cf. *Artists of Northumbria* (2005) p. 127.

3   Ibid. p. 128. This mezzotint was sold by Philips auctioneers in Leeds in November 1994 for several hundred pounds.

4   In a few cases, a longer time elapsed, but his caption usually distinguishes these, an indication of how carefully he situated each one in time and space.

5   This latter figure rose modestly to fifty-six in the town as a result of the 1832 Reform Act, according to the Poll Book of 1841.

6   In his introduction to the two-volume reissue (Birlinn, 2007) Alan Bell describes Kay's work as 'formalised but not posed . . . lying at ease on the border between portrayal and caricature'.

7   Dempsey's collection of fifty-one watercolours was rediscovered in Tasmania in the 1950s. It covers, like Forster's, the 1820s and 1830s and like his is fully labelled and dated (Hobart Museum).

8   cf. Ruth Richardson, *The Making of Mr. Gray's Anatomy* (OUP, 2008).

9   cf. Ariella Azoulay, *The Civil Contract of Photography* (2008).

10 Alan Thomas, *The Expanding Eye* (1978). Both Daguerre and Fox-Talbot made their quite separate discoveries public in January 1839. The latter acknowledged his debt to earlier artists in his 1844 lecture 'The Pencil of Nature', while claiming a place among them with 'photogenic drawing' (cf. Asa Briggs, *A Victorian Portrait*, 1989). But only the daguerreotype followed the artist in that its image could not be reproduced mechanically, as calotypes could, and were.

11 A process made universal by the inventions of Kodak by George Eastman after 1888. Even in the 1900s, Jacques-Henri Lartigue, a wealthy and gifted amateur pursued the same type of image-inquiry that had preoccupied Forster in the 1830s.

12 He did include other drawings, agricultural implements, such as the grinding wheel and the cheese press; but one cannot build an argument on that, nor the elaborate keys of St Mary's and St Michael's Church – unless it is a far-fetched reference to the keys of St Peter, 1829 being the year of Catholic emancipation.

13 William Davison, *Alnwick* (1822) 1st edition, 2nd edition, 1826 and 1829, 3rd facsimile edition 1973.

14 J. Michelet, *Ouvres Complets*, XXI, p. 268, quoted by Anderson, *Imagined Communities*, p. 198.

15 His skill can be described as mimesis, intimate engagement by the viewer with the subject, as if literally getting under the skin, to bridge the gap between experience and understanding. Yet this is not definitive, for different viewers across a long cycle may draw out different inferences. (cf. Howard Cannatella, *The Riches of Art Education*, 2008)

CHAPTER TWO:
INHERITANCE AND TRADITION

1   Although the Scottish Highland clearances had already begun, until the 1830s the only part of Scotland where the population actually fell were the Border counties whose families might leave for Glasgow or Tyneside and the Durham coalmines, if they chose industry, or stay in North Northumberland as agricultural labourers or domestic servants. According to the 1831 Census, many of Alnwick's servants (who totalled 313 women, 28 men) gave their birth places as Roxburgh or Berwickshire.

2   Rowlinson Report to the Board of Health 1849, done during the last cholera epidemic. These can be compared with parts of Lambeth at the time, belonging to the Archbishop of Canterbury. (Conzen, p. 67)

3   M.R. Conzen, Alnwick, *A Study in Town Plan Analysis*

(1960) p. 4 charts its growth, the historic layout of its streets, the rapid rebuilding of its medieval core, and the extensions 1750–1850. Two maps, Thompson's (1760) and Wood's (1827) point up the town's spread.

4 According to *Pigott's Directory* Hulne Park, where Percy Forster's family lived, constituted a 'township' of nine farms plus the ancient Abbeylands.

5 Conzen. p. 63.

6 See Arthur Young's *Travels*, the *Scottish Border Surveys* of the 1790s, and Cullen's publications.

7 The early-seventeenth-century Earls had in the late Renaissance historical tradition embellished Alnwick Castle's battlements with carved stone figures of Roman warriors. More than a century later, some of these being eroded or damaged, they were restored again in the local grit stone. But by then the myth had grown up that they had been placed there in antiquity to frighten off marauders from Scotland.

8 See Jenny Uglow, *Berwick, Nature's Engraver* (2006).

9 Thomas Davison, 1st edition, 1820, revised 1823, reissued with plates in 1829. It is the latter that is used here. See also George Tate, *History of Alnwick* (2 vols) 1868.

10 For a recent history of their many rises and falls, see Alexander Rose, *Kings in the North: The House of Percy in British History* (2007).

11 1803 figures included 33 children under five, 46 between five and ten, and 165 persons over sixty years of age.

12 The opening ceremony pp. 295–8 and grandiose references to Rome, Paris and London, was matched by H.C. Selby's 1814 monument at Swansfield House, near the end of the Napoleonic War, claiming Britain's real and glorious responsibility for the 'nations of the Continent' exemplifying 'the roles of Nelson, Wellington and Pitt and the British Empire itself'.

13 Davison, pp. 386–91. The eulogy was somewhat spoiled by the local legend that Brizlee Tower's design 'had originally been made of pastry by a French cook'.

14 John Sykes, *Local Records or Historical Register of Remarkable Events* (2 vols) 1833.

15 Sykes, Vol. 1, p. 196–7; Vol. 2, p. 302.

16 Alnwick Castle archives 187A/131.

17 cf. Alan Everitt, *Landscape and Community in England* (1985) especially the section on carters and hauliers. 'Among the carriers themselves . . . there was often a strong sense of community . . . fostered . . . by their meetings week by week at the inn' (p. 303).

18 *Ibid*. p. 321–9.

19 The main formative writings on English and regional identity can be seen in the contemporary accounts of Arthurian and Anglo-Saxon mythology, above all, as far as Alnwick's intellectuals were concerned, Thomas Percy's *Reliques of Ancient Poetry* (1765), Sharon Turner's *History of England from the Earliest Period (1799–1805)* and the novels of Walter Scott. Thomas Arnold's Inaugural Lecture, arguing that the English were racially mixed but culturally pure, came later (Oxford, 1841), and the bias against the Irish and the Welsh later still (Robert C. Young, *The Idea of British Ethnicity*, 2009) – but Sir Francis Palgrave, prolific historian of 'the continuity of English life', was widely read in the 1830s. Existence of the idea of a *common history*, matching a common language, even if religious affiliation differed, had been established in Forster's mid-life.

20 Sir Keith Thomas' recent study *The Ends of Life* (OUP, 2009) makes this point mainly for the seventeenth century and the Civil War. The quest for self-fulfillment can be started there, because earlier than that, it is hard, even with such scholarship, to pin down what men and women sought as goals, what gave inner meaning to their lives. But Thomas' answers: military prowess, work, wealth, reputation, personal relationships, and the afterlife, need modification for the 1830s, since the scope of the first had become professional and the last a matter of permanent dispute.

CHAPTER THREE:
WORK OR OCCUPATION

1 Davison, using the previous Census of 1821, gives agricultural families 174, compared with 186 in 1831; families in trade, manufacturing and crafts 512 (591), others 718 (817). Population in the whole vast parish rose from 5,426 in 1811 to 5,927 in 1821, and 6,788 in 1831, a steady but gradual rate.

2 Pigott: *Directory for Northumberland* (1822) pp. 565–70 and (1829) pp. 560–70; Parson's *Directory and Gazette for Durham and Northumberland 1827–8* (Vol. 1) pp. 300–97. Later on, White's *General Directory* (1847) pp. 659–76.

3 George Culley (1775–1825) *General View of the Agriculture of Northumberland, etc.* (1805) laid down the principles

of farming improvement in the fertile Millfield plain north of Alnwick.

4 George Ewart Evans, *In the Farm and the Village* (1968) indeed argued that, in his own East Anglian experience, there still existed 'a rural culture which had extended in an unbroken line at least since the early Middle Ages, and which possessed innumerable direct links with much earlier times' – but which were mostly to be extinguished by the mid-twentieth century.

5 Norman McCord, *The North-East*, p. 27.

6 Davison p. 243 gives the six-year average of the mid-1820s as 553 black cattle, 4,973 sheep and lambs, 527 calves (veal being a local speciality), hundreds of pigs, uncounted numbers of poultry.

7 The famous Stockton-Darlington line, run by steam engines from 1825, was actually only an extended wagon way. Railway lines were often delayed by landowners' objections and promoters' inability to meet these except by local bargaining. Thus the 1839 Newcastle to Carlisle line had to sign an agreement with Charles Bacon of Styrford Hall that the railway buildings should not be seen from his mansion (McCord, pg. 34). The London–Euston line to Gateshead was completed in 1844 but only extended once the Newcastle high level bridge had been built, reaching Tweedmouth in 1847, Edinburgh in 1848. This north eastern line was only fully ready by 1850.

8 Alan Everitt, *Landscape and Community in England* (1985) p. 27.

9 The Northumberland Arms, the George and Dragon, the Angel, the Four Horseshoes, the Golden Fleece, the Turk's Head, the White Hart, the Nag's Head, Gray's Inn, the Half Moon and the Crown. Six of these were still in existence in the 1950s.

10 A.W. Purdue, *Squires, Scholars and Soldiers* (2000).

11 Davison took over from his original partner John Catnach *c*.1810 and proved to be a commercial polymath. To printer, publisher and bookseller, which was the usual range, he added auctioneer and share broker.

12 Before the coronation of Charles X, he had already spent 500 francs on two pairs of pistols by Lepage, much jewelry and Sevres porcelain, and in August 1825 he paid a London goldsmith Rundall of Bridge and Rundall £5,770 for a massive diamond 'from the King's crown set into the Duke's necklace' (Castle Letters, vol. 6). The latter sum would have paid for the building of a fair sized mansion.

13 c.f. Keith Thomas, *The Ends of Life* (OUP 2009).

14 Napoleon, a stallion 2 guineas each mare and 2/6 for the groom. Trusty, another, a mere guinea a time.

15 County Archives, ZMD1 Davison notes, 1829.

16 No English town followed Glasgow's lead of 1800 in establishing its own police *force*, until London in 1831.

17 For the Borough list, see Tate, vol. II, pp. 440–52. A man could only qualify if he was the son of a Freeman or if he had served seven years apprenticeship to a Freeman. Admission of the latter involved a sort of marathon, a procession led by the town's Waits playing fiddles up Freemen Hill where lay a deep pond dammed and laced over with straw ropes. The water being well stirred up to mud, the novices in white clothes had to swim or wade its entire length, change into dry clothes and run or ride home for the festivities (Robert Middlemas, 'The Freemen of Alnwick' *c*.1930).

18 The author's great grandfather Robert Middlemas was still performing these functions in the 1860s and 1870s.

19 Susan Lawrence *Charitable Knowledge Hospital Pupils and Practitioners in 18th Century London* (1997) argued that hospital practice helped to remold medical authority. By 1800 most provincial hospitals had become institutions for exporting sound medical knowledge and reliable doctors, together with a new sort of medical reporting based on European enlightenment and Royal Society publications. Doctors in Newcastle, even Alnwick, became leaders in two senses, via scholarly output (lectures, pupils, practical demonstrations) and through the public's dutiful acceptance of what they were introducing.

20 But it was in Newcastle, where on a Thursday patients were instructed to attend 'at eleven o'clock in the forenoon to return thanks to the gentleman of the house committee, for the benefit received from the charity' (quoted in McCord, *The Northeast*, p. 102).

21 My great grandfather, son of a mining drainer in 1831, crossed this barrier at the age of twenty-three.

22 Northumberland County Archives: Insurance agents file.

23 Davison, *Alnwick*, p. 246.

24 *Lord Goderich and the Country Bankers*, Alnwick Castle archive, ZR1/34/2. Some correspondents complained that the Bank of England had chosen only the best local ones as survivors, while rejecting 'even the best bills and most unquestionable securities of inferior parties, many of whom were ruined'.

25 Who mattered most can be gauged from the proclamation of William IV's ascent to the throne, 1 July 1828 led by Charles Bigge, chairman of the County, four leading magistrates, all gentry, the under-sheriff, the militia staff, and the County bailiffs.

26 According to Pigott 1830, its revenue (distinct from Poor Rate) had for years been kept a secret, but it was forced to disclose the sum of £680 in 1819, £640 in 1822, against expenditure of £350. Where the residue went is not clear.

27 McCord, *North-East*, p. 74–5.

28 Despite this, Rowlandson's *Report of 1850* on sanitary conditions in Alnwick (McCord p. 78) revealed just how much remained to be done, albeit from a higher critical standpoint.

29 J. Rewcastle, *Newcastle As It Is* (1854) p. 13 and McCord, p. 70a.

30 What emerges from local newspaper reports, mostly very attenuated, is that the combination of how the accused was charged and the knowledge local juries had of him, materially affected the sentence: the Magistrates did not sit unchecked. Forster's sketching years 1820s and mid-1830s, witnessed a notable change not so much in severity of sentence to those found guilty, but in the extent of acquittals – not unconnected with the anti-slavery campaign and mistrust of paid informer-witnesses. Juries had, after all, to balance their responsibility to their own community against the propriety of what they understood the law to be: justice, as distinct from law, required them to distinguish between a criminal occupation and a poor man or woman's desperation.

31 See Alan Everitt, *The Pattern of Rural Dissent in the 19th Century* (1972).

32 Castle Archives, 187A/127, 24 August 1833.

33 Colonel Peter Hawker, *Shooting Journals* (1990 edition, *passim*).

34 By an Act of 1818, informers could be paid as much as £40 if their evidence led to conviction; but this caused juries to treat all such witnesses with a certain suspicion which in turn let many off the hook.

35 Castle Archives, *Beeby Diary* 187A/735. By the 1820s the regiment was being run down, and in 1830 its soldiers had to make due at annual camp with a small compensation payment rather than the usual 'uniform suit'.

36 Davison, *Alnwick*, p. 221.

37 By the 1840s, illegitimacy had risen from 6 per cent all births in the late eighteenth century to 7 per cent; a rate which was much exceeded in the Border counties and the North East (E. Royle, *Modern Britain*, 1997, p. 53).

38 J.M. Golby and A.W. Purdue, *Popular Culture in England 1750–1900* (1984).

39 A.W. Purdue, *Merchants and Gentry in North-East England 1650–1800* (1999) p. 250.

CHAPTER FOUR:
THE EDUCATED MIND

1 George Tate, *Alnwick* vol. 2, p. 206.

2 Tate, *ibid.* vol. 2, p. 169.

3 Although child death rates remained high (35 per cent of all burials 1813–20 being under 5) those under 18 constituted more than half, perhaps 60 per cent of Alnwick's parish, with a higher proportion of girls than boys.

4 This reached an absurd level with the claims made by Resurrectionists (alias grave robbers, selling corpses to anatomists) to 'their power in raising disembodied spirits', according to the papers of William Donkin, Alnwick solicitor.

5 This did not apparently detract from the distinct cultural aspirations of what two leading historians of popular culture call *The Civilization of the Crowd* (Golby and Purdue, 1984). But the prevalence of literacy and numeracy of the 1820s did shape the ways in which popular culture developed (c.f. Alan Everitt, *Landscape and Community in England*, 1985), reinforcing perhaps, from a better-educated standpoint, the sense of sturdy working class independence.

6 In 1830, the town gave the United Association Congregation minister 'silver and various useful articles worth £50' for his new home, 'for that spirit of candor and liberality which he has shown to all denominations of Evangelical Christians'.

7 I have in my possession a clay peg tile, taken from a

Sussex barn built in about 1820. It is deeply inscribed by the maker with the word *Liberty* in a fair hand. The point is that this was done on the underside, so that it would never be read – a mute protest, using only the one revolutionary word, not equality or fraternity.

8   Robert Middlemas, an early scholar, quoted in the *Duke's School* (1990) p. 91.

9   As argued by Everitt, p. 66.

10 Castle Archives, 187a/160.

11 The proceedings of St Michael's Vestry in the 1820s and 1830s demonstrated that under the vicar William Proctor, the four church wardens, all local farmers or retailers, were at the same time Overseers of the Poor and heavily represented on the Town Council: the effect being a powerful restraint on the wider aspects of Evangelism and any extension of the school's curriculum.

12 c.f. *Civilization of the Crowd*, p. 129.

13 E. Mackenzie, *View of the County of Northumberland*, vol. 2, p. 484–5 (1825).

14 Hugh Cunningham, *The Invention of Childhood* (2006).

15 Catnach moved south attracted by ever greater opportunities, setting up a printing works in London's Seven Dials. In 1815, he claimed, he could print 100,000 pamphlets in 24 hours – more than even Davison imagined possible.

16 Davison's idea was to fold local news in a general format printed for him in London. But rivals in Newcastle and Berwick, each only three or four hours away by coach, had all this at the same time, which limited his market. cf. Morris Milne, *Newspapers of Northumberland and Durham* (1981) and P.G. Isaac, *William Davison of Alnwick* (1968).

17 *Berwickshire Naturalists' Club*, vol. XXIII, p. 315–37.

18 Wendy Griswold, *Regionalism and the Reading Class* (2007).

19 County Archives, Davison collection, ZMD 167.

20 BNC History, 1876–8, p. 373, obituary by Robert Middlemas.

21 George Johnston (1797–1856) a farmer's son brought up at Ilderton, 20 miles from Alnwick, educated at Kelso and Edinburgh University, author of *Flora of Berwickshire*, *Natural History of the Eastern Borders*, etc.

22 Castle Archives, 187A/131.

23 See M.R.G. Conzen, *Alnwick: A Study in Town Plan Analysis* (1960).

24 *Lady Ridley's Diary*, Northumberland Archives.

25 William Leithead's brother, John had a mistress, Mary Middlemas from a Berwick family, who was able to urge the old solicitor to give her Alnwick nephew the chance of taking Articles and becoming a partner within seven years.

26 Apropos the Private Bill 'for paving and improving this town', E. Mackenzie commented 'aided by his Grace the Duke, will soon render this one of the cleanest, most convenient and pleasant county towns in this part of the kingdom'. *View of the County of Northumberland*, vol. 2, p. 484 (1825). Cleanliness needs to be emphasised: all the evidence about personal hygiene suggests that the English grew dirtier from the sixteenth to the eighteenth centuries and washed less; but that their foul habits changed in the second half of the eighteenth century, partly because the arrival of Irish linen meant that sheets and shirts could be washed more often. Alnwick certainly had a better water supply by the 1820s, and most of its new late Georgian houses had indoor lavatories. Washing children had by the 1800s become a sign of affectionate parenthood.

CHAPTER FIVE:
SPORT AND LEISURE

1   A typical night at the Old Theatre by the Nag's Head, 27 February 1829: tightrope dancer, *The Virginians* by Sheridan, *Pilot and Storm at Sea – A Farce*, Pizarro, *Babes in the Wood*, *Man of the World* by Macklin (satire), *Maria Marten* or *The Red Barn* (murder), and *Rob Roy McGregor*. Boxes 2/6, Pit 2/-shillings, Gallery 1 shilling. Some programmes have thinly-veiled undertones: *King of Queer-O-Mania*, and *A New Way to Pay Old Debts*.

2   *The First Modern Midnight Steeplechase* (printed by Ackerman in 1825) shows a gang of motley, half-drunk young men racing for a wager over hedges by moonlight.

3   The Alnwick Subscription Assembly, No. 3 'particularly requested that tickets may be procured as no money will be received at the door'. (*Newcastle Courant*, 18 April 1829)

4   Tate records the last session of Bull-baiting in the marketplace around 1820. Both were forbidden by law in the mid 1830s.

5   Northumberland Archives, Hunting, letter of 1924.

6   Not even the 1835 Cruelty to Animals Act or its

1845 successor barring cock-fighting were wholly successful. Badger baiting seems to have been completely unaffected. Conversely, lotteries had been abandoned by the mid-1820s and Sabbath observance (400 societies across Britain) built up the force which did finally assault gambling in the 1850s.

7 The English habit of sketching mountains, castles or historic ruins amazed and amused French countrymen and even town-dwellers, the enthusiasm and skill of their amateur art being almost an unknown pastime in the *pays* (Graham Robb: *The Discovery of France*, 2008, p. 196).

8 Castle Archives, 187A/131.

9 R. Mullen and J. Munson, *The Smell of the Continent: The British Discover Europe* (2007).

10 Alnwick had two armourers, one of them Davison's brother, and with the changeover from flintlock to percussion cap did good business in this period. Top of the range of course were the London gun makers, heirs to Durs Egg such as John Manton.

11 For the main studies, see E.W. Bovill, *The England of Nimrod and Surtees 1815–54* (1959) and *English Country Life 1780–1830* (1962).

12 Castle Archives Z113.

13 Bovill, pg. 122.

14 Castle Archives 187A/183.

15 Castle Archives 187A/127.

16 Grouse shooting began two weeks before the legal day 12th August —as it still does, to ensure that ripe birds sit on the table in London restaurants.

17 As late as 1840, Robertson complained to the Duke about the shortage of foxes due to overhunting. 'In another season, if yr Grace thinks proper to direct your keepers not to use man-traps, for they destroy the Foxes often, without intending it . . .' The Duke's agent seems to have complied, following the practice of his neighbour the Duke of Roxburgh and Lord Elcho, and ignoring protests from Lord Tankerville's keepers.

18 Even the Duke of Northumberland advertised to neighbouring gentlemen not to shoot in Alnwick Park, 'the rides and woods in the vicinity of the Castle nor in Aydon Forest . . . it is requested that gentlemen should refrain' unless they had a three-guinea license, while tenants were ordered to usher them off if not. (*Newcastle Courant*, 7 February 1829).

19 Total entries came to 653 of whom 400–500 actually lived in the town. Dodds' hinterland covered Bamburgh, Morpeth, Rothbury, a 20-mile circle and some orders were even sent south to London. (Northumberland Archives, MSS Dodd, 2 vols.)

20 cf. Alison Adburgham, *Shops: Shopping 1800–1914* (1964) also Judith Flanders, *Consuming Passions* (2006). Even in the eighteenth century, Dr Johnson had noted that shopping had drifted from necessity to pastime. By 1851 of course, two clear distinctions, about the spur of international competition to the British market, and between the stimulus to educate as opposed to satisfy and provide entertainment, had grown up 'to improve the taste of the common man'.

21 This is how Alfred Marshall explained the revival of the Napoleonic legend in the 1850s: those who had experienced the glories of his empire before 1815, passed on their memory to their grandchildren.

22 cf. *Civilization of the Crowd*, pp. 190–2.

23 Thomas Brassey, foremost contractor in the world, building the first mainline railway in France, Paris to Rouen in the late 1830s, found the local labourers so stunted and physically inadequate that he had to import Irish and English navvies, habituated to two pounds of meat a day.

CHAPTER SIX:
THE BALANCE OF POWER

1 It was arguable that Alnwyck borough had originally been summoned to Parliament. But even if accurate, this right had been lost through disuse and unwillingness to pay for a member in the later Middle Ages.

2 Tate vol. 2, p. 288–92.

3 Castle Archives, J2 Class I, Division II, 1–17, 26. 40–2.

4 Davison p. 320.

5 E.J. Hobsbawm and George Rudé, *Captain Swing* (1968)

6 Tate vol. 2, p. 350.

7 Castle Archives, J2.1 Division 2, passim.

8 Ibid. His license cost one shilling per annum for twenty years.

9 Norman McCord, *The Northeast*, p. 82–4.

10 Castle Archives, Hugh 3rd Duke, Letters 1827–8.

11 *Ibid.*

12 Newcastle Public Library collection, 2 vols. 1793–1880.

13 Northumberland Archive, Donkins Papers.

14 In Castle Ward, Liddell 450, Bell 434, Beaumont 349, Howick 202. Overall, Liddell 1562, Bell 1380, Beaumont 1335, Howick 977.

15 In his diary, R.W. Hodgson, a nearby landowner, wrote early in 1831, 'the mode of taking votes has to be in districts, which is certainly a very essential improvement and will tend to keep away all that disgusting bustle of passion, which is the concomitant of a contested election at present' (Northumberland Archives, March 1831).

16 McCord p. 17.

17 Tate, vol. 1 p. 346.

18 As reported in the *Newcastle Courant*, 4 June 1832.

19 Quoted in T. Devine, p. 273. Scotland's number of parliamentary seats rose from forty-five to fifty-three.

20 Thomas Raikes, *Diary*.

21 Quoted in Devine, p. 275.

22 For the full printed version: Castle Archives, p. 141 *et seq.*

23 My grandfather Robert Middlemas, in a lecture on the Freemen in October 1950, wrote 'the history of this transaction furnishes a striking illustration of class legislation'. But which class or classes?

24 1827–30 had already witnessed a dispute over the best route for the London to Edinburgh mail service, the General Post Office being in favour of the Wooler-Greenlaw road, the opposition being for the coast one via Berwick.

25 Council Minutes 16 April 1847.

26 For a stimulating account, see Graham Robb, *The Discovery of France* (2008).

27 The competition being between Wetherby Wooler on one hand and York Alnwick Berwick on the other (Castle Archives, Mail, 10 July 1828).

28 Under the old system, sometimes referred to as Speenhamland, from a particular example, outdoor relief had been cheaper than work houses; but this only worked properly in rural areas where the parish authorities presided. The Royal Commission of 1832 led to the 1834 Poor Law, under which work houses were run by new Guardians. Harsher in the end, these did not come fully into operation in Northumberland till about 1840 (1845 in Scotland) coinciding, to popular fury, with the next deep depression.

CHAPTER SEVEN:
ALNWICK'S REAL COMMUNITY

1 Historians have for centuries focussed on *England*, more rarely on *Scotland*; but they have almost universally played down the Border region as a distinct element (that is, unless they study the early medieval kingdom of Northumbria). Yet throughout the Middle Ages and more especially after the Civil War, there were, for all the enactments against cross-Border migration, settlement and marriage, underlying similarities which distinguished it from the Lowlands and the Yorkshire-Lancashire axis. Alnwick, in the middle of what James VI of Scotland, I of England, called his 'Middle Shires', inevitably faced both ways, after the 1603 Union and more importantly after the full legal Union of 1707. It is perhaps not a coincidence that the compilers of the history of Northumberland (which followed the pattern of the Victoria County Histories) omitted Alnwick, leaving that to Tate in his two volumes.

2 Charted recently by J.M. Golly and A.W. Purdue in the *Civilisation of the Crowd: Popular Culture in England 1750–1900* (1999).

3 See for example, JP's treatment of cases of game poaching in Aydon Forest (Castle Archives, JII.46).

4 For Tate's encomium, see *History of Alnwick* Vol. 2 pp. 369–70.

5 Indeed Engels, keen fox-hunter and friend of the upper class, had no time for utopian levellers: 'living conditions will always evince a certain inequality which may be reduced to a minimum but never wholly eliminated'.

6 *Civilisation of the Crowd*, p. 100.

7 It was the Vicar of Norham W.S. Gilley who wrote *The Peasantry of the Border: An Appeal on their Behalf* in 1841 in the circumstances which Thomas Bewick remembered from around 1800: 'These cottagers were of an honest and independent character while, at the same time, they held the neighbouring gentry in the greatest estimation and respect, and these again in return did not overlook them but were interested in knowing that they were happy and well.' (Thomas Bewick, *A Memoir Written by Himself* (1862, p. 24), quoted in McCord, *North-East England*, p. 95)

8 Witness the family of William Wightman, solicitor in Wooler, half of whom took ship there in 1828 and did

not return: they prospered there.

9   One case study, however, of murder in mid-eighteenth century Rye does, as a by-product of its main detective theme: P.C. Monod, *The Murder of Mr Grobell, Madness and Civility in an English Town* (2006).

10 M.R.G. Conzen, *Alnwick, Northumberland: A Study in Town Plan Analysis* (1960).

11 R.C. Young, p. 34.

12 *Ibid.*, p. 166.

13 *Ibid.* p. 169.

14 cf. Richard Brock, *The Romantic Economist* (2009).

15 R.C. Young, p. 240.

16 To quote a modern scholar: 'Notions of "home" and the desire to belong represent fundamental human needs. Decisions about who is an "insider" and, conversely, who remains an "outsider" or stranger to the community, underlie both the theory and practice of citizenship . . . Citizenship defines who can become a full political subject (even if not a voter) who possesses both the formal rights to membership of the community, and the capacity to access and indeed exercise these rights – and who does not.' (Professorial Lecture by Barbara Einhorn, University of Sussex, 9 June 2009.)

17 In a philosophical argument about the nature of community in a complex society, Adam Fergusson puts a similar proposition about how and why a community can continue to function *Principals of Moral Philosophy* (1792, p.510–12).

18 Cf. Scott L. Newstok, *Quoting Death in Early Modern England: The Poetics of Epitaphs* (2008).

19 In a more literal sense, Forster's characters too will have a permanent home in the Northumberland County Archives Museum.

INDEX